T5-ARJ-917

Client/Server Accounting

Subscription Notice

This Wiley product is updated on a periodic basis with supplements to reflect important changes in the subject matter. If you purchased this product directly from John Wiley & Sons, Inc., we have already recorded your subscription for this update service.

If, however, you purchased this product from a bookstore and wish to receive (1) the current update at no additional charge, and (2) future updates and revised or related volumes billed separately with a 30-day examination review, please send your name, company name (if applicable), address, and the title of the product to:

Supplement Department
John Wiley & Sons, Inc.
One Wiley Drive
Somerset, NJ 08875
1-800-225-5945

For customers outside the United States, please contact the Wiley office nearest you:

Professional & Reference Division
John Wiley & Sons Canada, Ltd.
22 Worcester Road
Rexdale, Ontario M9W 1L1
CANADA
(416) 675-3580
1-800-567-4797
FAX (416) 675-6599

Jacaranda Wiley Ltd.
PRT Division
P.O. Box 174
North Ryde, NSW 2113
AUSTRALIA
(02) 805-1100
FAX (02) 805-1597

John Wiley & Sons, Ltd.
Baffins Lane
Chichester
West Sussex, PO19 1UD
UNITED KINGDOM
(44) (243) 779777

John Wiley & Sons (SEA) Pte. Ltd.
37 Jalan Pemimpin
Block B # 05-04
Union Industrial Building
SINGAPORE 2057
(65) 258-1157

Client/Server Accounting

Reengineering Financial Systems

Stewart McKie

John Wiley & Sons, Inc.

New York • Chichester • Weinheim • Brisbane • Singapore • Toronto

This text is printed on acid-free paper.

Library of Congress Cataloging in Publication Data:

McKie, Stewart.
Client/server accounting : reengineering financial systems / by Stewart McKie.
p. cm.
Includes bibliographical references and index.
ISBN 0-471-15784-8 (cloth : alk. paper). — ISBN 0-471-16882-3 (paper : alk. paper)
1. Accounting—Data processing. 2. Client/server computing. I. Title.
HF5679.M3755 1997
657'.0285—dc20 96-30767

Printed in the United States of America

10 9 8 7 6 5 4 3 2 1

Contents

Preface

This book is a resource for business managers who want to understand the background, concept, and application of client/server accounting technology. Client/server accounting is the term used to describe business accounting software applications designed for use on the client/server computing platform. Client/server is a computing architecture, in which the hardware and software resources are distributed across a local- or wide-area network instead of being concentrated on a single machine such as a mini- or mainframe computer. Here, accounting is used in a generic sense to include the financial, supply chain, manufacturing, and human resource areas of business management.

The book is focused on corporate-level accounting software applications. For many years these applications have been regarded primarily as transaction processors and to some extent treated as a necessary evil by business management. Accounting departments are managed as cost centers, making them a prime target for corporate downsizing and reengineering efforts. Client/server accounting is a catalyst for changing this scenario by providing the tools to leverage more value from accounting data.

Client/server accounting is an architecture that is extending the reach and expanding the capabilities of accounting systems. By incorporating electronic commerce, workflow, document management, OLAP, software agents, and other technologies into the accounting process, client/server accounting is transforming the design and potential of accounting software. Client/server accounting gives the accounting department the tools they need to make a more positive contribution to the overall management of a business and unlock the potential of a key corporate information asset.

WHO SHOULD READ THIS BOOK?

The book is intended for business people who need to understand the concepts and application of client/server accounting. The book does not describe specific software or hardware features in detail. The aim is to provide the information business managers need to help them decide how client/server accounting can add value to their management systems. Consequently the book is not overly concerned with in-depth descriptions of technology or products but with the application of such technology in a business setting. The following people will find this book useful:

- Strategic business managers such as Chief Executive Officers, Chief Financial Officers, and line-of-business Vice Presidents
- Functional business-systems managers such as Controllers, Accountants, and accounting Supervisors
- Technical business-system managers such as Chief Information Officers, and Systems and Business Analysts
- Systems-integration specialists such as Big Six staff, vendor-marketing and support staff, value-added resellers, and independent consultants

WHY READ THIS BOOK?

Many businesses are currently evaluating or undergoing the transition to client-server computing. After the initial pilot projects are completed, accounting systems are a popular choice for selection as the first major application that is switched to the new platform. This is often because the accounting software in use is over a decade old and reaching the end of its useful life or because new technology directions in other functional departments demand that accounting be kept synchronized.

The client/server accounting software market is currently in an explosive growth period as new products are released by startups and old products are rewritten by established vendors. Furthermore, a range of complementary technologies such as workflow, OLAP, electronic messaging, and commerce are all adding value to accounting systems. Consequently, the marketplace is characterized by vendor hype and customer confusion. The aim of this book is to provide business managers with a client/server-accounting base of knowledge so they can cut through the hype and make more informed decisions in their evaluations of the technology.

WHAT CONTENT IS COVERED ?

The book is divided into five parts as summarized below:

Part One Introduction

- **Chapter 1 The Business of Change** outlines directions in business strategy and tactics, and technology trends that have influenced the introduction of client-server accounting technology.
- **Chapter 2 Models of Accounting Systems** outlines the various system topologies that have characterized computer accounting systems prior to the introduction of client/server accounting.
- **Chapter 3 Host-Centric Computing** discusses the advantages and disadvantages of centralized accounting systems running on computer hosts such as mainframes and minicomputers.

Part Two The Client/Server Architecture

- **Chapter 4 Client/Server Concepts** introduces some key terms and concepts of client/server as a computing platform for running business applications.

- **Chapter 5 Client/Server Systems** discusses the hardware and technology components of a client/server architecture when it is deployed to run business applications.
- **Chapter 6 Client/Server Applications** discusses the construction of client-server applications and the importance of databases and data access.

Part Three Client/Server Accounting

- **Chapter 7 Client/Server Accounting Concepts** introduces some key terms and concepts of client/server accounting as an architecture for business management applications. The aim is to define what client/server accounting means and to differentiate it from traditional business accounting systems.
- **Chapter 8 Client/Server Accounting Software Design** discusses what is different about the design of client/server accounting software. The aim is to communicate the potential of these new designs for delivering added value solutions for financial systems.

Part Four Reengineering Your Accounting System

- **Chapter 9 Making the Transition to Client/Server Accounting** discusses migration strategies for legacy accounting users, preparing your people for the new client/server environment, ensuring the technology foundation is in place, and revising the software selection process.
- **Chapter 10 Reengineering Accounting Transaction Processing** discusses transaction processing problems, reengineering approaches, and resources.
- **Chapter 11 Reengineering Accounting Decision Support** discusses decision support reengineering in the same manner as Chapter 10 treats transaction processing engineering.

Finally, at the end of this book resources have been provided. They are designed to provide a wide range of useful references for readers who want to find out more about client/server accounting. These resources include:

- A contact data listing for leading client/server accounting vendors
- A glossary of client/server accounting acronyms and terms
- A short bibliography

Please note that the vendor and product names referred to as resources do not imply any endorsement by the author of these vendors or their products, but rather that they are representative of the resources used to deliver the reengineering solutions discussed. The resources list is not exhaustive, but rather a means to point you in the right direction. You should note that in most cases the vendors will also bring in other system integrators or consulting resources to help implement these reengineering solutions.

PART ONE

Introduction

CHAPTER 1 THE BUSINESS OF CHANGE

The strategies and tactics that businesses adopt in order to remain competitive have an impact on the design and use of the computer systems they use for business management. Computer-accounting systems are no exception, and a wide range of popular strategies and tactics can all be seen as impacting the design and use of these systems. Furthermore, changes and advances in the technology on which computer-accounting systems are based also have an impact on their design and use so that the function of a computer-accounting system may be expanded and extended by inclusion of these new technologies.

CHAPTER 2 MODELS OF ACCOUNTING SYSTEMS

Accounting systems are designed for deployment in at least five levels of business organization, each with different characteristics reflecting the increasing complexity of the business-management problems addressed. These five models are: desktop, workgroup, subsidiary, corporate, and enterprise. What is interesting about client/server accounting is that it has the potential to embrace all these models. This makes it fundamentally different from traditional accounting solutions that were often associated with a particular computing platform and size of business.

CHAPTER 3 HOST-CENTRIC COMPUTING

Most enterprise-level accounting systems in place today are based on the host-centric computing model. This is the centralized computing characterized by mainframe and minicomputer-based accounting systems, now known as legacy systems. While host-centric accounting systems are both advantageous and necessary for certain businesses, there are many reasons why they may not be an appropriate model for managing modern, rapid-growth businesses. As users looked for alternatives to host-centric accounting systems, vendors responded with a variety of short-term fixes to the problem that rehosted parts of the application without any fundamental redesign of the application functionality.

CHAPTER ONE

The Business of Change

1.1 INTRODUCTION

Every business is in the business of change, a fact that is confirmed by the research and published works of many past and present management gurus. The prescriptions of these gurus themselves are one driving force behind the dynamic of business change, while another is the relentless pace of technology innovation. For today, every business is also in the business of managing technology for competitive advantage. Poor technology management can reduce competitive effectiveness, have a negative impact on the bottom line, make the company a takeover target, or simply put it out of business. Excellent technology management is a factor in preventing these scenarios and securing a long-term business future. Managers of accounting departments are beginning to realize that they too must become technology savvy, if only to understand how technology is reshaping their working world and the role they play in it.

1.2 BUSINESS STRATEGY

Most of the world's leading corporations have at some time over the last decade attempted or succeeded in implementing some of the strategic, business-wide initiatives listed below. Implementing these strategies impacts what is expected from accounting systems, so in each case the strategy is briefly defined and its implications from an accounting system perspective is noted:

Best Practices

- Best practices are the methods used by an industry leader in order to achieve optimum results from a given business process. Organizations are seeking out these process leaders, whether they operate inside or outside their own market segment, in order to emulate their success. Best practices benefit from a workflow-based rather than departmental view of business-process management in which each function is viewed as the customer of the next in the chain, as espoused by Richard J. Schonberger in his books *World Class Manufacturing* (The Free Press, 1986) and *Building a Chain of Customers* (The Free Press, 1990).
- In terms of accounting systems, best practices are usually studied to reduce transaction-processing time and therefore the cost per transaction, for example through faster customer billing or electronic purchasing. In order to compare and implement best practices, financial management systems need the capability to produce statistics about transaction volumes and the time it takes to process a transaction from start to finish. Systems must also offer the capability to model the software functionality around the business process in order to map the software feature set directly onto best practice process templates.

Continuous Improvement

- Continuous improvement (*Kaizen* in Japanese) is the attempt to improve every aspect of a company's operations through small, incremental steps. *Kaizen* can be used for the tactical implementation of a best-practice strategy and was one of the practices adopted by the Japanese as a result of the teachings of W. Edwards Deming in the early post-war years.

- For financial management systems to assist with continuous improvement they need to offer the same capabilities as for best practices above plus the ability to model processes and store those models in a repository. These process models can then be recalled and modified as the basis for the incremental improvements that characterize continuous improvement initiatives. Thus the model of a best-practice purchasing cycle, for example, can be recalled from the process-model repository and refined to deliver the next level of quality advantage.

Downsizing

- Downsizing is the backlash from the big-is-beautiful attitude that characterized the operations of many of the world's largest corporations from 1950 to 1980. In practice, downsizing focuses on reducing corporate headcount, particularly in what are considered as low-added value areas such as clerical and middle-management positions. The consequence of downsizing is often that more demands are put on the people and systems that remain in the organization.
- Accounting departments are a prime target for downsizing because they are composed of two prime targets of downsizing initiatives: white-collar middle management, and clerical staff. Consequently financial-system managers should look for systems that are either more efficient—to shoulder the burden of less headcount—or more able to deliver greater business intelligence—to make the accounting staff more productive and their roles more valuable.

Empowerment

- Empowerment is an attempt by management to give workers more autonomy and responsibility, as discussed by Rosabeth Moss Kanter in her book *The Change Masters: Corporate Entrepre-*

neurs at Work (Simon & Schuster, 1983). From a systems perspective, empowerment means giving workers access to the data and software tools they need to do their job more effectively. Empowerment is expected to deliver a qualitative rather than quantitative improvement in information processing.

- Financial systems need to deliver flexible query and reporting tools with features such as data drilldown in order to empower accounting users with the tools they need to do their jobs more effectively. For the accounts payable clerk to resolve a vendor inquiry about an unpaid bill they may need access to payables, purchasing, and cash-management systems using query and reporting tools designed for navigating this interconnected data.

Extended Enterprise

- The extended enterprise recognizes that the boundaries between an organization and its suppliers and customers are getting fuzzier. In essence, an organization can be viewed holistically as comprising these three parts: the organization itself, its strategic partners, and its outside service providers. This is the basis of the Shamrock Organization described by Charles Handy in his book *The Age of Unreason* (Harvard Business School Press, 1990).
- Technology is a key enabler of the extended enterprise through electronic commerce using Electronic Data Interchange (EDI), e-mail, and lately the Internet. Financial systems must support electronic commerce and messaging functionality in order for an organization to effectively communicate with its extended enterprise partners.

Global Trading

- Global trading is no longer the preserve of the world's traditional multinational conglomerates. The efficiencies and low cost of widespread digital communication systems mean that a one-person consulting firm can just as easily engage in global trading as a traditional multinational conglomerate. Along with global trading comes the realization that acting locally pays dividends, so many of the leading international businesses are actively pursuing a think-globally, act-locally operating strategy.

- Financial systems must be ready and able to handle the basic requirements of global trading, namely: multicurrency management, revaluation, consolidation and translation reporting, and multinational statutory compliance, document, and report production. At the same time these systems should allow managers to act locally by deploying software that is sensitive to local language, terminology, tax structures, and business processes.

Mergers and Acquisitions

- Mergers and acquisitions (M&A) remain a primary vehicle for business growth, largely as a consequence of easier access to capital and the pursuit of market dominance by the world's largest organizations. The polar opposites of M&A—demergers and spin-offs—are also part of this dynamic. M&A forces the merging or integration of technological infrastructures and may place a greater processing or functional burden on the financial systems of either merger party.
- M&A demands systems that can easily integrate into alternative system architectures and accounting software that may be scaled up to meet the higher processing or more complex functional needs required to manage the post-merger scenario.

Service-Centric

- Service-centric business management recognizes the fact that businesses prosper by both gaining and retaining customers and by managing the relationship with their suppliers. This is achieved by a number of methods that depend on knowing exactly who your customers and suppliers are, what their needs are, what expectations they have, and what defines satisfaction from their perspective. In other words businesses have to understand their customers and suppliers better and communicate with them more effectively.
- Financial management systems, especially receivable, order-

entry and billing systems, payables, and purchasing contain a great deal of useful information about customers and suppliers and their preferences. Consequently managers are looking for the data-mining functions that enable them to unlock that information in order to leverage it to improve customer and supplier relationships. Also, as the Internet matures as a medium for electronic commerce, accounting systems will be expected to provide self-service functionality that allows customers and vendors to maintain and query their own data in third party accounting systems.

These are just some of the business strategies being used or adopted by contemporary organizations. Even at this macro level, it is clear there is a considerable trickle-down impact on accounting systems. This impact influences the design of the accounting software that is utilized to help implement and manage these business strategies.

1.3 BUSINESS TACTICS

The strategic business directions outlined above are being realized through a range of tactical business practices that also have a bearing on the design and use of accounting systems. A selection of these tactics is outlined below. As in the case of the previously listed business strategies, each case's tactic is briefly defined and its implications from an accounting system perspective are noted here:

Activity-Based Costing (ABC)

- Activity-based costing is the mechanism for determining the true cost of a product or service. This means combining the direct costs of production of the product or service with indirect costs such as overhead, distribution, and head office or subsidiary support services.
- For a financial system to handle ABC it must deliver three functions as a minimum:
    1. To capture analysis at the transaction level in order to tag transactions to activities for recognizing activity costs

2. To query across functional modules in order to gather the information needed to truly represent a cross-functional activity
3. To allocate costs on a rule-driven basis against activities in order to build an accurate picture of the total activity cost

Business Process Reegineering (BPR)

- In order for businesses to adapt faster to change it has been argued that the analysis, restructuring, and continuous improvement of business processes, business process reengineering, is a necessary prerequisite. BPR is a tactical implementation of a continuous improvement strategy. Although back office processes, including accounting, are typically low added value processes from a profitability perspective, they are often easy to identify, model, and reengineer. This promise of a quick win has meant that accounting processes have become a prime target for reengineering efforts, especially when businesses use the adoption of a new accounting system as a catalyst for initiating BPR in the organization.
- Financial systems that have been designed to be molded around business processes, usually those with a strong workflow component or delivered with high functional granularity, are the types of applications that can take best advantage of BPR efforts.

Case Management

- Case managers are individuals who provide a single point of contact for a specific business process from start to finish. The idea is to prevent customers, vendors, or employees being given the runaround when they deal with an organization. Case management is a tactical implementation of a service centric policy and staff empowerment.
- Case management is a tool for use in the conversion of accounting staff from transaction processors into knowledge workers. As such, case management demands systems that give users the ability to manage all aspects of a transaction from end to end through

superior query and reporting tools that cross functional software modules.

Cross-Functional Teams

- Cross-functional teams are workgroups that cross the functional boundaries of a business. Cross-functional teams are a hallmark of the extended enterprise because they recognize that an extended enterprise is less of a whole than a sum of parts. From the perspective of an accounting system, cross-functional teams mean workgroups whose working "world" crosses application boundaries and combines functionality from multiple modules. The payables team may need to use functions from general-ledger, accounts-payable, purchasing, and inventory modules, for example.
- To support this style of working, the financial system must allow the assembly of functions around a user workgroup. This is achieved either by limiting user access to a subset of functions through use of security controls or through the assembly of software granules (functional components) around specific cross-modular business processes.

Just In Time (JIT)

- Just-in-time production is a Japanese quality control principle for eliminating waste in inventory by ensuring a constant flow of items. This avoids the peak-and-trough effect of inventory overstock and understock. JIT is a tactical example of a best practice strategy, having been invented by a Toyota executive who recognized the value of supermarket inventory planning for application to the auto industry. From a systems perspective, JIT means being able to identify at any point in time the current state of a transaction, particularly when a transaction has reached the completion of its business process.
- JIT demands accounting-systems functionality that provides the ability to query and manage the status of a transaction irrespective of the application module that currently owns the transac-

tion. It also requires close integration between modules such as sales ordering and purchasing to create back-to-back transactions for faster response to customer demand.

Outsourcing

- Outsourcing is the replacing of internal services or products with external services or products, usually for cost cutting purposes. Outsourcing is an implementation of the extended enterprise and downsizing strategies and reflects the attempt by a business to focus on core competencies.
- The only reason outsourcing is mentioned here is because accounting systems may become the next big outsourcing prospect for those organizations that have already outsourced other departments. After all, many businesses formerly ran their accounting systems using timeshare or bureau services and many still do, especially for payroll processing. New technology such as telephony, the Internet, and database replication is set to revolutionize the accounting process and may make outsourcing accounting departments the norm rather than the exception.

Shared Service Centers

- Shared service centers are the result of global enterprises recognizing that the recentralization of certain shared services makes sense from the business process perspective. Shared service centers are often used to centrally manage an organization's cash, receivables, payables, or purchasing, for example, and are often a tactical response to the complexity of managing global, distributed systems.
- For use in shared service centers, financial systems must offer multicurrency processing and reporting facilities combined with sophisticated consolidation reporting, data-transfer, and intercompany transaction management. Shared services demand that functionality can be decoupled to support combinations of distributed and centralized business processes such as distributed requisitioning and centralized purchasing.

Once again, as with the broader strategic business trends, tactical business practices have an impact on the design and use of accounting software. Accounting systems must be selected to match the demands that will be put upon them when used by businesses implementing these and other strategies and tactics.

1.4 TECHNOLOGY TRENDS

While business strategies and tactics have been a major factor in the dynamic of the business of change, technology trends have also played their part, continuing to move the goalposts for many businesses. A simple example of this is the communication of business data. Fax systems experienced explosive growth during the 1980s and largely replaced older technologies such as the Telex. However, the fax is now expected to become a marginal business by the end of the 1990s due to the rapid adoption of electronic messaging (primarily electronic mail) by businesses worldwide. Conversely, the Internet, largely a haunt of academics and computer programmers during the 1980s, is now the springboard infrastructure for a whole new generation of electronic commerce providers in the 1990s. Technology development has become the lens through which business entrepreneurs focus their vision.

Amongst the many technology trends that have gathered momentum and gained commercial acceptance over the last decade, those outlined below are some of the most influential from an accounting system perspective:

Open Systems

- Open systems is the movement away from proprietary computer hardware and software toward systems that are not controlled by one vendor but essentially open to any vendor or customer to use and enhance. The move toward open systems has come to be associated primarily with the migration of business systems from proprietary mainframe and minicomputer computing platforms, dominated by large hardware vendors such as International Business Machines (IBM), Hewlett-Packard (HP), or Digital Equipment Corporation (DEC), toward systems based on the UNIX operating system. The core specifications and source code for UNIX are in the public domain, qualifying it as a truly open operating system on which applications can run.

- The consequence for accounting systems was that many vendors ported their mainframe or mini-accounting applications for use on hardware running the UNIX operating system. The result has been more choice for customers and more cost-effective accounting systems in many cases due to the improved price/performance ratio of UNIX based systems versus the accounting platforms they replaced.

Relational Databases

- The 1980s saw the commercial realization of the relational database management system (RDBMS), some years after Dr. E. F. Codd's original definition of the relational model based on research conducted during his tenure at IBM. Today, the RDBMS dominates the database marketplace as the model of choice for new implementations and application software that utilizes databases such as accounting.
- Most of the current versions of the world's leading accounting software now manage data almost exclusively on RDBMS technology. The move to relational accounting has homogenized the storage of accounting data by replacing a variety of hierarchical and network databases or index-based file management systems with a single data storage model.

Graphical User Interfaces

- The ground-breaking graphical user interface (GUI) of the Apple Macintosh computer achieved commercial success in the mid-1980s. This began the momentum towards the GUI becoming the desktop interface of choice, for users of applications on personal computers or workstations. Now, in the mid-1990s the desktop interface standard is Microsoft's Windows 95. More than any other product, Windows has been responsible for homogenizing the look and feel of desktop software applications.

- While accounting software benefits from many aspects of the GUI, some people remain skeptical of its use in heads-down transaction processing. Still, despite initial inertia, almost every accounting software vendor has now released versions of their software sporting a graphical user interface and is concentrating their development resources on a single user "front end" for their products.

Client/Server Computing

- Client/server is a computing architecture that is designed to take advantage of distributed resources connected by local or wide-area networks. Part of the reaction to proprietary systems was a proliferation of local-area networks set up at the workgroup level, which were outside the control of central information systems departments. Consequently, many businesses found themselves with a mixture of system platforms and architectures, many of which were disconnected from each other. Client/server is a means of integrating different hardware architectures, operating systems, and applications by dividing them into clients or servers and connecting them together through networking. For one reason or another, client/server has taken hold of the imagination of many business information system departments and now is rapidly gaining widespread popularity.
- Between 1990 and 1995, almost all significant accounting software in the U.S. marketplace was rewritten for use on client/server architectures. Many vendors have dropped or marginalized their non–client/server accounting versions and are concentrating their development efforts on their new client/server application suites.

Electronic Commerce

- Electronic commerce, used here in its broadest sense, is the use of electronic messages and documents in order to manage and transact business. This includes technologies such as e-mail, document management, electronic document interchange (EDI), and the Internet. Electronic commerce is used for the distribution and dissemination of information using electronic means as opposed to paper-based letters, documents, and reports.

- The long-term consequences of electronic commerce will be a significant reduction in transactions processed by human operators and the virtual elimination of paper-based output from accounting systems. While e-mail, document management, and EDI are commonly found in many leading accounting software suites, Internet accounting is the latest of the electronic commerce options finding its way into client/server accounting applications.

Workflow

- The popularity of business-process reengineering has led to the rapid growth of workflow as both a software market niche and a functional requirement of accounting software. Workflow can be defined as the automation of business processes through software. Workflow is also a technology that acts as a form of glue by connecting functions, modules, and/or whole applications together to deliver process-driven virtual applications that may be both multivendor and multiplatform.
- Many of the leading vendors of enterprise accounting have embraced workflow and are offering increasingly sophisticated workflow management functions as part of their standard accounting functionality.

Object-Oriented Technology

- The perennial problem faced by businesses needing new software applications is whether to make them or buy them. Making them gives the most flexibility and control but at significant cost. Buying them takes advantage of lower acquisition and ongoing maintenance costs at the price of a close fit to the business needs. Object-oriented (OO) technology, defined as software programming methodologies and application development tools for building reusable software objects, promises to eliminate the make-or-buy decision. Customers are looking for ways to customize software more closely to their business while taking advantage of packaged applications. Vendors are looking for ways to accelerate their time to market with software breadth and depth and lower their ongoing maintenance costs. Software built to OO designs is intended to deliver reusable object components that can be assembled into applications.

- A few leading-edge accounting software vendors are delivering applications built using OO technology, and this trickle is expected to become a flood in the remainder of the 1990s. Component accounting is the next wave of business accounting application design and a natural successor to and exploiter of client/server accounting.

These are just some of the technology trends that have impacted the design and deployment of accounting software in the last decade. All of these technologies and their integration into accounting applications are covered in greater depth in Parts three and four of this book.

1.5 CONCLUSION

By any standards, the range of strategies, tactics, and technology trends that modern business is expected to manage is almost overwhelming. At some point these factors bring pressure to bear on the information systems used to manage businesses of all types and sizes. The result is often that a new computing paradigm is adopted to manage this impact. The adoption of client/server computing can be regarded as one such paradigm shift.

CHAPTER TWO

Models of Accounting Systems

2.1 INTRODUCTION

One of the first uses for business computers was for accounting. Until the early 1970s, virtually all business accounting software was written and maintained by either in-house teams of programmers and analysts, or by similar teams of outside vendors. Generally these vendors were the same people that supplied the hardware, peripherals, and other services that were the foundation of a business computing system. Business software was written for specific combinations of mainframe central processor units (CPUs) and operating systems.

(a) Timesharing

The expense of developing and maintaining this mainframe software plus the associated expense of the hardware required to run it had a number of consequences:

- Only the largest businesses could afford to run their accounting on an in-house computer.

- Even the largest businesses had to monitor the use of in-house computing resources very carefully.
- It was fiscally imperative to ensure that the software and hardware assets were leveraged for as long as practicable to ensure a justifiable return on investment.

For many businesses, accounting in house was simply out of the question. They were forced to share computing resources with other businesses or business units (timesharing) or hire computing resources from third parties (bureaus). Despite the many technological advances over the past two decades, timesharing and bureaus are still used today for various accounting tasks. For example, much of the world's payroll is still run by external bureaus, and New-Jersey-based Automatic Data Processing (ADP) is a multibillion dollar leader in this market.

(b) Mainframe Accounting

The market for packaged accounting software did not truly surface until the early 1970s when the first packages were released for use on mainframes. Pioneers in this market included McCormack & Dodge (M&D), Management Science America (MSA), and Walker Interactive Systems. Mainframe accounting packages allowed more businesses to justify bringing their accounting in-house. Also, the release of packaged software for mainframes was an impetus for increasing the number of timesharing and bureau service providers, because it lowered the cost of entry into this market.

Early mainframe-packaged accounting software was a step up from writing from scratch, but it was still expensive to buy, maintain, and modify. It required full-time specialists to manage and customize the software; it frequently took many years to install and many more to modify the software to fit the business. The software was usually leased rather than licensed as is the norm today.

From this mainframe heritage, the first few decades of packaged accounting software history can be directly linked to developments in programming languages, computer hardware, and operating systems. Some of the key events that influenced this development are shown in Figure 2.1.

(c) Events and Directions

(i) COBOL

COBOL is a programming language designed for building business application software that subsequently became the most popular language used to develop packaged accounting software. As the language itself was ported from mainframe operating systems for use on mini-computers, personal computers (PCs), or UNIX operating systems, accounting packages written in COBOL could eventually be run on a wide range of operating platforms. COBOL remains the foundation for many of the leading legacy accounting packages in use today. When people refer to legacy accounting systems, they usually mean systems running COBOL software. In reality what they mean is heritage systems, because COBOL is a crucial part of accounting software heritage. COBOL remained a major force in accounting software until the mid-1980s when it was overtaken by C, a programming language associated with the rise of the UNIX operating system. Today almost all new accounting software is developed in or uses C or its successor C++.

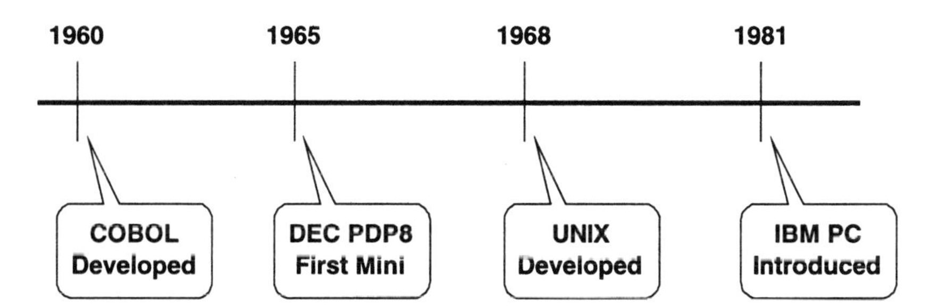

Figure 2.1. Key Technological Events.

(ii) Mini-computer Accounting

Mini-computer accounting dominated the 1980s. Minis were the logical successors to the mainframe: They provided the same host-based computing architecture but offered these advantages:

- They were physically smaller and required less precise operational environments.
- They could be installed and maintained more easily and cheaply than mainframes.
- The acquisition cost was less, as was the cost of software and peripherals such as printers.

There were dozens of minihardware vendors at the height of the mini boom, but these hardware families proved most popular with accounting software vendors as platforms for their applications:

Vendor	***Family***
IBM	System/34, /36, /38
Digital Equipment	PDP11, VAX
Hewlett Packard	3000 Series

Minicomputing helped move accounting out of the mainframe glass house. Many businesses that used time sharing or bureau services for their accounting could now afford their own mini-based accounting system. Many larger enterprises could now afford to departmentalize their accounting or take smaller subsidiaries off the mainframe and onto their own minicomputer. This opened up new markets for accounting software vendors to exploit.

(iii) PC Accounting

PC accounting provided the next major impetus for the accounting software market following the introduction of the IBM PC in 1981. Compared to mini- and mainframe platforms, the PC was very cheap to buy and develop applications for, providing a low entry cost for developers and a potentially vast market for accounting software entrepreneurs. The result was a flood of new accounting software packages. They lacked the heavyweight functionality of mini- and mainframe packages, but they were more than an order of magnitude less costly and much easier to install, implement, and use.

PC accounting software was initially designed for single-user, low-volume accounting, reflecting the design constraints of the PC. This was a big change for accounting software. Previously, whether on mainframes or minis, accounting software and data were the exclusive preserve of the corporate information systems (IS) departments. These departments acted as the guardians of the accounting data: i.e., they restricted access to the data and maintained its integrity. PC accounting software moved accounting to the desktop and effectively into the hands of the accounting user. If this was an early warning bell for events to come, it was largely ignored by most mainframe and mini-accounting software vendors. PC accounting also extended the reach of accounting software into the small business market that had previously had to pay CPAs to manage their accounting.

(d) Market Segmentation

In the early 1980s the accounting software market could be categorized into three distinct segments: mainframe, midrange, and PC. Each segment had clearly defined market leaders with packages linked to specific hardware families within those segments. Although some vendors provided products that crossed segments, this was the exception rather than the rule. Where crossover existed it was up or down one segment. No leading mainframe vendors offered a PC product and no leading PC vendors offered a mainframe product. This crossover pattern meant that accounting software was sometimes scaleable downward but seldom upward.

The result was a rather cozy status quo in which packaged software pricing, functionality, and ease-of-use were largely a reflection of the market segment the vendor occupied, with mainframe software being the most expensive, richest in functionality, and most difficult to use. In particular, software pricing was essentially processor-based. Software for a CPU that handled 20 million instructions per second (MIPS) was often simply twice as expensive as the same package for a 10-MIPS CPU. There was no notion of value-based pricing that reflected how customers actually used the software or how many users were connected to it at any given point in time.

(e) PC LANs and UNIX Accounting

The rise of computing architectures based on the PC local area network (LAN) and the UNIX operating system during the mid- to late 1980s can now be seen as a primary catalyst for changing the accounting market's status quo. In their early days, LANs were used simply to link small groups of PC users together in order to provide basic file- and printer-sharing services. Similarly, UNIX was associated with powerful desktop workstations loosely linked together and used for specialist applications like computer-aided design (CAD) that demanded more powerful processing and graphics handling than PC systems offered at the time.

As multiuser PC LAN- and UNIX-based computer systems became more reliable they began to be considered as viable alternatives to the mini-computer as a platform for accounting. Once again lower, initial, and ongoing costs were a primary attraction, plus software for these platforms was generally newer and therefore easier to use. Both of these computing platforms promised to deliver an accounting solution that essentially crossed the PC and the midrange segments.

PC LAN- and UNIX-based systems were also ideally suited for the more decentralized, workgroup-oriented accounting departments becoming popular in the decentralized corporate world. PC LAN- and UNIX-based accounting software packages were typically upscale versions of packages from vendors positioned in the PC market: As a result, what they lacked in functionality they gained in ease of use, relative to their midrange and mainframe competitors. Although this was less obvious at the time, the rise of accounting on PC LAN- and UNIX-based systems heralded the subsequent platform shift to client/server accounting in the 1990s.

Table 2.1 provides a timeline that shows when some of the leading accounting software vendors in the mainframe, midrange, and PC/LAN/UNIX categories were established. These vendors represent leading accounting software suppliers in the U.S. marketplace today on a revenue basis. Some of the early leaders were subsequently acquired as the industry consolidated during the 1970s. For example, Dun & Bradstreet Corporation acquired McCormack & Dodge (M&D) in 1983 and Management Science America (MSA) in 1989 to form the nucleus of Dun & Bradstreet Software's business accounting portfolio.

Non-client/server accounting software from all of these vendors is still in use today and being purchased to add to existing imple-

Table 2.1. Some Accounting Software Vendors Founded between 1966 and 1985.

Platform	*1966–1970*	*1971–1975*	*1976–1980*	*1981–1985*
Mainframe	M & D MSA Walker Interactive	American Software Integral SAP AG		
Midrange		Lawson Software Ross Systems	CODA JD Edwards Marcam	Computron Software Global Software Hyperion Software Software 2000 SSA
PC LAN/UNIX			Solomon Software	FourGen Software Great Plains Software Platinum Software Systems Union

mentations. Many businesses are running on software that is at least a decade old in design, sometimes two decades old. A great deal of new technology has been introduced in the interim. Consequently, the design of much of the accounting software in use today is effectively obsolete and out of step with current software. The move to client/server accounting in the early 1990s has led to a thriving client/server accounting software market in 1996 and a useful shot in the arm for the accounting software industry. It provides an opportunity for vendors to redesign their software around a more modern and productive technology infrastructure in order to deliver a wider range of benefits to business users. For the first time the impetus for redesigning is not simply a change of hardware platform but a whole new paradigm for business computing.

The aim of the following sections is to provide an overview of five typical accounting-system deployment scenarios as they existed before the introduction of client/server accounting. These scenarios are categorized as: (1) SOHO, (2) workgroup, (3) subsidiary, (4) corporate, and (5) enterprise. In each case the essential and typical characteristics of the scenario are defined using the structure explained in Figure 2.2.

2.2 SOHO ACCOUNTING

SOHO accounting is the simplest of all accounting deployments and the standard for the sole proprietor, small office or home office busi-

Characteristic	Description
Volumes	The transaction and user volumes managed
Platform	The computing platform for the deployment
Module Breadth	The range of accounting tasks managed
Functional Depth	The depth of functionality provided
Special Features	Special considerations relative to this deployment
Market Position	Example vendors, products, pricing, and implementation time scales

Figure 2.2. Accounting Market Segment Criteria.

ness with revenues up to $500,000. These systems are used at a single location.

Volumes

SOHO accounting is single-user and low-transaction volume, processing less than a few hundred transactions of all types per month.

Platform

SOHO accounting is based on IBM-compatible or Apple PCs running single-user operating systems such as MS-DOS or MacOS. The packages use a file system, rather than a database management system (DBMS), to manage the accounting data.

Module Breadth

SOHO accounting focuses on the core financial modules (GL, AR, AP) and billing, sometimes including inventory, job costing or payroll. Modules are fully integrated and designed to be used as a single integrated application on a single computer.

Functional Depth

SOHO accounting systems are deliberately designed to their price point and the expectations of their intended user market. For this reason, they are not expected to manage high transaction volume, offer sophisticated functionality such as intercompany allocations or larger business modules such as human resources (HR) or manufacturing.

Special Features

SOHO accounting systems are designed to make the accounting process as easy and jargon-free as possible. In fact, many SOHO accounting systems have set the pace for ease-of-use design in accounting software. Some functions, such as the on-screen check payment, or transaction entry register in Intuit Quicken, or the accounting process maps found in BestWare Mind Your Own Business (MYOB), have still not found their way into high-end accounting suites costing a hundred times the price of these packages. Because SOHO packages are single-user and ease-of-use-oriented they offer real-time posting of data and are unencumbered by the need to process batch updates between modules.

Market Position

Packages such as Intuit Quicken and Quickbooks, or Peachtree Accounting for Windows are market leaders and the price point is typically less than $200 for a suite of applications. This market is further segmented into starter packages and full suites. The starter packages are typically priced below $50 and in comparison to the full suites, offer fewer modules or reduced functionality. SOHO accounting can be implemented in a matter of days and is sold by mail or retail.

2.3 WORKGROUP ACCOUNTING

Workgroup accounting is the first step up from SOHO accounting and the standard for the small business sector with revenues up to $5 million. These systems are typically used at a single location with no remote users.

Volumes

Workgroup accounting is multiuser with a transaction volume of less than a few thousand transactions, of all types, per month. Workgroup accounting is required when the transaction volume of the business or the functional sophistication of parts of the business demands that the accounting tasks be allocated to more than one person. A typical workgroup would include between 2 and 10 persons including a division between receivable and payable accounting staff for example. This arrangement requires a multiuser system in which each module may be used stand-alone while still maintaining essential integration with the other modules in the suite. A workgroup would usually require a system administrator or manager.

Platform

Workgroup accounting is based on local area networks (LANs) consisting of IBM-compatible PCs or Apple PCs running a network operating system such as Novell's Netware or Microsoft NT Server. It may also be based on low-end UNIX servers, such as those running versions of SCO's UNIX operating system, where dumb terminals or PCs are connected to a central UNIX server. Apart from the added sophistication of multiuser accounting, workgroup accounting software usually offers a more sophisticated file system for managing the accounting data. Most of the leading packages in this segment use the Btrieve file manager from Pervasive Inc. as the data manager embedded into their applications. Btrieve offers more sophisticated transaction management facilities than the simpler file systems that may be used by SOHO accounting systems, and it has better scalability to handle transaction volume. Btrieve is also a more open data management system because its file structure is accessible from a wide range of third-party query and reporting tools. This opens up the accounting data by giving users more options for querying and reporting the data.

Module Breadth

Workgroup accounting focuses on providing the core financial and supply chain modules with the addition of specialized modules such as fixed assets, payroll, and cash management. Modules are fully integrated but may also be used stand-alone, sharing data using batch interfaces. It is unusual to find workgroup accounting software that also provides human-resource or manufacturing modules.

Functional Depth

Workgroup accounting systems build on the functionality of SOHO accounting, offering a richer set in each module, and always support bookkeeping for multiple legal entities. The packages offer more flexible query, reporting, and document-formatting tools. They may also allow some limited customizing features for changing the look and feel of data-entry screens. The chart of accounts allows a multisegmented code block of at least three segments to allow for more sophisticated reporting and transaction analysis. More advanced features such as multicurrency, allocations or intercompany processing, for example, are seldom provided.

Special Features

Workgroup accounting is designed to be used in a multiuser environment, which means that it offers the file locking and use of shared printers and peripherals that characterize multiuser applications. Application security is more sophisticated, allowing system administrators to restrict access through passwords to modules, entities, or application functions. The application may include better assistance with the recovery of data after a system or network crash in order to reduce rekeying of data.

Market Position

Packages from vendors such as Great Plains Software, Macola, Platinum Software, State Of The Art, and Solomon Software are market leaders, and the price point is typically less than $1,000 per module, for a multimodule suite of applications. Modules may be purchased separately or as a suite. Workgroup accounting can be implemented in a matter of weeks and is sold retail or by value added resellers and consultants.

2.4 SUBSIDIARY ACCOUNTING

Subsidiary accounting is used to describe accounting for subsidiaries of or departmental accounting within larger corporations managing revenues up to $50 million. These systems are single-location but may be connected locally or remotely to another accounting site and may support remote users.

Volumes

Subsidiary accounting is multiuser with a transaction volume of less than 10,000 transactions of all types per month. Subsidiary accounting is required when corporations or enterprises have decentralized their accounting and allow receivables or payables departments, or smaller operating companies and divisions, to manage their accounting locally. A typical subsidiary system would support between 10 and 50 persons divided up into workgroups responsible for different aspects of the accounting process. A subsidiary system would always require an individual to be designated as the system administrator or manager and may require additional business analysts and programmers.

Platform

Subsidiary accounting is based on local area networks (LANs) consisting of IBM-compatible PCs or Apple PCs running a network operating system such as Novell's Netware or Microsoft NT Server. It is also often based on UNIX systems where dumb terminals or PCs are connected to a central UNIX server. In the past these systems may have been run locally on minicomputers or remotely by connecting to the corporate mainframe. Because subsidiary accounting may be subject to corporate standards, it may require the use of a specific database management system or operating platform. It may also use accounting software that is overly sophisticated for the user's needs because a software site license agreement has been negotiated centrally by a head-office information-systems department and applied across the enterprise.

Module Breadth

Subsidiary systems offer combinations of the full range of accounting modules in a suite including: financials, supply chain, manufacturing, HR, and payroll. Subsidiary systems may also be focused on a more vertical accounting application such as fund accounting, project accounting, or treasury management.

Functional Depth

Subsidiary systems are often used for the subsidiary businesses or departments of multinational organizations. Consequently, more specialized functionality such as multicurrency, intercompany, and allocation processing will be required. Subsidiary systems require more flexible charts of account to provide segments to capture transaction analysis for group and local management or statutory reporting. An account code of at least five segments is likely to be required. A subsidiary system may be used by a shared service center in which case-specific modules, such as accounts receivable and billing, may offer a higher-than-normal level of sophistication in the functionality set provided.

Special Features

Subsidiary systems will offer more complex report writers that may require the help of a part-time specialist to master. Application security will include the ability to switch on or off specific functional components and include some basic rule-driven security at both user and workgroup levels. Customizing capabilities may include the ability to hook in specialist functions or to build and integrate new data tables and the screens to maintain them. Subsidiary systems often offer multilingual and multiplatform versions.

Market Position

Packages from European vendors such as Systems Union and Scala are popular subsidiary systems because they include strong multinational accounting features that are often important for subsidiary accounting. The price point is from $2,500 per module and up, pricing being based on a combination of computing platforms, database engines, and the number of users connected. Modules may be purchased separately or as a suite. Subsidiary systems may be implemented in a matter of months and are sold through value-added resellers or directly by the vendor.

2.5 CORPORATE ACCOUNTING

Corporate accounting is used to describe accounting for medium to large corporate entities in which the accounting is either centralized in a single site or spread across a few major regional sites. Corporate accounting manages businesses with revenues up to $500 million. These systems may be single or multilocation and almost certainly support local and remote users.

Volumes

Corporate accounting is multiuser with a transaction volume in the tens of thousands of all types per month. Corporate accounting is required when corporations or enterprises have centralized their accounting departments or smaller operating companies and divisions are remotely connected to a head office or regional accounting system. A typical corporate system would support between 50 and 250 users divided into entity-based workgroups responsible for different aspects of the accounting process within each operating entity. A corporate system would always require more than one systems administrator and may also be supported by business analysts, full-time programmers, and a database administrator.

Platform

Corporate accounting is based on mini-computers, mainframes, UNIX-based platforms, or sometimes a combination of these platforms mixed together in a heterogeneous computing environment. Corporate accounting systems are usually selected by teams representing the corporation's accounting and MIS departments and the platform standards for software and hardware to which they adhere. Corporate systems always require the use of a sophisticated database engine to ensure the transaction integrity and volume scaleability required. Most corporate systems utilize databases from the leading relational database vendors such as Oracle, IBM, Sybase, and Informix.

Module Breadth

Corporate systems offer combinations of the full range of accounting modules in a suite including: financials, supply chain, manufacturing, HR, and payroll. Corporate systems may also include specialist vertical modules built for specific industries or sectors such as healthcare or government. Some corporate systems deliberately focus on a subset of modules, such as financials or manufacturing, in order to offer best-of-class functionality across this limited range of modules.

Functional Depth

Corporate systems are used for managing the accounting of larger domestic and multinational organizations. Consequently, more specialized functionality such as multicurrency, intercompany, and allocation processing is provided. Corporate systems deliver more flexible account charts to provide segments to capture transaction analysis for group and local management or statutory reporting across multiple domestic and foreign entities. An account code of up to 10 segments is likely to be standard.

Special Features

Corporate systems are either written in an application development tool that users can also use to customize the package or provide a toolkit module for user customization. In either case, corporate systems allow extensive customization of the core modules and offer hundreds of add-on modules from third party vendors. Corporate systems may include other specialized functionality such as workflow, document management, or electronic commerce options such as electronic data interchange (EDI).

Market Position

Because of their functional breadth and depth, packages from the top-20 U.S. accounting software vendors, for example, would all qualify as corporate systems. The price point is from $50,000 per module and up, pricing being based on a combination of computing platforms, database engines, and the number of users connected. Modules may be purchased separately or as a suite. The software may take a year to implement fully and is sold directly by the vendor or through major systems-integration firms such as Electronic Data Systems (EDS).

2.6 ENTERPRISE ACCOUNTING

Enterprise accounting is used to describe accounting for large, usually multinational enterprises in which the accounting is centralized in a number of major regional sites. Enterprise accounting manages businesses with revenues over $500 million. Fortune 1000-level companies are the primary target for enterprise systems. These systems are multilocation and support local and remote users.

Volumes

Enterprise accounting is multiuser with a transaction volume that may exceed a million of all types per month. A typical enterprise system would support over 500 users connecting to one or more physical computer systems. An enterprise system requires more than one systems administrator and the support of business analysts, full-time programmers, and one or more database administrators.

Platform

Enterprise accounting is based on minicomputers, mainframes, UNIX-based platforms, or a combination of these platforms mixed together in a heterogeneous computing environment. Enterprise accounting systems are always selected by teams of representatives from the accounting and MIS departments of the enterprise and often with the help of advice from a major systems integration or Big Six accounting firm. Enterprise systems may utilize databases from the leading relational database vendors such as Oracle, IBM, Sybase, and Informix, or they may use non-relational databases running on mainframe platforms.

Module Breadth

Enterprise systems offer a full range of accounting modules covering all aspects of enterprise management including: financials, supply chain, manufacturing, HR, and payroll. The breadth and depth of modules is a key differentiator between enterprise and other accounting systems.

Functional Depth

Enterprise systems are functionally equivalent to corporate systems in most cases, except that the same level of functionality is offered across a broader range of modules.

Special Features

Enterprise systems may offer specialized system administration features over and above those of corporate systems, reflecting the multisite nature of their deployment.

Market Position

Packages from the world's largest accounting vendors such as SAP AG, Dun & Bradstreet Software, System Software Associates, or J. D. Edwards would all qualify as enterprise systems. The price point is often from $100,000 per module and up, pricing being based on a combination of computing platforms, database engines, and the number of users connected. Modules may be purchased separately or as a suite. The software may take more than one year to implement fully and is sold directly by the vendor or through major systems integration firms. Implementing an enterprise accounting system may cost far more than the acquisition cost of the software itself, varying from $3 to $5 of implementation cost per dollar of acquisition cost.

2.7 CONCLUSION

Understanding the fit of your business relative to the accounting system models outlined above should help you to select accounting software that is positioned for your level of needs. Selecting software designed for an accounting model above your needs may ensure you room for growth, but may cost much more than you need to pay to acquire, implement, and maintain software with functionality you might never use. Conversely, selecting accounting software based strictly on current functionality needs may force you to change your system sooner, incurring unnecessary additional costs and organizational disruption.

CHAPTER THREE

Host-Centric Computing

3.1 INTRODUCTION

The first two decades of business computing were essentially host-centric. Host-centric computing means that the processing is centralized and concentrated on a single (or cluster) of computer hosts to which all users are connected. This is the opposite of distributed computing, in which computing resources are spread across a number of computers of varying levels of processing power connected by a network. Host software applications, like accounting, were monolithic, which means that the application or individual application modules were not designed to be partitioned and deployed across more than one computer.

The most common host platform is a mainframe or mini-computer that shares these characteristics:

- A central host computer with single or multiple CPUs, or a cluster of connected host computers shared by many local and remote users simultaneously
- A single disk drive or cluster of disk drives that centralizes the management of all application data utilized by users connected to the host

- Local and remote peripherals such as line printers, modems, and terminal controllers directly connected to the host
- Nonintelligent user terminals that are simply screens for data input and display directly connected to the host
- Intelligent user terminals that connect to the host using an emulation program (a program that makes these devices emulate a dumb terminal) directly connected to the host
- Operating system, database, and user application software all resident on the host computer(s)
- Centralized system management software that is used for managing all aspects of a host, its operating and applications software, and its connected peripherals
- Comprehensive security that controls access to applications and data through a central security console
- Transaction processing monitors that manage transactions flows to ensure that they can be scheduled, processed efficiently, and completed successfully

3.2 ADVANTAGES

Whether this was a mainframe, midrange, or UNIX-based host makes little difference. Host-centric computing is not platform-specific, but rather an architecture that defines a way of managing information. The architecture does offer a number of clear benefits:

- Concentration of information management resources at a single site and on a single computing platform to maximize the value of IS staff and concentrate knowledge
- Single sourcing of most of the system hardware and software components that enables a homogenous environment less prone to finger pointing among vendors
- Closer integration between hardware and software for more efficient leveraging of the hardware and software architecture and better overall system performance

- Cradle-to-grave system support typically provided by a large, well-financed, multinational vendor that gives system users a greater sense of security and confidence and reduces the support burden on internal IS departments
- Sophisticated system management and performance tools refined over many years and optimized for the host platform, which allow IS staff to tune and manage systems more effectively
- The ability to manage the processing of very high transaction volumes with round-the-clock availability and reliability due to ability to share clusters of processors and utilize sophisticated fail-safe features for managing processor or disk failures

These are just some of the benefits of host-centric computing. Many of these benefits can only currently be realized from a centralized computing architecture using mature software and hardware systems refined over decades, so many businesses are not able or willing to give up them up. Critics of host-centric systems must concede that many of the world's largest businesses continue to manage their information on host-centric systems.

3.3 DISADVANTAGES

Despite the benefits outlined above, a host-centric computing architecture introduces a number of problems that have limited the way businesses can leverage their information assets, for example:

(a) Most host-centric systems are proprietary in nature and as a result:

- Customers are locked in to a specific vendor and the vision of that vendor going forward.
- Customer choice of peripherals and software that are compatible with the host is restricted.
- Customers could be subject to price gouging because all aspects of the platform are controlled by one vendor.

(b) Most host-centric systems are victims of their own sophistication and complexity.

- Like a delicate plant, the host often required housing in a purpose-built, climate-controlled environment for optimum operation.
- Hosts need nurturing by an army of specialists, each of whom is responsible for a specific piece of the host architecture.
- The complexity of host software helped to cause significant IS delivery backlogs in response to increasing user requests for more and higher quality information.

(c) Most host systems offer stepped scaleability for coping with business growth.

- Scaleability is achieved through a series of stepped processor upgrades with fixed price points that could only be sourced from the same vendor.
- Scaleability may also be achieved by clustering host processors that force purchasing more processors but only from the same vendor.
- Scaleability may not be focused to meet the demands of one particular part of the processing needs.

(d) Concentrating all resources on the host introduces serious potential system vulnerability.

- Host systems offer little flexibility in their configuration because operating systems, databases, applications, and system-management tools are run from one location so that problems cannot be easily contained without system-wide implications.
- Failure of host-centric systems is generally catastrophic due to their star configuration—a hub (host) with many spokes (terminals and other peripherals).

- If any aspect of the host-centric processing becomes overloaded, all connected users suffer from performance degradation. Because the host runs all the operating system, application, and database software, all aspects of user interaction with the host from dumb terminals may be negatively impacted.

(e) Software for host systems was built specifically for the host processor family and operating system.

- Software was seldom portable to other operating systems and so became a nontransferable asset.
- Choice of software was limited to offerings from vendors who had committed to the host platform.
- Software pricing was processor-based rather than based on the number of users or other value-based pricing schemes that benefit users in flexible business operating conditions.
- Software was inward-looking and not designed to interact easily with other complementary applications. The same could be said for many of the hardware peripherals designed for use with a host system.

(f) Because the initial and ongoing investment required for host-centric systems was so high, the need to leverage the asset could negatively impact information management.

- Software that needed to be replaced or moved to lower-cost platforms remained on the host.
- Software that could have been run on cheaper platforms was purchased for the host instead, because it was there.
- Purchasing software for other platforms than the host was resisted by IS departments to preserve jobs and reduce support headaches.
- Purchasing software for other platforms than the host was resisted by finance managers who insisted on fully leveraging the host hardware and software assets.

While host-centric computing was not specifically at fault, the architecture also commonly got blamed for many other problems, related more to the design of accounting software running on host platforms rather than the host architecture itself.

(g) The software was not easily fitted to the business.

Very few accounting software packages fit the needs of a specific business exactly. In most cases modifications are required, even if a business is prepared to fit its processes around the package. Most early accounting software provided either limited customization tools or none at all. Some vendors countered this by offering source code. However, modifying source code effectively is a tricky business to manage and maintain when the core software is frequently upgraded. The result is that much accounting software in use is a poor business fit or has cost many times its original price in modifications to achieve a closer fit.

(h) Accounting was perceived as an information island.

Most accounting software in use today is virtually an information island because it was not designed to interoperate with other applications. This has made getting information out of accounting systems into desktop productivity tools such as wordprocessors and spreadsheets a cumbersome, time-consuming task. It has also meant that the financial modules from a financial software vendor do not easily interface to the manufacturing modules from a manufacturing vendor. When customers buy from one vendor for the integration benefits, they often end up compromising on functionality.

(i) Accounting data was not available in real time.

Traditional accounting software is batch-oriented, a direct reflection of designing for host systems. By processing transactions in batches, more efficient use can be made of the host processor's time. As a result many accounting modules pass information between themselves in batch mode. Passing accounts-payable data to the general ledger is an example. This means that systems are not operating in real time. Real-time processing demands that transactions are posted immediately and all modules impacted by the data are updated simultaneously. Real-time processing means that system data is more accurate and the information more complete when an accounting query or report is run.

(j) Transaction processing dominated decision support.

Transaction management and auditing has been the primary focus of early generations of accounting software. As a result, decision support has often been a secondary design consideration. This has led to a great many businesses making excessive use of spreadsheets to provide the basis for their decision support activities. Corporate accounting departments spend inordinate amounts of unproductive time transferring or rekeying data from accounting systems into spreadsheets for further analysis and reporting. Most corporate accounting systems are surrounded by these worksheet bandages, necessary only because the accounting software lacks integrated decision support tools or does not provide access to the data from other applications.

(k) When accounting systems crashed the result was unpredictable.

Many accounting systems use relatively simplistic file management—as opposed to database management—systems to store their data. This simplicity makes data entry and posting faster. However, it can also lead to problems with data integrity. Lack of more sophisticated database management facilities makes it easier to corrupt the transaction data and cause inconsistencies in the accounting results. This leads to many basic reconciliation problems and frequent system downtime fixing corrupted files and indexes.

These same file systems also lack any form of transaction control. This is the capability of the database management software to ensure that only complete transactions are posted to the accounting database. This is achieved by recording all transaction activity in logs so that the database can always be returned to a consistent state. Without such transaction control, any form of system crash means that the data has to be restored from the last backup, and data entered since that backup is lost. A frustrating rekeying of data is the only option for the accounting department.

(l) Accounting systems lacked the scaleability needed for business growth.

Most businesses operate in a mode that assumes growth. In contrast, most accounting software is not capable of growing with the business because it is not scaleable. Accounting software is often not designed to handle three types of growth scenario:

- Increased transaction volume
- Increased user connectivity
- Increased user activity

Increased transaction volume and user connectivity is usually a direct consequence of business growth either through increased market share, entering new markets, or absorbing acquired businesses. Increased user activity is often caused by day- or month-end processing peaks or the seasonal activity spikes common to consumer-oriented businesses.

These and other problems that are related to the use of specific accounting software or specific hardware platforms mean that many accounting software users and managers are frustrated with their current systems. Many businesses have realized that one of their primary information assets—their accounting system—is not delivering the quality and quantity of information they need in a timely manner.

3.4 MARKET RESPONSE

One direct consequence of the problems of host-centric software systems and the limited vision of their vendors was the move toward so-called open systems from the early 1980s onward. The UNIX operating system provided the software foundation for this movement. The academic roots of UNIX meant that this operating system was not associated with any specific vendor; it was freely available or sold at low cost and was easily extensible. UNIX was seen as a viable alternative to proprietary host-centric operating systems from IBM, DEC, and others. As UNIX gained commercial credibility, all the main computer hardware firms developed a UNIX-based server range and offered it as an alternative to their proprietary hardware families. UNIX was dubbed an open system for these reasons:

- The specifications and source code for the core UNIX operating system was placed in the public domain.
- Commercial implementations of UNIX were not associated with any one specific vendor, and offered a choice of operating platforms.
- UNIX application software was portable across multivendor hardware families, allowing customers to mix-and-match vendor equipment.

Open systems proved popular both with business users and software vendors. This is because open systems removed that locked-in feeling associated with proprietary host-centric software and offered a larger potential market to software developers. The move to open systems opened a window of opportunity quickly exploited by a new generation of hardware vendors such as Sun Microsystems and Silicon Graphics, among others.

(a) The Short-Term Solution: Rehosting

Before vendors took the plunge into developing true client/server accounting applications, they used a variety of short-term measures to try to alleviate user frustration with their software. These measures can be termed rehosting, because essentially the design and function of the applications software itself did not change, merely one aspect of its deployment. These measures can be characterized as short-term because in each case they only solved a part of the overall problem. The real problem was that accounting software was out of step with the technology around it.

(i) Rehosting the Server

Rehosting the server was the reaction of many vendors to user concerns about the cost and openness of their accounting software. Rehosting the server means moving the whole accounting application onto another computer platform. Providers of IBM mainframe accounting software introduced versions of their packages that could be rehosted onto cheaper and more flexible IBM midrange platforms, such as the AS/400 family. Providers of midrange software on proprietary platforms such as the DEC VAX family introduced versions of their software that could be rehosted onto UNIX platforms. In all cases the software remained essentially the same; it was simply ported to a new server platform. For many customers this rehosting alone could mean substantial savings. Moving from Dun & Bradstreet's M-Series IBM mainframe software to its Millenium Series UNIX-hosted software could allow a mainframe to be switched off or redeployed. This in turn could mean that the reduction in ongoing service and maintenance costs would pay for the rehosting exercise within as little as a year or two.

(ii) Rehosting the Database

This was another rehosting option to increase system productivity or accessibility. Rehosting the database meant remaining on the same server platform but rehosting only the accounting data. In this scenario, a vendor would provide the ability for their accounting software to store data in alternative database management systems. On mainframe platforms this meant rehosting data from proprietary file formats such as IBM's VSAM to a more open relational database management system (RDBMS) such as IBM's DB2. On midrange platforms such as the DEC VAX, this meant moving from DEC's proprietary RMS file format to a third party RDBMS such as ORACLE from Oracle Corporation. Productivity rather than cost benefit was the main impetus for data rehosting because more and cheaper system development and decision support tools could interact with the new RDBMS than the previous database or file system.

(iii) Rehosting the Application Interface

This answered concerns about ease of use. To some extent a reaction to the rapid success of Microsoft's Windows graphical user interface (GUI), vendors began changing the look and feel of their applications. Initially this was called screen scraping. The original green-on-black terminal screens were literally scraped away and replaced with more colorful, graphical screens. These made the system look more interesting and provided some compatibility with the other GUI-fronted applications appearing on desktop PCs. Screen scraping did not require local processing resource and could still allow users to operate with dumb terminals.

Soon screen scraping was replaced with more graphical front ends, locally resident applications that offered a GUI compliant with IBM's common user access (CUA) specification. As more and more terminals were replaced by desktop PCs, more sophisticated GUIs became practicable from the availability of local CPU, RAM, and disk power to run the more resource intensive interfaces offered by the Apple MacOS or Microsoft Windows.

3.5 CONCLUSION

New business strategies and tactics, the pace of technology change, and the search for an alternative to host-centric computing are all part of the foundation for the rise in popularity of the client/server computing model, which in turn provided the impetus for the development of a new generation of accounting software. This was recognized as early as the late 1980s by client/server application pioneers such as PeopleSoft Corporation, which was founded in 1989 and is now a leading player in the client/server accounting market. Part two discusses the client/server computing architecture in more detail to show why this new platform holds such great promise for delivering new and improved accounting software to add value to your business management systems.

PART TWO

The Client/Server Architecture

CHAPTER 4 CLIENT/SERVER CONCEPTS

Client/server is a computing architecture, a way of computing that is fundamentally different from the centralized model that characterizes host-centric computing. While the term client/server appears to indicate a simple two-part architecture of clients and servers, in reality client/server is more complex when it is deployed for managing business applications. Client/server is defined by a number of concepts that position the architecture as new and different when compared to the traditional host-centric computing architecture.

CHAPTER 5 CLIENT/SERVER SYSTEMS

Client/server systems can be characterized by a computing architecture that uses combinations of clients and servers in a collaborative architecture distributed over a network. This chapter details the role played by clients, servers, and networks in client/server computing.

CHAPTER 6 CLIENT/SERVER APPLICATIONS

Client/server applications are different from the monolithic software applications of the past. The applications can be partitioned into at least three tiers: presentation or user services, business-rule or application services, and database services. The role of databases and structured query language (SQL) is discussed as they are utilized by client/server applications.

CHAPTER FOUR

Client/Server Concepts

4.1 INTRODUCTION

There are certain concepts that are fundamental to client/server computing that are mentioned when discussed either as a technology or as an application-deployment architecture. The purpose of this section is to briefly discuss some of these concepts in the context of accounting systems.

4.2 DISTRIBUTED, PARTITIONED APPLICATIONS

Client/server systems are distributed and run applications that can be partitioned across clients and servers. Distributed systems spread the processing load across multiple computers and balance that load by moving data and processes around these computers using a network. Users of distributed systems may be located locally or remotely to these resources. The applications they use may be running locally or remotely; the data they enter or access may be stored locally or remotely. This is a computing architecture that is fundamentally different from a host-centric design in which all resources are concentrated to one place, applications are always run remotely, and data is always accessed remotely.

Client/server applications are partitioned, which means that they are designed to allow discrete application components to be distributed and located wherever it makes sense for the business' use of the application. The presentation of a client/server application may be separated from the business rules and the data management. Each of these application layers or components can be located on their own separate and dedicated resource. Genuine client/server applications are highly granular in design. As a result, the Internet is an ideal architecture for deploying client/server applications because the application and data can be run from an Internet server (remotely) or from a local desktop PC (locally) and the client/server application can be deployed to accommodate either mode of Internet computing.

4.3 SERVICE-DRIVEN, DESKTOP-CENTRIC

Client/server is fundamentally a distributed architecture, which means that resources are not typically concentrated to one place but spread over multiple computing platforms and locations. The architecture is conceptually like a consumer warehouse, where consumers wander the warehouse shelves picking and choosing the products and services they want to purchase. In client/server the consumer is the desktop client and the warehouse is the range of services provided by servers on the network. Just as consumers flock to warehouse outlets with the widest range of products on their shelves, so client/server systems are more or less information rich depending on the range of services provided by the networked servers.

It could be argued that client/server has turned mainframe computing on its head, as depicted in Figure 4.1. Instead of a mass of largely dumb terminals slavishly attached to the powerful mainframe host, client/server offers a number of willing servers accessible from a desktop workstation. The center of power is not the server, which may only provide one of a number of specialized services, but the

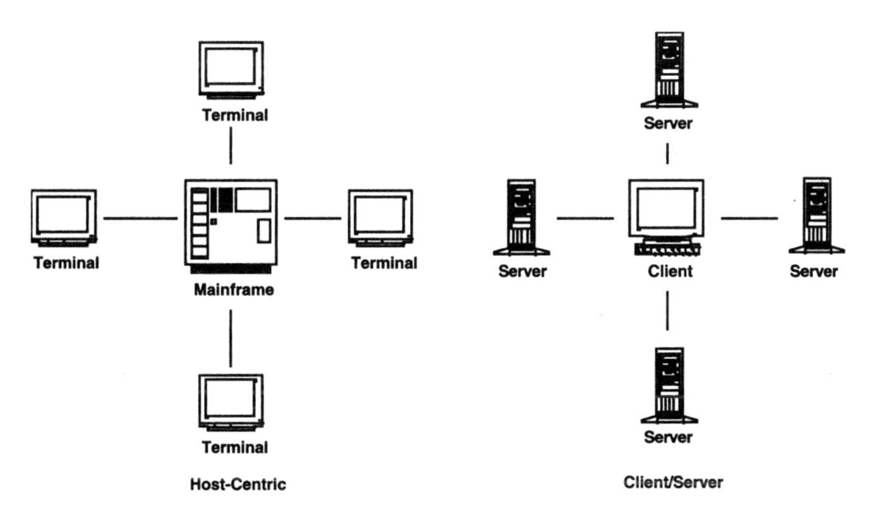

Figure 4.1. Turning Computing on its Head.

desktop client that can pick and choose between the services it wants to use. This can come as a culture shock to many corporate information systems departments who may resist the change to their mainframe's omnipotent status and by extension the change in the status of their relationship with the users who are their customers.

Accounting-system managers benefit from this change because instead of an information systems architecture focused on nurturing a central host computer, client/server introduces an architecture focused on the users and the services necessary to performing their jobs more effectively.

4.4 WORKGROUP-FOCUSED, NETWORK-DEPENDENT

The host-centric computing model centralizes all application software, data, and systems management on one or more host computers. All users, whatever their information domain—such as accounting, manufacturing, or sales administration—and wherever they are physically located, are all managed by the same resource and are all subject to the availability and reliability of that resource. If the resource is lightly loaded, performance is not an issue; if the resource is heavily loaded, all information domains may suffer from degraded performance irrespective of whether they are the cause of that degradation or not. If the host crashes for any reason, all users dependent on that resource are impacted and information processing effectively stops. Here the bottleneck is the ability of the host to manage the processing load at any point in time and to deliver maximum availability.

Client/server encourages system managers to focus on providing resources of two types, connected by networking:

- Resources exclusive to a specific workgroup
- Resources shared by many workgroups

In client/server computing, each workgroup may make use of its own specific server resources on the network and may share other resources. So users in the accounting domain may be accessing their own dedicated database and application servers while sharing the cross-workgroup e-mail, print, and fax servers, for example. By keeping resources discrete in this way, each workgroup feels less impact from the rise and fall of another workgroup's processing load and is insulated from downtime due to failure of another workgroup's resources.

However, this introduces a new problem because the central host resource is now replaced by the network bandwidth. The bottleneck potential is the ability of the network to manage varying levels of traffic efficiently. If the network itself crashes, it is no different from the host computer crashing: All users are still affected. Many information systems departments are not yet convinced that networks are fully mature enough to replace host systems entirely, especially in large, geographically dispersed environments.

4.5 RIGHTSIZED APPLICATIONS

Downsizing, upsizing, and rightsizing are all terms associated with client/server computing, but in reality have little to do with it. From an accounting-system perspective these terms are usually defined as follows:

- Downsizing is moving accounting systems from proprietary to open-computing platforms and using the new cost and processing efficiencies to redeploy or cut head count. Downsizing has developed a negative connotation because of its association with job losses and the turmoil of change.
- Upsizing is a term used to describe moving a PC LAN-based accounting system onto a more scaleable server platform running a variant of UNIX or Microsoft NT while moving accounting data from a flat-file storage system to an RDBMS. Upsizing may deliver cost savings in the medium to long term but is expensive in the short term.
- Rightsizing is the term used to describe moving accounting systems onto the most appropriate platform for the processing load. Many accounting systems were put on mainframes simply because they were there and it made sense to further leverage the value of the asset. However, when these accounting systems are serving 10-to-20-user workgroups it usually makes more sense if they are rightsized to a more appropriate computing model, such as PC LAN, a small UNIX, or Microsoft NT-level system.

Rightsizing is the most important of these three terms because it focuses on the question: What is the right computer platform for my accounting system? If this question is answered correctly, cost and productivity benefits will almost certainly follow. Rightsizing acknowledges that everything between the SOHO and Enterprise accounting models has its place, and that over time businesses should move up or down between the various accounting system models. Rightsizing focuses on delivering the right solution for the dynamic relationship between issues such as:

- Software functional needs
- Number of users connected

- Transaction processing loads
- Ease of use required
- Integration with other systems
- Hardware price/performance
- The projected future of all of the above

Downsizing, upsizing, and rightsizing have come to be associated with client/server for three reasons:

- Client/server computing has coincided with a general corporate momentum towards establishing more competitive benefit from their information technology.
- Client/server has provided a technology platform that enables downsizing, upsizing, and rightsizing initiatives to be undertaken.
- A decision to implement client/server computing is used both as a catalyst and an excuse for downsizing, upsizing, or rightsizing.

4.6 PROCESS REENGINEERING

Like the buzz words discussed in the previous section, reengineering, as an exercise in organizational transformation has also become a popular corporate strategy, particularly over the last decade. From a technological perspective, the interest in reengineering can also be seen as having simply paralleled the rise of client/server computing. In addition, the tools of reengineering, used for business process reengineering (BPR), such as process modelers, workflow, and document management systems, have also benefitted from the interest in client/server.

This is because client/server has offered a lower cost platform for delivering these tools to a wider market, thereby ensuring that the technology can reach a wider range of reengineering practitioners. In this sense client/server has helped increase the momentum of reengineering and continues to fuel this momentum as more vendors and products address this market. Without client/server, BPR vendors and products might have remained focused on mainframe platforms, reducing the prospective market for the tools and limiting the influence of BPR to the world's largest businesses.

Accounting departments have been easy targets for reengineering initiatives because many of their processes are easy to define, not mission-critical, and ripe for improvement. Consequently, many accounting software vendors are including some form of workflow technology into their new client/server accounting systems. As a result, the decision to investigate client/server accounting is often used as a pretext for BPR simply because it makes sense to leverage the change of system for this purpose—sweep out the old and bring in the new. Because client/server is a genuine shift in information technologies and attitudes it provides an ideal catalyst for a reengineering effort.

4.7 OLTP VERSUS OLAP

On-line transaction processing (OLTP) and on-line analytical processing (OLAP) are terms often mentioned in the client/server context. OLTP is the domain of financial services, utilities, airlines, retail, telecom providers, and others. These are the businesses processing high volumes of year-around transactions reflecting regular use of their services by a wide range of consumers. OLTP is focused on performance issues such as how many transactions can be processed per minute or second and how reliable and secure the transaction processing system is in operation. Just managing these transaction flows is an enormous processing and management task in its own right and demands the use of state of the art hardware and very large databases (VLDBs). Although it is making great strides, client/server computing has not yet replaced host-centric computing in many of the largest OLTP driven sites. In client/server computing OLTP is associated primarily with the use of an RDBMS for data management.

OLAP is a marketing term, coined in a white paper (i.e., a piece of marketing collateral) sponsored by Arbor Software, which has now achieved a life of its own. OLAP systems are concerned not with transaction processing but with information analysis and decision support. True OLAP systems depend not on relational but multidimensional databases that use a data structure more suitable for on-the-fly and ad hoc analysis consistent with decision support. The OLAP software market is developing rapidly, and many accounting software vendors are acquiring or incorporating OLAP technology as a means of differentiating their accounting suites and making them appeal to the business analysts and executives who need decision-support technology to increase their productivity.

The essential differences between OLTP and OLAP are:

Characteristic	*OLTP*	*OLAP*
Transaction type	Predictable	Unpredictable
Transaction duration	Short, repetitive	Long, ad-hoc
Transaction structure	Mixed-data elements	Dimensional data elements
Transaction Volume	High, at detail-atomic level	Low, at summary aggregation level
System Focus	Data entry	Data inquiry and reporting
System Users	Clerical	Analysts, managers
System Platform	Relatively high cost	Relatively low cost
System Deployment	Widely used	Narrowly used

4.8 CONCLUSION

Client/server is a different paradigm for computing than the host-centric paradigm it is replacing. It is a distributed architecture that is desktop centric and network dependent. Client/server provides an opportunity for businesses to rightsize applications, to reengineer business processes, and to focus on the differing needs of transaction processing versus decision support. Chapter 5 discusses the technology components of client/server computing in more detail.

CHAPTER FIVE

Client/Server Systems

5.1 INTRODUCTION

This section describes some of the key components of client/server systems when used to manage business applications, namely:

- Architecture: the overall client/server architecture
- Clients: local information processors
- Servers: remote service providers
- Networks: connectivity infrastructures

One simple way to view client/server versus the traditional host-centric model is to consider client/server as an architectural explosion of the mainframe. In other words, all the functionality that was once centralized and managed by the mainframe processor(s) has been distributed across multiple processors linked by a network, as depicted in Figure 5.1.

While this distributed architecture can introduce a number of benefits for business application users, it is also undoubtedly more complex to manage from an information systems perspective. So it is worth remembering that while client/server may appear easy to users of the technology, it is often a very difficult technology to

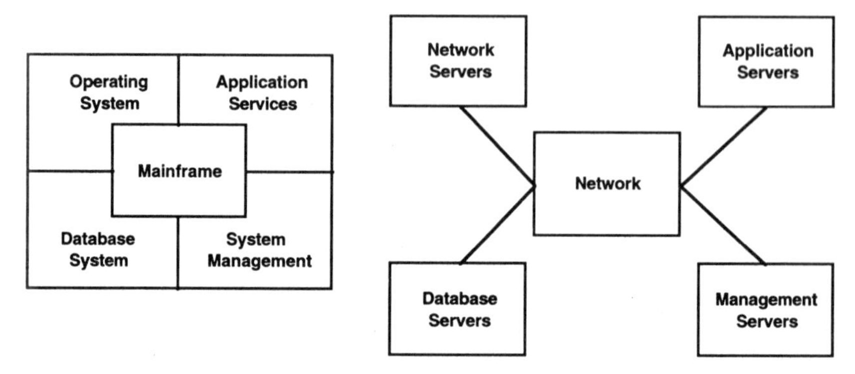

Figure 5.1. Exploding the Mainframe.

manage successfully for the people required to implement and maintain client/server systems.

5.2 ARCHITECTURE

Client/server is an architecture that partitions software applications and distributes the software components across logical devices called clients and servers that are connected by a communications mechanism, usually some form of network. A key point to understand is that client/server is not associated with any one vendor or hardware platform. It is not a proprietary architecture, but rather an open architecture. Client/server systems are heterogeneous: They may combine hardware and software from many vendors, which of course is why client/server can be complex to deploy and manage.

Also, client/server is an embracing architecture, especially from a hardware perspective. As vendors realize the attraction of its architecture to business application managers and users, they are moving to make sure that their hardware platforms can be embraced by client/server. Consequently, traditional mainframe and midrange computer vendors are working to integrate their hardware into client/server architectures that can already embrace PCs and other specialized Intel- or RISC-based hardware servers. Client/server is not a them-and-us situation of mainframes versus PCs, or UNIX versus AS/400; it is possible and desirable for all these platforms to perform their own role as clients or servers in a client/server architecture.

Client/server offers a very flexible information-processing architecture for these reasons:

- By partitioning software applications into smaller, more granular pieces, system managers have more choices as to how those pieces may be assembled for deployment and on what computing hardware they can be deployed.
- Because each software granule is essentially discrete, it may be enhanced or scaled independently of other pieces to provide more flexibility to cope with the changing pace of business demand.
- This granularity allows system managers to deploy client/server applications to small specialized workgroups or large generalized user communities by combining more or less computing resources together.
- The architecture encourages a mix-and-match computing deployment in which best-of-breed software and hardware from many vendors is combined to reach an ideal combination of functional fit and price/performance.
- The openness of the architecture makes it easier to plug in new technology as it becomes commercially available in order to keep systems in step with the relentless march of technological innovation.

Conventionally, client/server can be deployed either as a two- or three-tier architecture. The configurations outlined below show four typical deployments of client/server accounting systems. These are often described as two- or three-tier client/server configurations. The terms two tier and three tier refer to the way in which an accounting application may be partitioned for use in a client/server architecture. The three tiers are:

- Presentation services that manage the display and manipulation of data

- Application services that manage business rules and logic
- Database services that manage the raw application data

A two-tier application is simply a client/server application that is deployed in two layers:

- User-presentation services localized on the client
- Database and application services stored remotely on the database server

The distribution of the application services determines whether the system uses fat or thin clients. If the majority of applicaton services are located within the client application code, this is termed a fat client. Conversely, if the majority of application services are stored in or close to the database itself, a thin client configuration is all that is needed. A fat client requires more local resources than a thin client, which means the workstation must be configured with a faster processor and more free memory and disk space.

A three-tier application separates the business rules, or other business-process services such as batch processing and report production, from the database server by locating their application components on a physically separated application server. Separating application services in this way can deliver these benefits over a two-tier client/server.

- It centralizes business rules for easier administration.
- It creates a business-rule hub accessible to all applications for improved consistency.
- It offloads business-rule processing onto a dedicated server for better performance.
- It creates a more flexible deployment for more efficient resource management.
- It provides better scaleability to cope with the need for increased functional complexity.

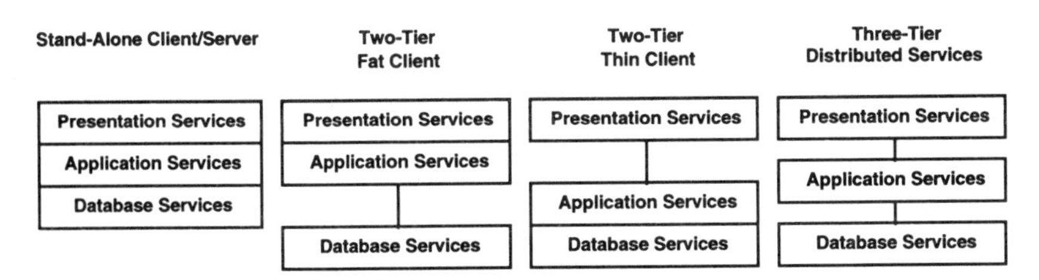

Figure 5.2. Four Client/Server Deployment Configurations.

Client/server systems can be very flexibly deployed either as a two- or three-tier homogenous (one vendor) or heterogeneous (multi vendor) solution. For example, an accounting system can use servers and clients all based on Microsoft's NT operating system, or a mixture of Microsoft Windows 95 clients connecting to Microsoft NT, UNIX, Novell Netware, or AS/400 servers if required. The four most commonly tiered deployments of client/server accounting applications are shown in Figure 5.2.

5.3 CLIENT

Essentially, the role of the client in a client/server architecture is to request and process information. To fulfill this role, the client depends on servers and the ability to manage communications between it and its supporting servers, usually through a network. The role of the client is summarized below:

Role	*Client*
Relationship	Data requester
Processing	Information processor
User location	Local
Software	Application-centric

Although client/server can be deployed on a single computer, for managing business applications the client is almost always separated from the servers and connected either locally through network cabling or remotely through dedicated or public-telephone dial-up lines. Clients are often depicted as desktop PCs, but in reality can be one of many types of devices as shown in Figure 5.3.

The range of potential client devices is expanding all the time. Computing clients can of course include laptop computers, dumb terminals, or other servers that can both provide services to a group of clients and be a client of another server. More specialized devices such as automatic teller machines (ATMs) and self-standing information kiosks may also be clients. We are also on the verge of seeing televisions, VCRs, and other home-entertainment devices also becoming clients on client/server entertainment networks. However, it is fair to say that for most business accounting software users, the client will be a PC running a version of Microsoft Windows, a UNIX workstation, or an Apple Macintosh PC.

For accounting users, client application software is primarily concerned with data entry, data presentation, and data manipulation or analysis. Because the actual client application software may need to be stored locally and the data it manages may be voluminous and

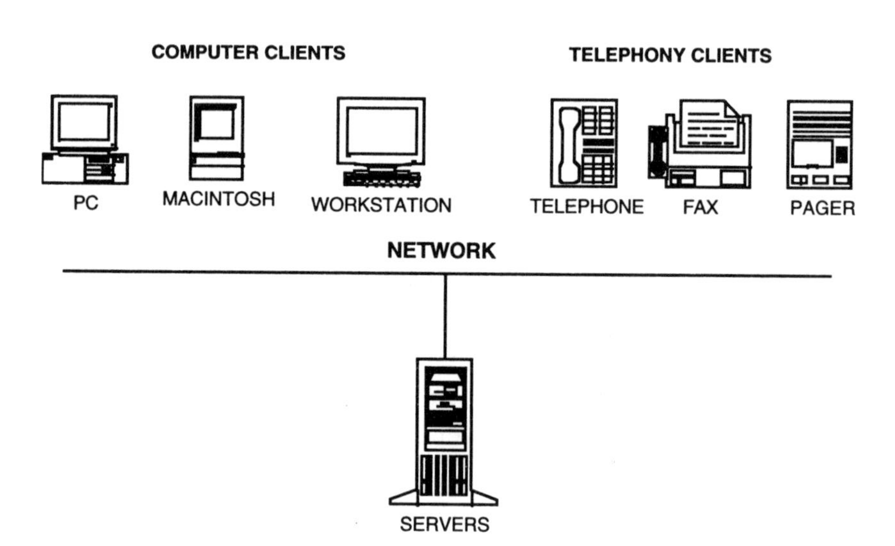

Figure 5.3. A Range of Clients.

need to be recalled after a client machine is switched off, clients must offer local storage in the form of a hard disk. Also, because most client/server software uses a graphical-user interface that typically demands high available memory to perform effectively and makes use of many connectivity drivers to manage communication with the servers, clients also need higher random-access memory and faster processors than average. This demands that a client PC typically be configured with an Intel 486 processor or better, a 500MB disk drive or better, and 16–32MB of RAM.

Consequently a client can cost up to ten times the price of a traditional dumb terminal linked to a mainframe. While many organizations can convert their existing desktop PCs into clients, there are also many businesses that will need to scrap hundreds of terminals and retool with state-of-the-art PCs. Even those with PCs on the desktop may need to upgrade their specification or reassign low-specification PCs to other departments that do not yet use client/server applications and purchase new PCs for accounting. The essential message here is that nobody should imagine that client/server architectures are cheap to setup and maintain.

5.4 SERVER

Essentially, the role of the server in a client/server architecture is to manage and deliver data or to provide other application services to clients. To fulfill this role, the server depends on an ability to manage communications between itself and the clients that it supports, usually through a network. The role of the server is summarized below:

Role	*Client*
Relationship	Data provider
Processing	Data repository
User Location	Remote
Software	Database-centric

In a client/server architecture there are three main types of server, and each performs different roles:

Role	*Description*
Network Server	These servers provide the networking and other infrastructure services shared by all users of the accounting system: for example, file, print, e-mail, and remote-access services.
Database Server	This server hosts the RDBMS engine used by the accounting system to manage the accounting data. The database may also store the business rules and logic of the accounting application encapsulated in database objects such as stored procedures or triggers.
Application Server	This server can be used for any combination of these three purposes: 1. To manage the accounting rules and logic when this information is separated from either the client or the database server 2. To manage transaction-intensive processes such as batch processing and financial reporting in order to offload processes from either the client or the database server 3. To manage ancillary services that are complementary to the accounting system such as workflow, image, or document management servers.

In client/server environments, network servers are shared by many applications, not just accounting. However, a client/server accounting application will always have at least one database server. If it is a three-tier application it may also have one or more application servers. Currently, the most popular hardware platforms for running client/server accounting servers are:

- RISC hardware supporting variants of the UNIX operating system
- Intel or RISC hardware supporting the Microsoft NT operating system
- IBM AS/400 hardware supporting the OS/400 operating system

Novell's Netware and IBM's OS/2 are also viable server-operating systems but have proven less-popular choices by users or vendors as a server platform for accounting systems. The chart below shows how each of the most popular computing platforms is typically utilized as a server in a client/server accounting system:

Platform and OS	*Database Server*	*Application Server*	*Network Server*
Intel PC and NetWare	✓	✗	✓
Intel PC and OS/2	✓	✗	✓
Intel/RISC and NT	✓	✓	✓
Intel/RISC and UNIX	✓	✓	✓
AS/400 and OS/400	✓	✓	✗
Mainframe	✓	✗	✗

5.5 NETWORKS

Networks are the communication infrastructures of client/server computing, providing the means for requests and data to pass between clients and servers. Networks are the essential third man of client/server computing. A network may be used to link local and remote clients and servers together. Although a network may be configured to run like a host-centric system as a star, in which all the network nodes are attached eventually to the host, most client/server networks are configured as a bus with devices strung along the bus backbone as shown in Figure 5.4.

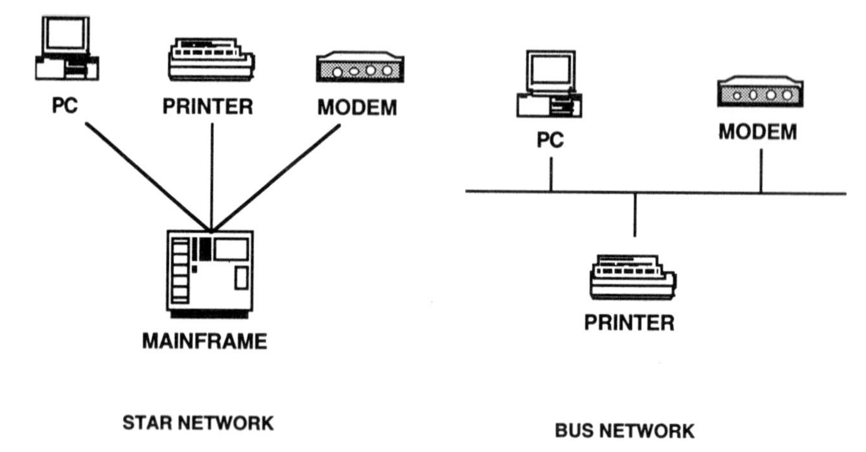

Figure 5.4. Star and Bus Networks.

There are a number of different network topologies, such as:

- Peer-to-peer
- Local area networks (LANs)
- Wide area networks (WANs)
- Value added networks (VANs)

Peer-to-peer is the odd man out in that it describes a network architecture in which each connected device is essentially equal and may communicate directly with another device. In other words each network node may act either as both a client and a server. Currently, peer-to-peer networking is used for small workgroups ranging from 2 to 10 users. LANs and WANs use dedicated-server computers to perform specific tasks that can be shared by the workstation nodes attached to the network. The basic tasks performed by network servers are to manage sharing among network users of:

- Data files and databases
- Printers and other output devices
- Other peripherals such as modems and CD-ROMs

While LANs and WANs both make use of dedicated servers there are a number of essential differences between the two network deployments, namely:

Property	*LAN*	*WAN*
Number of users	Lower	Higher
Location of users	Local/Focused	Remote/Dispersed
Types of network	Homogenous	Heterogeneous
Reach	Domestic/Internal	International/External
Complexity	Lower	Higher
Platforms	PC-dominated	Mixed

VANs (value-added networks) are a development of WANs in that they are wide-area networks but are usually designed to provide a service that is shared by the customers who use the network. Most of the traffic of electronic document interchange (EDI) is managed by VANs. The VAN is designed to allow suppliers and customers to interact with each other across a private network in order to carry out the business of document interchange.

The Internet and its sibling Intranet are also examples of VANs in that they are wide-area and provide a service over and above the networking itself. The Internet is essentially a public VAN, which is part of its attraction because it provides a free communication backbone that anybody can hook into without the steep fees associated with privately run VANs. The Internet and intranets are discussed in more detail in section 8.12 of the book.

There are many technologies and products that combine to deliver client/server networking in a corporate environment, but the emerging standard for transporting data across a network in the client/server environment is Transmission Control Protocol/Internet Protocol (TCP/IP). TCP/IP originated from the U.S. Department of Defense and has risen in popularity because of its association with the UNIX operating system and the growing need for interconnectivity between networks.

From a client/server perspective there are two areas of networking that are proving problematic. One is the bandwidth of current networks, the other is the sophistication of tools to manage the growing complexity of networks. Bandwidth affects the quantity of data that can be transported across a network. By increasing bandwidth one can either push more data through the network pipe or push less data faster. Increased bandwidth means that systems may either perform faster or handle greater data loads and different types of data such as sound and image. As the scope and complexity of multivendor client/server networks increase, the need for software tools to monitor and manage networks is becoming more critical. While clients and servers as components of client/server are easily scaleable, the issues of bandwidth and network-management tools may limit the scaleability of client/server networks for use in the world's larger businesses.

5.6 CONCLUSION

Client/server systems use a distributed architecture to deploy computing resources across clients and servers connected across a network. Client/server applications are also partitioned to allow them to be deployed in varying combinations across these clients and servers. Clients may utilize many types of computing and non-computing devices and may more or less localize processing resources. Servers may be performing one of a number of processing roles that represent individual pieces of the traditional, host-centric processing architecture. Client/server networks may be local- or wide-area based, and the availability of network bandwidth has a key influence on overall system performance. Because of the distributed nature of client/server resources and applications, two key benefits of the architecture are deployment flexibility and component scaleability.

CHAPTER SIX

Client/Server Applications

6.1 INTRODUCTION

Applications software written for client/server is different because it is not monolithic in design. In the past, most application software was written as one continuous source code that was deployed in the form of a single executable. Naturally a corporate-level, multimodule application such as an accounting or manufacturing system could be positively labyrinthine in the density of its programming code. Only powerful host computers had the resources to run and manage this type of program because it often demanded high amounts of available memory and disk capacity. There was no question of running this type of program on a desktop PC because the PC simply could not handle it. In this scenario, users of applications essentially never ran their accounting application at all: They simply interacted with the program running on the host through the window on their terminal.

Client/server introduces a whole new way of looking at how an application should be designed and deployed. As discussed already, client/server is a partitioned architecture that encourages the breaking down of computing resources into logical and physical components that can be distributed across a network. Consequently, client/

server applications can be exploded into smaller granular components and then distributed across a network. A typical client/server application would have four levels of partitioning granularity as shown in Figure 6.1.

Each of these broad categories of application partition can be further broken down into many more detailed subcategories. Potentially, individual application granules can be combined together and located either on clients or servers depending on what makes sense from a deployment perspective. Breaking down applications in this way makes them more manageable, flexible, and scaleable. However, while it can make applications more manageable from a development perspective, it can also make them less manageable when they are deployed because each of these pieces must know where the other piece is located and somehow manage communication among themselves. In this scenario applications become like data—they are broken down into smaller pieces and then reassembled as required when users demand access to specific combinations of functionality.

Although beyond the scope of this discussion, client/server introduces an ideal logical platform for the deployment of OO (object-oriented) software applications that are largely focused on the delivery of discrete, granular, and interactive business objects. This is one reason many business application vendors, including many accounting software vendors, are embracing OO development methods and releasing applications software based on the principle of building applications from reusable components.

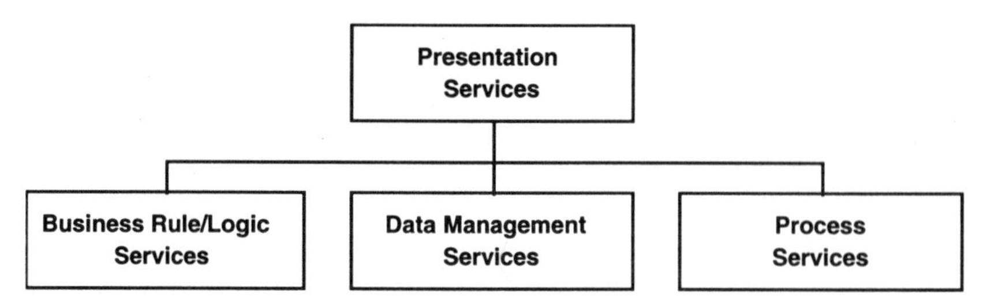

Figure 6.1. Client/Server Application Partitions.

6.2 DATABASES

Along with graphical-user interfaces, client/server is also linked to the rise of the relational database as the core of corporate information management. The range of database servers managed by a client/server system is an indication of the richness of the information available to clients who access those servers. Databases are an essential part of the client/server landscape because they act as repositories for:

- Textual and numeric data
- Sound and image data
- Document and software object data

(a) Flat Files

Many of the accounting systems used on mainframe and mini systems today do not use a database, but rather a file system. By comparison with today's database technology these file systems are relatively unsophisticated. File systems stored data in logical buckets called fields and records; physically the data was a long string of numbers and letters. Each file contained a number of record types: for example mixing account, transaction, and balance records into in one file as shown in Figure 6.2. For the accounting application soft-

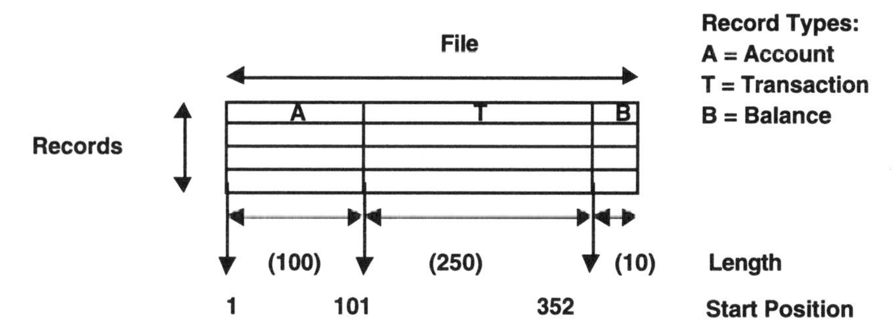

Figure 6.2. Positional File Structures.

ware to manage the file, it was very important to know what the record type was, where it began in the file, and how long it was.

This positional structure means that there are two key problems with file systems: They are inflexible and difficult to access. Inflexible because adding new record types or changing the length of existing record types caused havoc with the software used to manage, query, or report data in the file. Difficult to access because each file system was essentially unique; there was no standard means for accessing file data so every query and reporting tool was a one of.

The file systems used in accounting software are complex: Reorganizing data to meet changing information needs is not a trivial task. In addition, file systems were expected to operate statically on a host computer not dynamically across a network. This design means a simple information request from a network workstation, say for an account balance, may require whole ledger files to be transported from a server to the desktop PC. This is an inefficient way to manage data in a network environment.

File systems have some benefits. Because they are simple structures they can offer fast performance in a low-transaction volume site. File systems are usually bundled with the accounting software so there is no need to go out and buy a database engine. File systems require low maintenance—except when they go wrong—which means you may not need to hire a database administrator. However, the benefits of file systems do not outweigh the drawbacks unless the business using them is small or very simple.

(b) Relational Databases for OLTP

Over the last decade, the relational database management system (RDBMS) has become the technology of choice for on-line transaction processing (OLTP). This is the high-volume processing of predictable, structured transactions such as ATM withdrawals, airline reservations, or catalog orders. The structured query language (SQL) has become the standard for accessing data in an RDBMS, either in its native form or as utilized by emerging commercial data access standards such as Microsoft's Open Database Connectivity (ODBC).

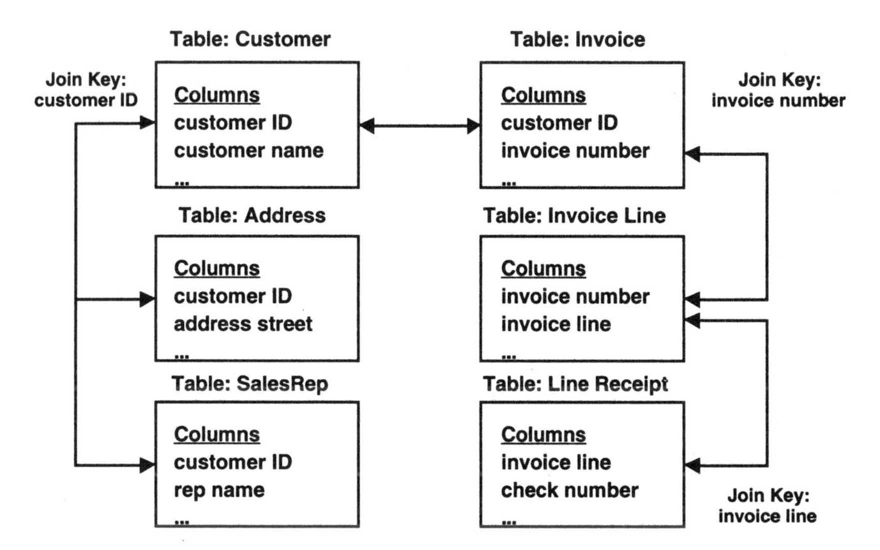

Figure 6.3. Joining Customer and Invoice Data.

The RDBMS and SQL emerged from research at IBM labs in the 1970s and the pioneering work of Dr. E. F. Codd. The commercial realization of this research was a database architecture that was both more adaptable and easier to access—solving two of the main problems of file systems.

Instead of a big file with multiple record types, relational database design demands a more atomic organization in which the data is broken down into smaller structures represented to users as tables and columns. To accommodate change you simply add new tables to the database or new columns to existing tables. To view the data differently you use joins to build a new logical view of the data by combining multiple columns from related tables together. Tables are related by a join key value, such as a customer identifier (ID) or an invoice number as shown in Figure 6.3. SQL provides the language for managing these tables, columns, and joins. Accounting data is in fact highly suitable for this type of structure.

When accounting data is managed in a relational database, system managers and accounting users can take advantage of a wide range of business benefits including:

Benefit	*Description*
Performance	Handling high volumes of transaction processing if required
Scaleability	Scaling up to handle increasing transaction or user loads
Security	Multilevel security for access to database structures and data
Accessibility	Data access from desktop tools through SQL connectivity
Adaptability	Database structures can be easily changed or expanded
Reliability	Reliable recovery from failure through use of transaction logs
Replication	Automatic copying of data from one database to another

However, there are more costs associated with using an RDBMS compared to a file system. Generally the database does not come with the accounting system so it must be purchased separately, and license fees can be steep. Most RDBMS engines benefit from a dedicated database administrator to set up, maintain, and tune the database for optimum performance. An RDBMS often requires database servers configured with very large amounts of spare disk and RAM in order to perform acceptably. On the other hand, dozens of inexpensive graphical query and reporting tools now support SQL and can connect to a wide range of popular RDBMS engines. This accessibility benefit alone is worth moving accounting onto a relational architecture for many businesses.

(c) Multidimensional Databases for OLAP

While the RDBMS maybe the king of OLTP, many analysts and users believe multidimensional databases are superior for on-line analytical processing (OLAP). OLAP is a marketing term for the kinds of queries and reports that managers and analysts need to do to manage a business and assist with decision support. One way to understand OLAP is to contrast it with OLTP:

OLTP	*OLAP*
Data-entry and input intensive	Data-inquiry and analysis intensive
Short duration transactions, often single table	Long duration queries using multitable joins
Regular transaction throughput	Random query requests
Predictable transaction load highs and lows	Unpredictable query load highs and lows
Rapid acceptance of transaction input	Rapid reanalysis of retrieved data
Single-application domain	Cross-application domain

OLAP uses the multidimensional database engine to provide the speed and data navigation capabilities that this type of decision support activity demands. The key difference between multidimensional and other database technologies is that it can provide a data value for every intersection of multiple dimensions represented in the data, as indicated in Figure 6.4. Let's say you are tracking actual sales dollars and you want to analyze these actuals by six dimensions: line of business (3), product SKU (1000), city (50), state (10), rep (20), and month (12). A multidimensional database would expect to be able to find a dollar value, or no value, for every intersection across all six dimensions—some 36 million or so values in any one year.

Because of this structure, and because small multidimensional databases can be held entirely in memory, you can expect very fast performance during ad hoc analysis of your sales information. Multidimensional structures provide an optimum architecture for data drilldown, focusing, and rotation. Drilldown is the navigation from summary data to detail transaction data. Focusing is the expansion

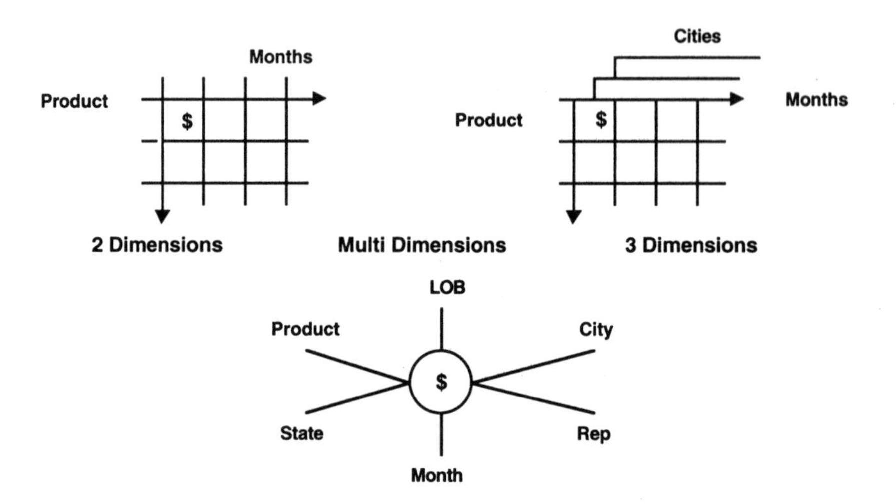

Figure 6.4. Two, Three, and Multidimensional Data.

and collapsing of data: from year to quarter to period for example. Rotation is the pivoting of the dimensional axis: switching from product sales by month to product sales by city for example.

Some information systems (IS) departments are considering or implementing a client/server accounting architecture that encompasses a relational database server for transaction processing and a multidimensional database server for decision support. Despite the cost and administrative burden of doing this, a dual database server architecture can ensure that decision support does not suffer at the expense of transaction processing. After all, inputting data into your database is costly, and extracting it is where the profit lies. Interest in OLAP from customers has stimulated the accounting vendors to introduce their own links to third party OLAP tools and to multidimensional database engines such as Arbor Software's Essbase.

(d) Object Databases

While the relational architecture dominates the client/server accounting software market and multidimensional databases gradually gain more popularity, others look to a future managed by object databases

(ODBMS). As an accounting system manager you may be familiar with the concepts of document imaging and workflow. Document imaging creates digital versions of invoices, checks, and other accounting documents. It allows the user to tag the document image to a specific accounting transaction so the source document can always be viewed on screen. These digital documents are a form of multimedia data that an ODBMS is optimized to handle. As workflow and process automation has gained prominence due to the popularity of corporate reengineering, the ODBMS may become a key database architecture for managing the transaction flows within an accounting system.

An ODBMS is designed to manage multimedia data objects—an object being a discrete piece of software that encompasses both data and its behavioral methods. So in the case of a document such as a sales invoice, the database stores not only the sales invoice information itself (its attributes), but also stores the code that determines how that information can be manipulated (its methods). This is usually represented as a kernel of data attributes surrounded by its manipulation methods, as seen in Figure 6.5.

In the future it is reasonable to assume that accounting systems will be expected to include the capability to manage documents, sound, and vision as well as workflow process maps. In fact, the accounting systems of the future will themselves almost certainly be assembled on the

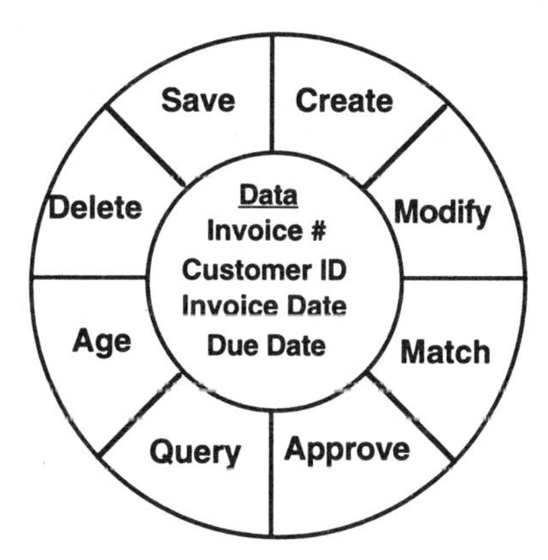

Figure 6.5. An Invoice Object Data and Methods.

fly from components called business objects that will be stored either locally on a client or on a local, remote, or Internet server. The most likely database technology to manage this component-based business management architecture will be an ODBMS.

(e) Select the Right Database for the Job

Clearly, there are many options for data management in a client/server system with at least three database technologies for managing different functional needs, as summarized below:

Accounting Mode	*Acronym*	*Database Technology*	*Acronym*
Transaction Entry	OLTP	Relational	RDBMS
Decision Support	OLAP	Multidimensional	MDBMS
Documents and Workflow	BPR	Object	ODBMS

There is no right database for client/server, only the right database for the functional need. A file system may not be as suitable as an RDBMS for managing the corporate database, but could be the right system for managing local data on a laptop that acts as a mobile client to the main database server. A RDBMS may be right for transaction processing but not the correct choice for managing documents and images or providing decision support services. The challenge is to fit the database architecture to the business need, not the other way around. Luckily client/server is an architecture that allows you to mix and match these databases and does not limit your choice of database architectures as so many proprietary architectures did in the past.

6.3 INFRASTRUCTURE AND MIDDLEWARE

Infrastructure and middleware software are part of the plumbing of information systems: seldom seen but essential to the smooth running of accounting applications. This type of software is managed by an information systems department.

(a) Infrastructure

Infrastructure software provides the tools for managing client/server systems from an administrative perspective. This software is used for managing and monitoring either network configurations, traffic, performance, and security, or application configurations, locations, and change management. Currently these tools are immature by comparison with mainframe infrastructure software that has been enhanced over a couple of decades. Naturally this makes the deployment of complex client/server systems more difficult or even impossible, from an IS perspective. The infrastructure software offered by popular up-and-coming client/server operating systems such as Microsoft's BackOffice suite is not yet as robust or extensive as those provided by operating systems with more longevity such as variants of UNIX, or IBM's OS/400. Nevertheless the sophistication of infrastructure software is expected to increase quickly, if for no other reason than this situation provides an ideal entrepreneurial opportunity for software developers.

(b) Middleware

Middleware is a confusing term that can be used in a number of different ways when describing software or hardware components in a client/server system. Here, the term is used to categorize some specific software components that provide services to client/server business applications. These three types of components are:

- Translators
- Routers
- Supervisors

(c) Translators

Translators translate from one computing language or dialect to another. This type of middleware is often essential to provide client/server applications a means of access to a variety of database services. The translator takes a client query and translates it into something with which a specific database can work, then translates the database response so that the client application can manage the result. This type of middleware can allow an accounting application client to access from many different databases, as shown in Figure 6.6.

(d) Routers

Routers are middleware products that route information through gateways to a specific set of recipients. For example Microsoft's mail applications programming interface (MAPI) is a gateway and router for messages, providing an electronic mail-routing facility for MAPI

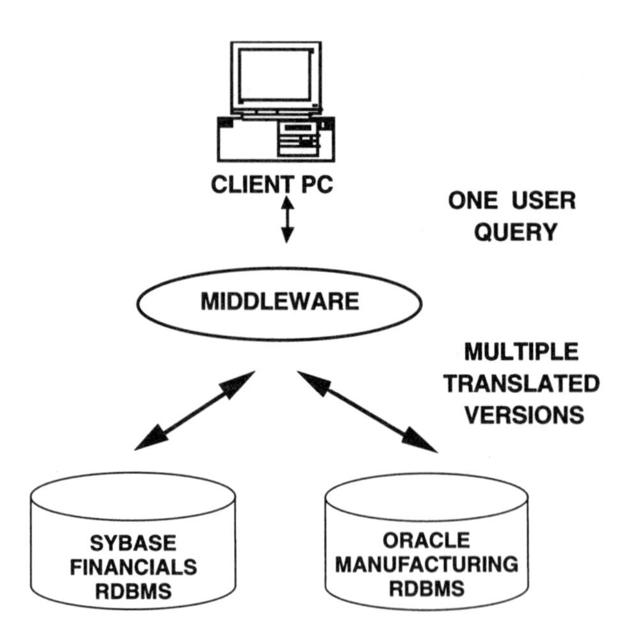

Figure 6.6. Mixed Databases Accessed by Middleware.

compliant applications. This type of middleware is used to disseminate information, such as financial reports, to persons outside the normal scope of an accounting system.

(e) Supervisors

Supervisors are middleware products that manage processes or transactions. Transaction monitors are examples of this type of middleware. A transaction monitor may be used to manage a complex accounting transaction that requires cross application or cross-platform processing. The transaction monitor acts as a form of traffic cop, directing the transaction to the best available resources, monitoring its progress until it either completes or fails, and keeping the accounting application informed of the progress of the transaction. Transaction monitors are essential for managing high-volume and complex transaction environments and are common on mainframe or UNIX platforms. This type of middleware is less mature for client/server systems, and at this time few client/server accounting systems can make use of this type of middleware.

6.4 SQL AND ODBC

Structured query language (SQL) and open database connectivity (ODBC) are both database access standards, the latter a superset of the former. Both are often important components of client/server applications. SQL has almost by accident become critical to the success of client/server as a business application platform. SQL was originally designed as a simple language for querying IBM mainframe databases and extending access to database information beyond the programmer. It subsequently became the primary language for creating, maintaining, and querying relational databases and has ridden on the commercial success of the RDBMS becoming an ISA and ANSI standard in 1986. While the language has many deficiencies and is by no means comparable to a generic programming language such as COBOL or C, it is being steadily enhanced by the standards committees and has been enhanced in numerous ways in its commercial variants.

However, the technical merits of the language itself are far less important than the fact that SQL has driven a data-access standard that has opened up relational databases to a wide range of desktop productivity software and put data in the hands of people who can turn it into information. Vendors have responded to the opportunity that SQL delivers by flooding the market with powerful but low-cost desktop query and reporting tools that are particularly useful for enhancing the value of accounting data. Even though SQL is typically implemented differently by different database vendors, SQL has now been packaged into so-called drivers so applications and users need not be concerned with which database they are trying to access as long as the appropriate database access driver is installed on their system.

This is where ODBC comes in. Although not an ISA or ANSI standard, and criticized for poor performance and its lowest-common-denominator approach, Microsoft's ODBC is quickly becoming the commercial database access standard for desktop applications. ODBC packages specific SQL-based database calls into a common interface to which application developers can write. As long as the appropriate ODBC driver is installed correctly on the desktop client, an ODBC compliant application can potentially interact with over a dozen different databases and file management systems, as indicated in Figure 6.7. While ODBC data access drivers may lack the speed and sophistication of native drivers, handwritten for a specific database, some client/server accounting software vendors are already using ODBC as their primary data-access technology. From a vendor perspective the benefit is that they only have to write code to one data-access interface but can then run a single version of their accounting application source code against one of many commercially popular databases.

SQL and ODBC have been crucial in delivering data to the desktop, giving vendors a common database access standard, and allowing users more choices in the database they can use as the founda-

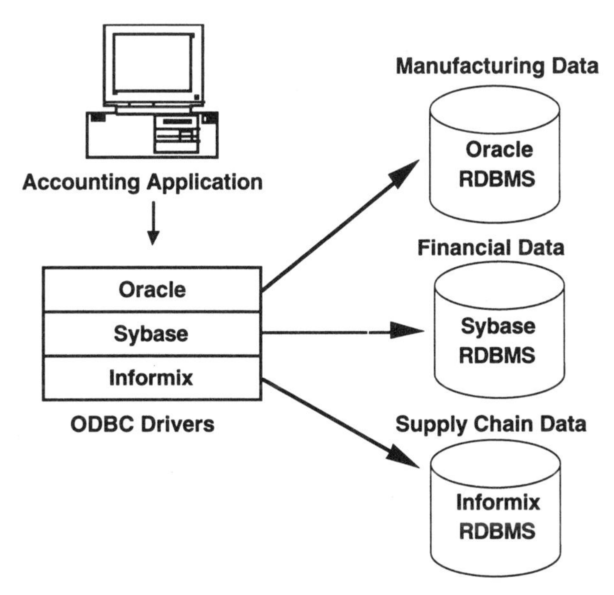

Figure 6.7. ODBC Database Accesss

tion of their accounting systems. Neither SQL or ODBC is necessary for a client/server system but both are commonly used in many client/server applications, especially database-driven applications such as accounting.

6.5 CONCLUSION

Client/server applications are different because they are designed to be distributed across network clients and servers for more flexible and scaleable deployment. Client/server accounting applications depend on database servers that may be running relational, multidimensional, or object-database management systems. To access and manage that data, client/server accounting applications may utilize a variety of middleware products and database access methods of which the most common are SQL and ODBC.

PART THREE

Client/Server Accounting

CHAPTER 7 CLIENT/SERVER ACCOUNTING CONCEPTS

Client/server accounting is the term used to describe accounting software applications designed to run on client/server computing architectures. There are many differences between traditional accounting applications and the client/server accounting applications that represent the new generation of accounting software. The aim of this chapter is to introduce some of the concepts and benefits of client/server accounting to provide a foundation for discussing how these concepts have been incorporated into the design of the new generation of client/server accounting applications.

CHAPTER 8 CLIENT/SERVER ACCOUNTING SOFTWARE DESIGN

True client/server accounting software is not just a port or conversion of mainframe or minicomputer accounting software to run on the client/server architecture, it is a ground-up rewrite and redesign. There are essentially three types of client/server accounting packages in the marketplace:

- Suites from new startup ventures that are still in the process of being rounded out with deeper functionality and a broader range of modules.
- New suites from vendors positioned in all accounting market segments that have been designed and written specifically for deployment on client/server platforms.
- Suites from vendors positioned in the mainframe and mini-accounting software segments that have been redesigned, but not necessarily rewritten, for use in a client/server environment.

In each case, new technologies such as electronic messaging, document management, workflow, and the Internet are rapidly being incorporated by vendors to enhance and differentiate their accounting applications. This chapter outlines how a wide range of complementary technology is impacting the design of client/server accounting applications.

CHAPTER SEVEN

Client/Server Accounting Concepts

7.1 INTRODUCTION

There are a number of concepts that can define client/server accounting. The aim of this section is to introduce the most important of them. The following nine concepts are introduced, discussed, and considered in terms of their business benefits.

- The use of relational databases for managing accounting data
- The use of graphical-user interfaces for presenting accounting data
- The deployment choices afforded by portable accounting software
- The use of granularity to deliver more flexible accounting software
- The ability of scaleable accounting software to accommodate growth
- The inclusion of tools to improve accounting software usability

- Development methods that make accounting software more adaptable
- Intelligent data transfer to make accounting software more cooperative
- The extending and expanding of the accounting information domain

7.2 RELATIONAL ACCOUNTING

Since the early 1990s, practically every accounting software vendor has moved the management of their accounting data onto a relational database management system (RDBMS). Even before the 1990s, pioneers of relational accounting such as Oracle Corporation and FourGen Software were delivering accounting applications on the ORACLE and Informix RDBMS engines respectively. To a great extent, the move to relational accounting does not reflect the superiority of relational databases over other options for managing accounting data but simply reflects the commercial success of the relational database as a tool for managing corporate data generally. As relational database technology has become a core component of corporate data management strategies, so information systems departments have pushed for accounting applications to be compatible with, or run on, the same database technology as other mission critical applications. Relational accounting has some drawbacks but also delivers a number of useful benefits for accounting systems.

(a) Relational Accounting Drawbacks

The first point to realize about relational accounting is that in most cases you must now buy the RDBMS licenses necessary to run the database itself, separately from your accounting software licenses. In the past, most accounting software came with a built-in proprietary database or file system that had either been licensed from a third party or built in by the accounting software vendor. The cost of this data management system was therefore bundled into the software price. Also, these built-in data management systems required little or no administrative overhead to maintain and tune. However, most RDBMS systems require a full- or part-time database administrator (DBA) on staff because extracting the best performance from a sophisticated RDBMS requires regular monitoring, maintenance, and tuning by trained staff. Relative to traditional accounting data management, relational accounting may cost more to acquire and maintain.

Because of the overhead required to deliver some of the benefits of relational accounting, an RDBMS may be slower than alternative accounting data management options in some cases. This is especially likely when posting new transactions or updating existing transactions in a low-transaction volume environment on low-specification equipment. A typical RDBMS is resource hungry—that is, it delivers its best performance when located on a multiprocessor server machine configured with high amounts of spare memory and disk capacity. This means that the server configurations purchased for a RDBMS-based accounting system are more expensive than for alternative data management options that require less memory or disk space. You can also expect to purchase one or more separate machines for the exclusive purpose of running the RDBMS: This machine is commonly known as a database server. Therefore in certain environments relational accounting may not deliver a performance gain and may require a more costly hardware infrastructure to support it.

(b) Relational Accounting Benefits

Despite these drawbacks, relational accounting delivers more advantages than disadvantages, especially for businesses that expect rapid growth or require better decision support functionality from their accounting system. The first point in favor of relational accounting is simply that accounting vendors are in the accounting applications business, not the database business. By separating the data management to a third-party product from another vendor—one focused on building database software—an accounting application vendor should be able to allocate more R&D money to its applications rather than maintaining a proprietary database or file system.

Riding on the back of the database vendor's R&D spend should mean accounting application vendors can deliver richer accounting functionality and have opportunities to leverage advantage from the RDBMS vendor's enhancing of its database product. A good example of the latter is replication, which is the ability of the database to automatically copy or publish data to another database, or receive or subscribe to such data from another database. All the leading RDBMS products now offer some form of data replication. Accounting applications can take advantage of this useful database feature, but the accounting vendors did not need to spend time and money developing replication functionality themselves, they can simply leverage the functionality offered by their chosen RDBMS.

(i) Relational Accounting: SQL

Every RDBMS uses some version of structured query language (SQL) to create, maintain, and query the database itself. Despite the known deficiencies of SQL for reporting accounting data and the variety of commercial implementations of the ANSI SQL standard, the fact remains that the applications software market has adopted SQL as its lingua franca for accessing RDBMS data. Consequently transaction data stored in relational accounting systems can now be directly accessed by a very wide range of desktop worksheet, query, and reporting tools. More than anything else, the commercial acceptance of SQL as a common database-access language has encouraged the market to develop a whole new generation of decision-support tools. Instead of limiting your choice of decision-support tools to those provided by the accounting vendor, you can now pick and choose from a vast array of inexpensive decision-support packages for enhancing the value of your accounting information asset.

By standardizing on SQL as their database-management language, RDBMS vendors have also done users of relational accounting applications another favor by giving them more options. In the past, accounting systems mostly offered just one option for their data management system, namely the database or file system embedded in the application. Many vendors, especially client/server accounting vendors, have constructed their applications so they can be connected to any one of a number of popular RDBMS products. Clearly this is less restrictive, but more importantly it allows a business two further advantages. First, an enterprise may use the same applications worldwide but use different RDBMS engines to manage the data in various locations for performance, cost, or local-support reasons for example. Secondly an enterprise may choose to change its RDBMS in order to benefit from a technology advantage or better-price performance offered by a competitive product without having to undergo a costly change to another accounting package because the same applications can be run against the new database.

(ii) Relational Accounting: Transaction Rollback

While purists can argue about whether the RDBMS is the optimal database architecture for accounting applications, the fact remains that most popular RDBMS engines offer specific features useful for managing accounting data. A key feature is transaction integrity. Through SQL, an RDBMS allows an application developer to ensure that only completed transactions are posted to the accounting database. If a transaction fails to reach its completion point, it is automatically rolled back to prevent the database from becoming out-of-balance.

Transaction rollback is made possible through use of a log in which the database manager automatically records all relevant activity. When a transaction fails, the database can undo all the changes made by working backwards through the log until it reaches the point immediately before the faulty transaction started. The same principle can apply in the event of a system crash. When the system restarts, the log is examined and all incomplete transactions are rolled back. Some systems offer roll-forward logs that replay the incomplete transaction back to the point at which the system crashed, which minimizes rekeying of data. As you might expect, the keeping of a log adds overhead to an RDBMS, especially when inputting new transactions or updating existing data. This typically makes an RDBMS slower at this kind of operation than a more simplistic file system without transaction rollback capabilities.

(iii) Relational Accounting: Replication

Replication is a database management feature that helps synchronize data between two databases. Essentially the database manager automatically controls the copying of data from one database to another so that at a given point in time they are synchronized. The sophistication of replication functionality varies considerably and may include:

- Uni- or bi-directional replication, from the parent to the child database, vice versa, or both
- Homogenous or heterogeneous replication between databases from either the same vendor or multiple vendors
- Publish and subscribe replication where it can be scheduled between the parent and child databases and limited to subscribing child databases
- Granular replication at database, business-object, table, or column level to reduce the replication load and improve performance
- Store and forward replication where changes to be replicated are stored in a queue that is flushed automatically each time a child database connects to the parent

Replication is useful in a number of scenarios, particularly for managing the relationship between a central accounting database and remote users of that database. Such a scenario might be a centralized sales-order, invoicing, and accounts-receivable relational accounting system that needs to provide information to a field salesforce equipped with laptops. Salespeople and territory managers can run a personal version of the central system RDBMS as an application on their laptop computers. The central system RDBMS can publish snapshots of sales-related data to the remote subscriber users in the field by allowing them to log in and download data. Data can then be replicated from the central database to the remote database. Clearly the same cycle can occur in reverse as field reps take orders that need to be uploaded and processed through the central receivables system. This moves data closer to its owners and avoids cumbersome and error-prone data imports and exports.

Replication technology is currently immature and its implementation varies widely across the leading relational database engines. However, replication has great potential for adding value to accounting systems. Intercompany journaling across databases and consolidation of month-end financial data are time-consuming accounting processes that could be significantly improved through the use of replication technology. Purchase-order data could be replicated from the customer's database to the supplier's database; or sales-order data could be replicated from the order taker's system to the supplier's system for handling drop shipments for example. We should certainly expect to see more advantage being leveraged from replication functionality by accounting applications over the next few years.

(iv) Relational Accounting: Database Access

The use of a relational database also encourages application developers to remove business rules, logic, and security from the application code and store it instead in the database. From a development perspective, the benefit of this is that the business rules are not duplicated and distributed over all the desktops running the accounting application but centralized in the database for easier maintenance. From a system management perspective, the benefit is that any application that attempts to access the accounting data is subject to the same security and constraints as a genuine accounting user, even though the application accessing the data may be a desktop worksheet, query, or reporting tool utilized by a nonaccounting user.

This means that casual accounting-system users such as analysts and managers can be given direct access to data, extending the reach of the system. In any case, if this is still not secure enough then IS can use SQL to construct views of the accounting data that restrict the depth and breadth of information accessible by these users. Views are virtual tables that the database creates based on a definition of tables and columns that should be displayed in the view. Users can then be limited to accessing these view tables rather than the actual data tables.

(v) Relational Accounting: Stored Procedures

Stored procedures are blocks of procedural code stored in the database that applications or database triggers (see *(vi)* on following page) can make use of to carry out a task. A stored procedure is different from regular program code because it is:

- Written in the language and variant of SQL that is specific to the RDBMS used
- Preparsed to ensure that it is syntactically correct and optimized for use
- Physically stored in the database and run by the database management system

Stored procedures are often used in accounting systems to run database-intensive tasks such as posting transactions or running reports; applying business rules and logic to processing; or managing basic tasks such as inserting, updating, and deleting database data. Stored procedures are very efficient ways to manage database data without using traditional programming code and require minimum amounts of memory and other processing resources. Because a stored procedure is parsed for correctness and its optimum execution plan stored when it is created and saved to the database, it is faster when it is run than raw SQL statements, which the system has to parse and optimize each time they are run. Typically a client/server accounting application that makes use of stored procedures—of which there may be many hundreds, even thousands—has been adapted more closely to a specific database environment. Stored procedures cannot be simply ported from one RDBMS to another, so some vendors have restricted use of this type of code in their applications specifically to make their applications more portable across multivendor RDBMS engines.

(vi) Relational Accounting: Triggers

Another feature of relational accounting common to most RDBMS products is the availability of triggers. A trigger is a piece of code that is stored in the database and automatically fired by the database manager in response to a specific database event, usually the insertion, updating, or deletion of a row or column in a database table. A trigger can also be used to fire off stored procedures that may carry out a complex set of functions—such as posting a batch of transactions or running a pack of financial reports. In any case triggers add value by allowing the database to carry out certain operations automatically such as:

- Recording the name of a user who tried to change an account code
- Recording the date and time a transaction was changed
- Ensuring that a transaction is in balance before it is posted to the ledger
- Alerting a manager to a budget overrun by sending a message
- Printing an audit trail automatically after a batch posting has completed
- Warning a user of unposted transactions before a report is to be run
- Checking that codes added to one table exist in other related code tables
- Deleting data from an address table when its customer owner is deleted

Triggers do impose an overhead on the database, which can complicate the database processing logic and impact performance, but they can also add significant value to an accounting system. Triggers can be used as the basis for managing:

- Referential integrity between tables to ensure that the accounting data and the relationships between the accounting tables stay accurate
- Auditing of the accounting system and user activity by logging who accessed what data and when and recording these audit trails in a separate table
- Business alert systems in which, due to a specific business rule being broken, the system can automatically generate a warning message and send it by e-mail

(vii) Relational Accounting: Views

SQL provides the ability to define logical views of data that allow users to work with a restricted set of data from one or more tables. A view is often used to combine data, for example, from an employee table and a payroll table to show different people different views of data that requires sensitivity in its availability. Views can be used simply to see information or to maintain data by inserting, updating, or deleting data from the view. A view is also stored in the database, which means that it can be a more efficient way of managing multitable data because the information required to join the tables and restrict the dataset retrieved is also stored as part of the view information.

In the 1980s relational accounting was an approach that only large organizations could justify and afford. Then, many questioned the ability of relational databases to provide the transaction processing performance expected from proprietary mini and mainframe accounting systems. Now relational accounting is a realistic proposition for almost every level of business and is offered by practically every mainstream accounting vendor. Benchmarks released by the leading RDBMS vendors suggest that exceptional performance can be expected from an RDBMS running on relatively low-cost platforms by comparison with mainframes. If you must have relational accounting on a mainframe platform, you can. Some client/server accounting packages offer the option to use IBM's mainframe DB2 RDBMS for managing their data.

While object and multidimensional databases will play an increasingly important role in many client/server accounting systems in the future, relational accounting is the name of the game for at least the rest of the decade. By converting to relational accounting you are no longer taking a risk but simply recognizing that database choice, scaleability, transaction integrity, centralized business rules, and other benefits provide a solid foundation for a business management system.

(c) Relational Accounting Checklist

Use this checklist to help determine the relative sophistication of the relational accounting offered by a client/server accounting package:

Database Support

- ☐ Does the software require use of an RDBMS?
- ☐ Does the software support a choice of multivendor RDBMSs?
- ☐ Can accounting data be utilized from more than one RDBMS?

Database Access

- ☐ Is data accessed using embedded SQL, database APIs, or both?
- ☐ Is data accessed using native database access drivers?
- ☐ Is data accessed using ODBC database access drivers?
- ☐ Can system managers select either native or ODBC database access?

Utilizing RDBMS Features

- ☐ Does the software integrate with the database security system?

- ☐ Does the software make use of stored procedures to insert, update, or delete data?
- ☐ Does the software make use of triggers for generating alerts or audit trails automatically?
- ☐ Does the software make use of views to isolate the user from the actual database tables?
- ☐ Can the software make use of any parallel processing features offered by the RDBMS?
- ☐ Can the software make use of any data replication features offered by the RDBMS?

7.3 GRAPHICAL ACCOUNTING

It has taken a few years, but finally graphical accounting is here for the corporate accounting system now that practically every major accounting vendor has released a true graphical user interface (GUI) for its applications. Of course, graphical accounting in some shape or form has been around for some time. Accounting software for the Apple Macintosh has always offered a graphical user interface and the SOHO packages (small office, home office) such as Intuit Quicken, Peachtree Accounting for Windows, and Sage DacEasy for Windows on PCs were early to market with Microsoft Windows GUI versions of their products.

However, converting the user interface of complex multimodule packages used by larger corporations and transnational businesses has been a slightly more demanding task. So it is only within the last three years that the leading business management suites have truly converted to graphical accounting. Oracle Financials, a relational accounting system released in 1988, for example, was only recently updated with a true GUI interface in 1995. In almost all cases graphical accounting has meant providing a Microsoft Windows GUI: less because this is the best GUI necessarily and more because it is the market leader on the corporate desktop. Generally, every client/server accounting vendor is focusing on Microsoft Windows 95, as the primary front end for their accounting applications.

For many users of so-called legacy accounting systems on minis and mainframes, graphical accounting meant a simple color choice between green-on-black or amber-on-black. True graphical accounting however makes much better use of color and graphical symbols or widgets, not just to make the user interface more interesting but to make it more intuitive and therefore easier to learn and use. Figure 7.1 and Table 7.1 illustrate and describe some of the more common graphical widgets from an accounting perspective.

(a) Graphical Accounting Widgets

Graphical widgets are the visual shapes, signs, and icons used to represent an interface to a user (see Figure 7.1). A typical GUI has

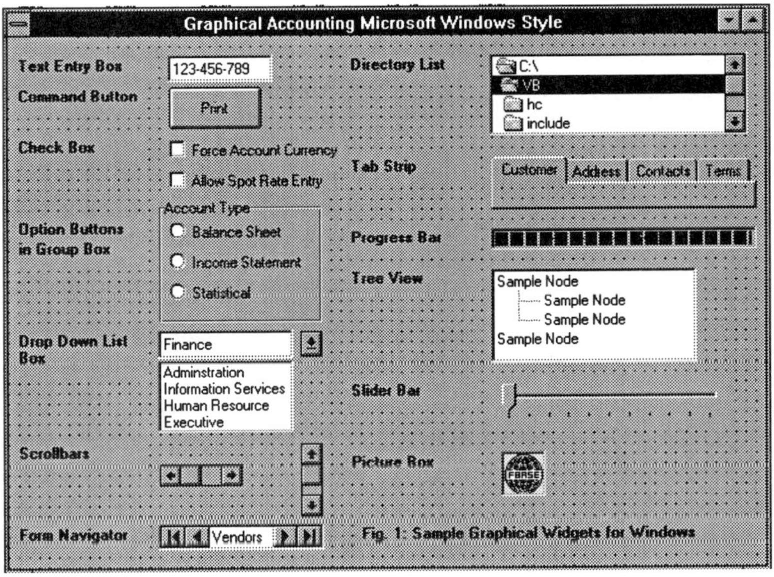

Figure 7.1. Some Sample Graphical Widgets.

Table 7.1. Graphical Widgets Explained.

Graphical Widget	*Description*
Text Entry Box	For entering text such as account codes, dates, descriptions, and so on. Usually you use the TAB key to move from box to box.
Command Button	By clicking the button with the left mouse button you may launch a process, such as printing a report or displaying a new data entry or query form.
Check Box	Clicking in the check-box marks toggles the condition between applicable or not applicable.
Option Buttons	Clicking a button sets the condition to one choice of the many options displayed.
Drop Down List Box	Clicking the arrow drops down a scrolling list of available choices, of which you click one to select it. Often you can key in the first few letters of a choice and the list box will jump to the nearest match in the list.
Scrollbars	Click the arrows to move data up or down or to the right or the left.
Form Navigator	Click the VCR controls to move forward and back or to the first or last records in a set, such as the chart of accounts.
Directory List	Displays a hierarchy structure using icons to provide a visual differentiator between levels.
Tab Strip	Click the tab to display a data-entry or query form with content specific to the tab title.
Tree View	Used to display a hierarchy. Double clicking on a row at a given level either expands or collapses the tree.
Progress Bar	Used to show the progress of a process such as posting a transaction or printing a report.
Slider Bar	Click the slider to increase or decrease a value or range to be recorded.
Picture Box	While the picture may be ornamental it may also be covering a hotspot. Clicking the hotspot can initiate a process or display another entry or query form.

dozens, even hundreds, of these widgets, which can be combined and displayed within a specific type of window or screen panel. Some of these widgets are shown in Figure 7.1. Windows may be full-screen, partial-screen, or pop-ups that contain messages or simple dialogues to which the user must respond. A graphical accounting system may display more than one window on the same screen at the same time. The user interacts with these windows and the widgets on them through use of either the keyboard or a mouse or similar pointing device, the mouse being the dominant device for communicating between the user and the GUI.

Apart from the difficulty of redesigning their product-user interfaces, many vendors resisted graphical accounting for other less-defensible reasons. Some pronounced Microsoft Windows a fad; some claimed accountants would never learn to use a mouse; and others that Windows was too slow for transaction entry. Windows' success in the marketplace has outdistanced the fad theory; accountants are as able to use a mouse as any other desktop application user; and transaction entry in a Windows application may be slower but there are ways around this drawback. In any case, there is a lot more to accounting software than capturing transactions and this is where graphical accounting delivers its benefits.

(b) Visualizing Graphical Accounting

The screenshot in Figure 7.2 shows a typical graphical accounting screen as it would look using the Microsoft Windows 3.11 GUI. The screen highlights a number of the standard look and feel aspects of graphical accounting, plus some of the more useful interface components that are becoming common in graphical accounting software. The screen shown is used to view and maintain a general ledger chart of accounts.

This screen shows the use of a number of popular graphical accounting styles using a main (parent) window that is also displaying a sub (child) window. Navigating the screen from top to bottom and left to right, these styles include:

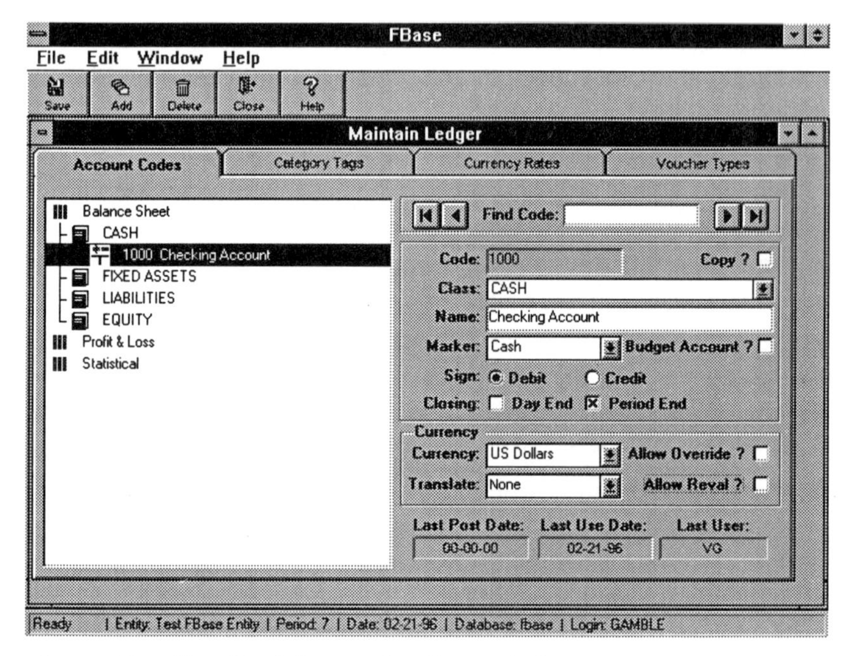

Figure 7.2. Graphical Accounting Example Screen.

Style	*Description*
Main Window Title Bar	The window title and buttons to close, minimize, and expand/collapse the window.
Menu Bar	Displays menu options and allows submenus to be pulled down to show multiple menu levels.
Toolbar	Buttons that can be used to manage common system or window specific tasks
Sub Window Title Bar	As main window above
Tab Folder	Clicking the tabs displays a different form within the current tab folder so the user can see or maintain related information.
Hierarchy Browser	A multilevel structure browser that allows you to navigate a complex data structure by expanding and collapsing data at each level
Form Navigator	A strip of controls that allow you to locate a specific data item (such as an account card) or to navigate the data from the first record to the last record

Maintenance Form	Allows you to view, insert, update, or delete data displayed when the tab is clicked
Status Bar	Used to display simple messages and data-entry prompts and to provide context information such as the current date or posting company for example

(c) Graphical Accounting: Benefits and Drawbacks

One of the most important benefits of graphical accounting is the homogenization of accounting user interfaces. In the past, accounting vendors essentially built their own interfaces. Apart from the development resources this absorbed by maintaining interfaces rather than functionality, it also resulted in a wide range of often bizarre interface designs. By and large, accounting user interfaces now look just the same as those of other popular desktop applications, and it can be hard to tell the difference between an accounting package and say, Microsoft Word or Excel. In fact many accounting systems now share menu structures very similar to most other Microsoft Windows compliant desktop applications. This makes accounting systems easier to learn and helps users become more productive faster.

Another benefit is that graphical accounting levels the playing field, because every vendor is essentially using the same standard interface. The advantage for users is that it becomes easier to compare apples to apples and therefore to spot good, bad, or innovative interface design. The advantage for vendors is that they can concentrate more time and effort on improving and expanding functionality to increase the breadth and depth of their accounting applications.

The breakdown of accounting systems can be represented by three main functional areas: (1) building structures, (2) transaction entry and processing, and (3) query and reporting. Graphical accounting delivers real benefits in all these areas.

Accounting systems are full of hierarchical structures: charts of accounts, organizations, sales territories, bills of material. Graphical accounting provides the browsers that allow you to efficiently maintain and navigate these hierarchies. Many accounting structures consist of logically linked categories of information. For example a customer card may link together customer account information, addresses, terms, and contacts, using a visual tab folder to view and maintain these different but linked customer items.

Many accounting transactions are not simple repetitive inputs, but rather based on documents such as invoices, requisitions, or orders. These documents have header, detail, and totals areas and can be represented very effectively as what-you-see-is-what-you-get (WYSIWYG) on-screen forms that users fill in. These forms can also be immediately output on plain paper and mailed or distributed without the need to use special, costly preprinted forms. While there is no doubt that there are faster ways to input transactions than through a GUI, at least the GUI makes it much harder for users to make simple input errors by providing more restricted choice and lookup list boxes. In any case we are moving into a world where more and more transactions will reach accounting systems through electronic commerce, so transaction entry may soon become a dying art.

Querying, reporting, navigating, and investigating data is where graphical accounting really shines. Query by form provides an intuitive way to build complex queries by simply entering query conditions, such as >500 or =debit, into the same boxes you enter data, in order to retrieve focused result sets. Query results can be manipulated in many ways. Balance queries can be used to start a drilldown, from summary to detail information, and all the way to the original transaction entry, using just the mouse to double click your way up and down the navigation path. The grid displaying the query data can be scrolled vertically and horizontally; and columns can be resized, reordered, and resorted on the fly. Ranges of data can be highlighted with the mouse and with a click on a toolbar button can be displayed as a chart or exported directly to a worksheet or cut and pasted onto a wordprocessor. Color can be used to great effect in order to highlight exceptions or to indicate differences such as positive and negative numbers making it easier to assimilate information.

Graphical report building provides a visual way to construct the contents of a report and to see how it will look when printed simultaneously. The report may also be populated with sample data as it is built so you can check whether the data is correctly formatted for your audience. Reports can be graphically previewed on screen before printing to check alignment, layout, or page breaking. Alternatively, reports may not need to be printed at all because they can be saved and viewed on screen and then sent by e-mail as message attachments to people who need to see them. Although complex report writing is still not simple, graphical accounting systems make report writing an easier and more approachable task.

Graphical accounting benefits from other ease-of-use features that are simply a part of the underlying GUI functionality. These include:

- Ever-present menu bars with pull-down multilevel menu systems that avoid the up-and-down-and-around-about navigation of old-style hierarchical or ring-menu systems
- Multiple document interfaces (MDI) that allow you to display more than one form at a time on screen so you can compare and contrast information easily
- Context-sensitive toolbars that gather the most frequently used functions on a button bar so these functions are always only a mouse click away

Graphical accounting does have some drawbacks. First, users must have the supporting GUI installed on their computers. For most desktop users this is not a problem but it does mean that current users of terminals need to be converted to PCs or workstations of some sort. Even Microsoft Windows graphical accounting is not completely homogenous so, for one reason or another, for better or worse, some vendors have deviated from the standards here and there. Look for official logos, such as Microsoft's Designed for Windows 95 compliance logo, to guarantee that the product has been certified with a minimum level of common standards.

Graphical accounting has not proven to be better than traditional non-GUI systems for rapid, heads-down transaction entry. Non-Windows proficient users may take time to become familiar with how to use Windows and a mouse—double clicking often takes a while to master. Some accounting systems are marketed as graphical yet are nothing but emperors with no clothes, so-called screen scrapes, ports of old mainframe-like screens, or simply wild deviations from the standards. These should be avoided. Some graphical accounting systems provide better keyboard support than others through the use of standard accelerator keys. Forcing users to mouse all the time is often not the fastest way to navigate a system.

On the whole, graphical accounting is a major step for accounting applications in terms of usability. It is also responsible for introducing many functional innovations in the navigation and maintenance of complex accounting structures, in drilling through data, in presenting data using more intuitive tabular or chart formats, and in the construction and presentation of reports. When evaluating a new accounting system, the GUI should be viewed with the same critical eye as other aspects of the system. After all, this is the part of the system design that all accounting operators will be forced to face and use every day.

(d) Graphical Accounting Checklist

Use this checklist to help determine the relative sophistication of the graphical accounting offered by a client/server accounting package:

GUI Support

- ☐ Does the software require use of a GUI?
- ☐ Does the software support a choice of GUIs?
- ☐ Can accounting data be accessed from more than one GUI?

Microsoft Windows GUI Support

- ☐ Is the software badged with the Windows Compliant logo?
- ☐ Is the software badged with the Designed for Windows 95 logo?
- ☐ Does the software make effective use of the full range of graphi-

cal widgets such as check boxes, option and command buttons, slider bars, or VCR navigation buttons?

Good GUI Design

- ☐ Does the application make use of tab folders to organize information?
- ☐ Does the application make use of expand and collapse browsers to navigate hierarchical structures?
- ☐ Does the software make use of drag-and-drop techniques to move data from one window or object to another?
- ☐ Does the software provide adequate keyboard support as well as mouse access to GUI features and menus?
- ☐ Does the software make effective use of colors, borders, icons, and group boxes?
- ☐ Does the software make effective use of standard toolbars and drop-down menus throughout the application?
- ☐ Does the software provide pop-up context-sensitive help for data entry fields and toolbar buttons?
- ☐ Does the software provide a visual status bar with useful information about your application context?
- ☐ Does the software provide a multiple document interface (MDI) to allow multiple windows on screen at one time?

7.4 PORTABLE ACCOUNTING

In the past, portability was regarded as a highly desirable feature because it meant that an accounting application could simply be recompiled, installed, and run on a different host platform. For example, as the COBOL programming language was ported as new compilers became available for platforms other than mainframes, accounting applications written in COBOL could be ported to HP,

DEC VAX, IBM AS/400, and other host computing platforms without much additional effort. This allowed vendors essentially to sell the same program in different markets and allowed users to deploy their accounting software on different platforms throughout the enterprise. This is referred to as server portability.

Client/server accounting packages have added more portability options as a consequence of the front-end and back-end design of client/server applications. Now portability encompasses:

- Server portability
- Database portability
- Interface portability

Server portability is the ability to run the server side of a client/server application's code on more than one platform. Computers running variants of UNIX or the Microsoft NT operating systems are the most popular server platforms for client/server applications whereas computers running Novell NetWare are the most popular platforms for running PC LAN-based accounting systems.

Database portability means the ability to run the data management of a client/server application on more than one database. While the RDBMS leaders such as Oracle, Sybase, and Informix are the most popular choices for accounting databases, some systems allow other choices such as IBM's mainframe DB2 RDBMS or Microsoft's SQL Server RDBMS.

Interface portability means the ability to run the client side of a client/server application using more than one user interface. While variants of Microsoft Windows are the most popular client GUIs for client/server accounting applications, many packages can use other GUIs such as the MacOS, OSG/Motif, and even non-GUI character terminals.

This three-level portability means that it is practically possible to use the same accounting application throughout an enterprise on many different combinations of servers, databases, and user interfaces. In fact in some cases, it is possible to mix servers, user interfaces, and database engines within a single discrete implementation of a client/server accounting application. This type of deployment flexibility gives client/server accounting system managers more choice to use the combination of server, interface, and database engine that provides the best price/performance for the functional need. It also increases the chances of being able to standardize on a single accounting system to handle the diverse needs of users throughout an enterprise computing environment. The mix-and-match potential of portable client/server accounting systems is show in Figure 7.3.

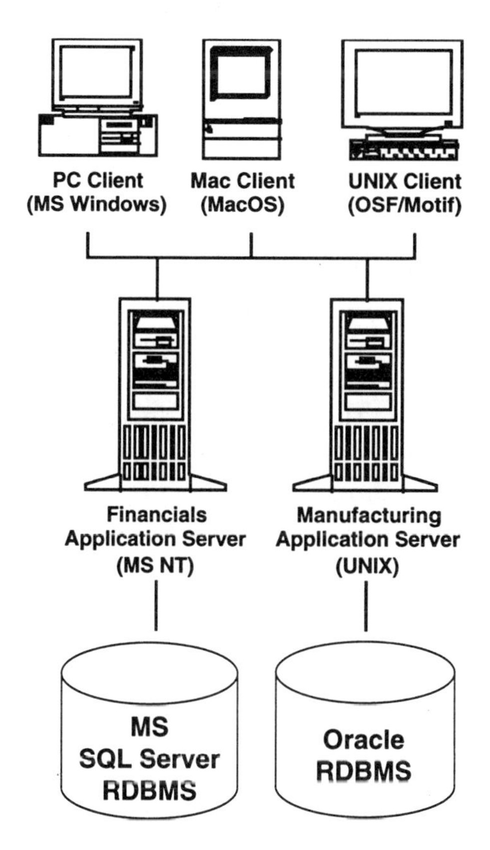

Figure 7.3. Mix and Match: Portable Client/Server Accounting.

(a) Portable Accounting Checklist

Use the following checklist to help determine the relative sophistication of the portable accounting offered by a client/server accounting package.

Portability Support

- ☐ Does the software offer a choice of server operating platforms on which to run the application?
- ☐ Does the software offer a choice of RDBMS engine for storing accounting data?
- ☐ Does the software offer a choice of GUIs for displaying information to the user?
- ☐ Can these options be mixed and matched within a single installation of the accounting system?

7.5 GRANULAR ACCOUNTING

Partitioning applications into client (front end) and server (back end) was the start of a general trend to introduce more granularity into accounting applications. This trend has a long way to go before we reach the goal of component-based systems that are assembled around business processes—a direction in which the accounting software industry is already heading. Nevertheless, the concept of software granularity is changing the construction, use, and deployment of client/server accounting software.

(a) Granular Software Construction

Accounting software has traditionally been monolithic in design. This means it was based on a massive block of source code, often running to hundreds of thousands, even millions, of lines of code. Code was maintained line by line or routine by routine within this morass.

Managing source code often became difficult and error prone. You could regard this maintenance task as similar to using an encyclopedia but without an index. It was not easy to break up and manage this type of source code to ease the maintenance burden. Instead source code is like a bound book as opposed to a ring binder with individual sections that allows you to take out specific content or reorder the content to meet your needs.

Taking a granular approach to software construction means that vendors break the software down into smaller, reusable, or shareable components, each of which performs a specific, discrete function within the application. These components are stored in a database repository and managed through some sort of hierarchical browser that graphically shows the dependencies between each component and provides a visual means of navigating the component structures. This type of granularity offers a number of benefits for the software developer:

- This approach tends to force developers to more rigorously analyze the functionality they are delivering in order to build true components.
- It is easier to locate, navigate, and manage than traditional blocks of source code.
- Code of this type encourages the practice of reusability that promises to reduce code maintenance and ensure greater consistency across applications.

(b) Granular Software Use

Most traditional accounting software was built to a modular level of granularity. An accounting suite consisted of modules such as general ledger and accounts payable, themselves fashioned on the traditional books of account or ledgers that characterized manual bookkeeping. Users had to switch between modules to manage business processes such as procurement, which crossed module boundaries, by exiting one module and entering another. Often this involved traversing up and down simple hierarchical menu systems, which is a tedious, time-consuming business. Even though security systems often allowed you to switch off menu options to hide them from users who did not use them, it was difficult to customize systems to reflect the way users actually used the software to manage business processes. Granular software design, however, delivers these benefits to users:

- It allows software to be assembled around a business process or around the functional world of individual users without needing to switch off menu options.
- It allows users to use software in a way that crosses traditional module boundaries and avoids excessive menu navigation.
- It allows managers to ensure that accounting users are focused on essential task flows rather than distracted by nonessential functionality.

(c) Granular Software Deployment

Because software is constructed in a granular manner it can also be deployed more flexibly in a client/server architecture. Process intensive functional components such as those that manage transaction posting, currency revaluation, or financial reporting for example can be split off from the main application and deployed on separate servers. This provides useful additional scaleability for the accounting system as a whole and allows individual processes to use their own dedicated resources. The fact that the accounting system can be deployed in pieces instead of only in modules provides these benefits for system managers:

- They can purchase only the system granules or components that they really need for more efficient purchasing and use of the accounting software.
- They upgrade the system easily by adding new components or upgrading only those that have been enhanced by the vendor instead of buying or upgrading whole new modules.

- They can decide to partition component processes onto dedicated servers for better performance or scaleability.

Granularity is set to become even more important as a system design feature in the future as vendors move further into the use of object oriented development techniques and the infrastructures for deploying and managing component based software mature.

(d) Granular Accounting Checklist

Use the following checklist to help determine the relative sophistication of the granular accounting offered by a client/server accounting package:

Granularity Support

- ☐ Can the software be purchased in separate, discrete granules rather than whole modules?
- ☐ Can user-specified accounting processes be run on their own dedicated server hardware?
- ☐ Can the software be deployed in thick, thin, or balanced-client mode that enables a three-tier client/server architecture?
- ☐ Can application activities be isolated and combined to fit the functional needs of the user or assembled around the business process?
- ☐ Can application activities be isolated from the main application and deployed as Internet or Intranet applications?

7.6 SCALEABLE ACCOUNTING

For larger enterprises and fast-growth businesses, scaleability is critical to the success of their information systems. Large organizations are faced with an operating environment that encompasses mergers and acquisitions, spin-offs, and buyouts, centralized and distributed management, seasonal information-processing spikes, and hiring bulges. Fast-growth businesses face all the same issues but over a compressed timescale. This dynamic operating model puts great pressure on information systems to be flexible enough to cope with these changes without forcing an expensive and time-consuming change of their system environment or software.

Because the acquisition cost of corporate or enterprise accounting systems is usually more than $2 of implementation cost to every $1 of software cost, changing an accounting system is a very expensive proposition. This also ignores the transition trauma that accompanies every accounting system change and can affect staff from the CFO downwards. Consequently, most organizations want to change accounting software as infrequently as they can and are therefore understandably conservative about undertaking major revisions of their accounting systems. In the past, this has been why many accounting-system managers bought applications software that was more powerful than they needed and ran it on platforms that required more resources than their accounting systems justified. They were simply being cautious because they did not want to be caught out by the scaleability trap.

(a) Defining Scaleability

There are three types of scaleability that should concern the managers of accounting systems: transaction, workgroup, and functional.

(i) Transaction Scaleability

When scaleability is being discussed, it is generally transaction scaleability that is being referred to. Transaction scaleability is simply the ability of the accounting system to handle increasing transaction volume. Transaction volume may grow for a number of reasons, including:

- A steady increase in the volume of business due to successful growth, the planned move into new geographical markets or expansion into new lines of business

- A sudden increase in the overall volume of business due to merger or acquisition, or the unexpected move into a high-transaction volume line of business such as telecoms or utilities
- A spike in the volume of a specific line of business due to seasonal variations, the introduction of new product lines, or wildly successful marketing campaigns

In each case a greater number of transactions must be input and managed by the accounting system. This puts pressure on three components of the accounting system:

- The database that stores the transactions
- The hardware platform and network that handles transaction throughput
- The application software that provides decision support against the transactions

For an accounting system to be able to handle transaction scaleability it must have an underlying database management system that is designed to provide predictable performance while managing increasing transaction volume. Some database systems were not designed to handle high-transaction volume and their performance degrades rapidly once certain transaction throughput thresholds are reached. Also, as database systems can take advantage of their hardware server resources, such as multiple processors, free memory, and disk space, their scaleability is effectively constrained by the range of hardware platforms on which they can run. Databases designed to run exclusively on Intel PC platforms simply cannot scale as well as databases designed to run on multiprocessor RISC platforms, or proprietary mini or mainframe platforms, because of known hardware and operating system limitations.

(ii) User Scaleability

For many of the same reasons that a business experiences transaction growth, it can also experience a growth in the number of users connected to the accounting system. Note that the increased number of users attached to the system does not necessarily mean that transaction volume itself increases significantly. New users can be connected to the accounting systems for a number of reasons, including:

- A redistribution of workloads such that the same transaction volume is being spread over more input users as part of the transformation of clerical types into knowledge workers or making existing knowledge workers responsible for their own transactions.
- The connection of more internal analytical, decision-support, or casual management accounting system users to provide greater accessibility to the accounting data.
- The connection of more external, extended-enterprise users such as customers, suppliers, and outsourcers who may have inquiry and reporting rights against the accounting system.

User scaleability also puts pressure on the underlying accounting database, but in a different way. As the number of users scales up, so does the possibility of data contention. Data contention is caused simply by more than one user competing for the same item of data in the database. This is seldom a problem except in large accounting systems with high transaction-input volumes and large numbers of connected users, but when it becomes a problem it can be time-consuming to diagnose and fix. In order to manage this contention and prevent the database integrity from being compromised, database management systems use some form of locking mechanism.

Locking is used to secure a data item from manipulation by other users while it is being inserted, updated, deleted, or viewed by a specific user. It is the granularity and sophistication of this locking that has a major impact on user scaleability (see Figure 7.4). Locking granularity in a RDBMS, for example, can be implemented from database through to column levels; however, many commercial RDBMSs do not offer either row- or column-level locking. Theoretically, the finer the level of locking granularity, the less data con-

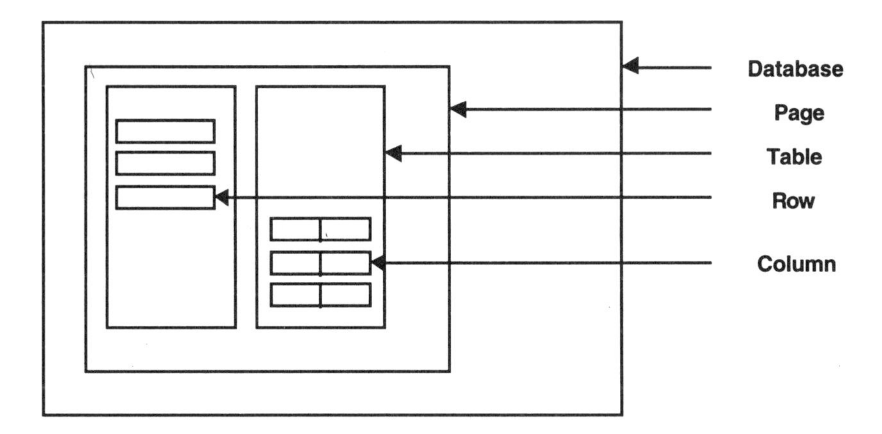

Figure 7.4. Database Locking Granularity.

tention should occur, and the more users a database can manage while offering the same overall performance.

The sophistication of the locking refers to whether the database lock management provides both write and read locks or uses versioning as a means of implementing its locking. The availability of only write locks means that data is always locked exclusively for the use of a specific user because the database assumes that an insertion, updating, or deletion of data is about to take place. If there are a lot of decision-support users running inquiries and reports against the accounting data, as well as a lot of transaction entry users, this can slow things down for both groups, especially the decision-support users. The use of a read lock means that access to the data item is treated as nonexclusive by the database until a write lock is applied. The use of read locks can reduce data contention and therefore improve performance if there are large numbers of decision-support users regularly accessing the database.

Data versioning is another means for handling locking that can be regarded as more like a read than a write lock. Versioning uses a before-and-after approach to accessing the database data. By keeping a snapshot of the data as it existed when it was first accessed by a specific user, the version manager can always get back to the before scenario if some unexpected event takes place. Versioning is a relatively expensive form of lock management because it demands first that the version manager copy data somewhere, and second that the data itself is stored temporarily either in memory or on disk. For this reason, versioning is usually used by systems that are managing complex data such as images, engineering plans, and drawings or documents. Versioning is not a common locking technique used in accounting systems at this time because it is not a common locking technique used by relational databases. However this may change as accounting systems are used to manage more varied data types than just text and numbers.

(iii) Functional Scaleability

Businesses do not just grow in size, they grow in terms of sophistication. Functional scaleability is the capacity of the accounting application to offer more sophisticated functionality without requiring a change of system. Functional scaleability depends on the breadth and depth of the accounting software chosen. There are many different types of functional scaleability that an accounting system may be required to handle. These include:

- Accounting reach
- Accounting scope
- Multientity
- International
- Line of business
- Management outlook
- Statutory compliance

Accounting reach is the functional scaleability required to extend the accounting domain beyond the reach of the accounting system itself to involve other nonaccounting participants in accounting processes. These participants may be internal line managers, business analysts, or executives, or they may be external partners such as customers, vendors, or outsourced service providers. Accounting reach is quickly becoming the most important type of functional scaleability to look for in an accounting system. Applications that deliver the functional scaleability of accounting reach typically provide support for:

- E-mail connectivity
- Workflow management
- Electronic document interchange (EDI)
- Electronic funds transfer (EFT)
- Electronic commerce on the Internet
- Telephony

Accounting scope is the functional scaleability required to expand the accounting domain beyond just the financials to fixed asset, inventory, treasury, project management or travel, and entertainment accounting for example. This type of scaleability demands accounting software with the functional breadth to offer the additional modules that support the demands of the expanded accounting domain. So-called best-of-class vendors who focus their software exclusively on one area—for example, financial accounting—do not have the breadth of offering to deliver functional scaleability of this type and force system managers to integrate with other packages. At this time such integration can be a costly business to achieve effectively.

Multientity is the functional scaleability required to effectively manage accounting across multiple entities. This is not just the ability to maintain separate sets of books for more than one entity on the same system. True multientity functional scaleability demands functionality such as:

- Consolidation reporting
- Intercompany processing
- Shared-service payables or receivables
- Cross-entity allocations
- Combined-entity inquiry and reporting

International accounting is the functional scaleability required to allow a business to manage both domestic and foreign transaction entry, inquiry, and reporting. The functionality to support international accounting includes:

- Multicurrency rate management
- Currency revaluation and gain/loss accounting
- Consolidation and translation reporting
- Compliance with local statutory regulations
- Multilingual application software
- Culturally sensitive terminology and symbols

Line of business is the functional scaleability required to adapt to changes in or additions to the lines of business managed by an organization. This primarily concerns the ability of the accounting system to handle new or different analytical demands on the accounting system. A product- or project-driven line of business each demands a different approach to the structure of the accounting system, especially the elements that determine how data can be input, balanced, queried, and reported, such as the design of the chart of accounts. To offer line-of-business scaleability the accounting application should offer either:

- A flexible, user-defined, segmented account code
- A structure for tagging transactions with user-defined analysis tags

Management outlook is the functional scaleability required to handle changes in the way accounting managers view the business. This is what allows managers to structure their system around a cost-centered or profit-centered outlook, a product- or project-driven outlook, or an activity-based or process-centric outlook. This type of functional scaleability demands that accounting systems can be structured to:

- Tag transactions to specific cost, profit, product, project, or process activities
- Monitor and audit the performance of specific business processes

Statutory compliance is the functional scaleability required to cope with changes in the demands of regulatory authorities for information from business accounting systems. In most countries the demands of statutory compliance bodies for more detailed reporting is increasing as tax systems become more complex and cross-border trading increases. To cope with these demands, accounting systems need to provide:

- Flexible data import and export capabilities for data transfer
- Ways to integrate with specialized statutory compliance or reporting systems
- Sophisticated report writers to handle the variety of statutory formats required
- Sophisticated document formatters to output correctly formatted statutory forms

The key to delivering this functional scaleability is not just the breadth and depth of the accounting application's functionality; it also depends on the design granularity of the application. By designing the software with a high level of granularity, functional scaleability can be deployed piece by piece by assembling components. Whether these components are combinations of traditional modules, new application granules, or cross-functional tools such as workflow management systems does not matter. What matters is that organizations may functionally scale their accounting applications to cope with the demands of business change, without either having to purchase more functionality than they need upfront or having to change systems midstream, by simply adding that functionality in small, easy-to-implement chunks.

(b) Scaleable Accounting Checklist

Use the following checklist to help determine the relative sophistication of the scaleable accounting offered by a client/server accounting package:

Transaction Scaleability

- ☐ Does the accounting system utilize a database that can run on UNIX, AS/400, or mainframe platforms?
- ☐ Does the accounting system utilize a database that supports sophisticated data cache techniques for faster performance?
- ☐ Does the accounting system utilize a database that can take advantage of parallel processing on multiprocessor hardware?

User Scaleability

- ☐ What locking schemas are offered by the databases supported by the accounting system: page, table, row, or column?
- ☐ Do the databases supported by the accounting system provide data-versioning functionality?
- ☐ How do the databases supported by the accounting system react to deadlocks caused by two users locking data in transactions that are dependent on each other?

Functional Scaleability

- ☐ Can the accounting system deal with multientity accounting in all its complexities?
- ☐ Can the accounting system deal with international accounting?
- ☐ Can the accounting code blocks deal with expanding and changing data-analysis or statutory-compliance needs?
- ☐ Does the accounting system provide sophisticated functions for importing data from and exporting data to third party systems?

7.7 USABLE ACCOUNTING

Because most systems claiming to be client/server accounting systems were rewritten for the client/server platform and for graphical-user interfaces they have been subject to a range of usability improvements. Usability is the term used to describe software features designed to make an application more intuitive and easier to use. Many large software vendors such as Microsoft Corporation and Lotus Development Corporation maintain usability labs where software can be tested by new or existing users who are observed by the application's functional and interface designers. The observations and statistics gathered from these sessions are used to determine if new or existing features meet the required levels of usability.

There are a number of usability functions that are already common in client/server accounting software, for example:

- Visual help systems
- User tutorials
- Graphical process maps
- Specific functional Cue Cards
- Setup and guiding Wizards

(a) Visual Help Systems

Visual help systems allow users to navigate the index and contents of an on-line manual organized by topics and stored on disk or CD-ROM. The navigation is achieved by searching for key words among the included help-system topics and jumping from one topic to another using hypertext links to navigate around the help system itself. Help is usually always accessible from a pulldown menu option, or by clicking a key such as the function key F1 to access Microsoft Windows help. Help may also be context-sensitive. That is to say if the F1 key is pushed while the user is currently entering an account code into an account code box on a data-entry form, the help system will load help text that is appropriate both to the box and function that define the user's current context. Visual help systems are becoming so comprehensive that paper manuals have truly become mere shelfware.

(b) User Tutorials

User tutorials are also common, typically as computer-based training (CBT) courses supplied on diskette or, more typically, CD-ROM. These courses provide a means for users to train themselves by following a series of electronic lessons guiding them through the functionality and use of the accounting software. CBT has not yet replaced traditional classroom training led by an application specialist but it has an important role to play for refresher training and as a means to provide an on-line tutor.

(c) Graphical Process Maps

Graphical process maps are visual maps of the main business processes that can be managed by the accounting software. This might be the payment process in accounts-payable or the cash-matching process in accounts receivable for example. These process maps demonstrate the logical flow of a transaction and show the specific functional options required to complete that flow using the system functionality. These are very helpful in giving the user a big picture of processes that may often involve many steps and require the use of many system options in a specific order. In some cases the process map itself may be live and act as a form of menu. By clicking on the icons depicting process steps you can launch the appropriate system function and then return to the map when you have finished the step activity. Graphical process maps first showed up in SOHO accounting systems and have been widely copied since.

(d) Cue Cards

Cue cards are popup screens that contain advice on how to carry out a specific task, usually by enumerating and describing the various steps and activities that make up the task. Cue cards supplement the visual help system by providing a focused summary of help for a specific functional option or process in the accounting system. In many systems, cue cards can be set to automatically pop up wherever they are available as a means of providing an electronic mentor that pops up to help the user wherever it can.

(e) Wizards

Wizards are screens that guide and prompt users through a specific process to ensure that it is completed as quickly and efficiently as possible. Wizards are usually created to lead users through processes that are either most frequently used, relatively simple to define, or easy to get wrong unaided. Most of Microsoft's Office suite of applications make extensive uses of wizards, as do many third-party packages. Applications for the Microsoft Windows 95 GUI are usually installed using a Setup wizard that ensures that an application can be installed with just a few mouse clicks by the user. Accounting systems are no exception to this rule and many accounting packages now include wizards for tasks such as setting up structures like charts of account, code-block segmenting, document entry forms, and report formats.

The combination of all these usability features means that client/server accounting software should be able to boast a higher usability rating than any previous generation of accounting software. However it is important to note that despite this, corporate and enterprise client/server accounting software is still costing some $2 to $5 to implement per $1 of actual software cost.

(f) Usable Accounting Checklist

Use the following checklist to help determine the relative sophistication of the usable accounting offered by a client/server accounting package:

Usability Functions

- ☐ Does the accounting system come complete with an on-line manual and context-sensitive visual-help system?
- ☐ Does the accounting system come complete with on-line and guided tutorials?
- ☐ Does the accounting system provide visual process maps to allow users to quickly see the big picture of an accounting process?
- ☐ Does the accounting system help new users conquer the learning curve through use of cue cards or similar functions?
- ☐ Does the accounting system speed up installation and the use of complex everyday processes through use of wizards or similar functions?

7.8 ADAPTABLE ACCOUNTING

The monolithic accounting software applications of the past, written in COBOL and destined for use on a specific hardware platform, were difficult to customize without extensive work deep in the program source code. As many of these systems had a life that spanned a decade or more, it is no surprise that source code became difficult to manage as successive generations of programmers supporting the accounting department exerted their own influence on the source code. In the past, customers would often purchase the source code at great expense for no other reason than to be certain that they could customize the package if necessary, or that their system could survive if the vendor went out of business.

The fact is that selecting an accounting system is like trying to hit a moving target. You have to project the direction your business will take in the future and try to ensure that the system you select is capable of adapting to unexpected changes in your business, your marketplace, or the technology you use. It is easy to miss a moving target, and it is equally easy to make a poor system decision based on the best of intentions. That is why so many accounting software evaluations stress customization as an important feature on the functionality checklist.

(a) Traditional Approaches to Customization

Customization has always been a thorny problem for vendors. One solution is not to offer it. Instead the most commercially attractive customer requests for modifications are simply built by the vendor and incorporated into the product source code. Everyone benefits; a single source code version is maintained; and the vendor avoids messy customer-driven modifications. Another solution is to sell the product source code as an option, and allow customers or resellers to modify the code as they wish. Of course the vendor can then distance itself if any problems result from source code modifications. As a result, the responsibility for supporting these application hybrids falls primarily on the customer or value-added reseller (VAR).

Both these approaches are represented in the marketplace. Vendors such as Computron and Systems Union stress their single-version no-modifications source code. PC accounting vendors such as RealWorld and SBT built their businesses on their ability to supply and support source-code licenses for their products. It is common to be able to buy the source code for PC and LAN accounting systems written in xBase, or for mini or mainframe systems written in COBOL. However, these approaches to customization are somewhat limiting—on the one hand dependent on the whims of the vendor, on the other demanding the customer or their VAR shoulder the support and maintenance burden.

More sophisticated solutions for customization include the exposure of user hooks in the product design in order to allow customers or vendors to build in their own custom routines. These routines make use of the hooks to insert, update, delete, or query data via functions included in the regular software. Order entry and billing are typical targets for this type of customization for handling business-specific procedures such as calculating customer prices, credit controls, line discounts, or sales commissions. Many midrange vendors, such as J. D. Edwards on the IBM AS/400 platform, use this approach. The result is that many third parties have built libraries of routines to hook into the vendor's code in order to surround their core modules with more specialized vertical market custom components.

(b) 4GLs and RAD Tools

A growing number of accounting vendors are moving away from writing their applications from scratch or developing their own in-house application development tools. Instead they are building their applications using commercially available fourth generation languages (4GLs) or rapid-application-development (RAD) tools. Current popular examples of these tools are Centura Software SQL Windows, Microsoft Visual Basic and Access, and Powersoft PowerBuilder. There are at least five reasons for this shift to 4GL development:

- The increasing robustness and sophistication of these tools compared to pioneering versions of these tools that appeared in the early 1980s.
- Commercially successful tools of this type have become widely installed and influential infrastructure components in large corporations.
- These same tools have generated a large after market of add-in and add-on components that vendors and customers can take advantage of when customizing applications built with the tool.
- Vendors can get applications more quickly to market, then more quickly deliver enhancements and new modules once the applications are installed.

- Customers can use the 4GL or RAD tool to apply their own customizations to accounting applications with a minimum of traditional source-code-level programming.

Many corporate buyers are attracted to accounting software written in a 4GL or RAD tool, especially if they already use the same tools in house. This approach provides system managers with a solution that can be integrated easily with other in-house applications: it can share the same look and feel, and allow MIS to modify and add to the packages using the development tool as a means of accessing the product source code. Part of the attraction of client/server accounting packages listed below is that they were written in a 4GL.

Vendor	*Product*	*4GL/RAD Tool*
Oracle	Oracle Financials	Oracle Developer 2000
SQL Financials	SQL Financials	Centura SQL Windows
Dun & Bradstreet Software	SmartStream	Powersoft PowerBuilder
Solomon Software	Solomon IV for Windows	Microsoft Visual Basic
Concepts Dynamic	CDI Control Series	Informix NewEra
Apprise Software	Apprise Financials	Progress 4GL

(c) The Accounting Engine Concept

Some of the shipping and forthcoming client/server accounting packages are emerging as a new type of accounting software application. They could be termed accounting engines and they offer a much more flexible approach to application customization. This approach fits well with the dynamic nature of most businesses, because the driving force behind the need for customization is the need to cope with business change.

These new accounting engines reflect a couple of differences between new-generation and traditional accounting software architectures. One difference is the client/server characteristic of separating the back-end data management and business rules from the front-end application logic and presentation. This allows vendors to provide a means for the front-end presentation layer to be highly modifiable by separating it from a core-set back-end transaction processing procedures and rules. Another difference is that object-oriented development methods have introduced more granularity into accounting software design. This allows applications to be easily broken down into functional components, which can effectively be reassembled by users for a closer business fit.

These functional components may be processes such as entering and approving an invoice or carrying out a month-end close. They may be high-level data entry or query forms, reports, or documents that can be accessed from a library of such objects. They may be individual widgets such as a Help button that pops up a message box, or a Find button that requests a key value to locate a record for display. In any case these application business objects are accessible for customization.

Vendors are offering a number of approaches to delivering this new level of customization functionality. One approach is to supply a special toolkit as a module that can be purchased like any other. This toolkit allows you to bolt new functionality onto the software and modify existing functions and processes. The second approach is to supply the software in a form that allows the user to build their own accounting system if they wish from a set of high-level functional objects. The third approach is to supply software designed for on-the-fly customization, through use of a user-accessible data dictionary, in which modifying the package is just another function on a menu.

(d) Ten Attributes of Accounting Engines

In order to qualify as an accounting engine, there are ten desirable attributes the accounting application should offer:

1. A 4GL-based front end
2. A toolkit module
3. An internal scripting language
4. A user-accessible data dictionary
5. Exposed application procedures
6. Object builders
7. Self linking and compiling capability
8. Process-definition builders
9. Infrastructure integration tools
10. Self-maintenance on upgrade

(i) 4GL-Based Front End

If the front end is written in a commercially popular 4GL, such as SQL Windows, PowerBuilder, or Progress, the application objects are usually open to modification in the 4GL development environment. For users already familiar with and using the 4GL, this can be a big plus by leveraging their investment in the tool.

(ii) Toolkit Module

Even if the front end is not written in a 4GL, a separate toolkit module may be supplied that offers 4GL-like functionality. Because this product is proprietary to the application, it may provide better accounting-aware functionality and faster performance in deployment than a generic 4GL.

(iii) Internal Scripting Language

If the toolkit includes a complete programming language, whether procedural- or event-driven, or both, this increases the flexibility of the package. Using a popular commercial language such as Microsoft Visual Basic (VB) is even better because this opens up the possibility of using a wide range of commercially developed custom controls, and many programmers are already skilled in VB.

(iv) Data Dictionary

A dynamic, user-accessible data dictionary is ideal. The data dictionary provides a repository for the definition of all system components including tables, forms, menus, processes, messages, events, and rules. This provides a complete road map of the application for developers who can customize the applications at various levels of sophistication.

(v) Exposed Application Procedures

An application procedure could be a stored procedure, trigger, script, or dynamic link library (DLL) that performs a key function within the system. Typically these are server-based. An example is a procedure for posting an accounting transaction to the database. Many internal modules may share this function and it would be essential that any new customized transaction-posting function should also use the same procedure. These procedures must be open, documented, and easy to hook into from external applications.

(vi) Object Builders

There are at least three types of application objects that define the presentation layer of an application: table objects that define the structure of the application data; form objects that define the user-interface and data-entry logic for the application; and message objects that provide for popup dialogues, error, validation messages, and user help. There must be a means for users to build new instances of these objects and modify existing instances.

(vii) Self Linking and Compiling

The package should include the means to link the new or modified objects into the application, for example through attaching them to menus or buttons. It must also recompile the application to reflect the changes without needing to access a traditional external compiler or running a separate compilation process.

(viii) Process Definition

If the application supports workflow concepts then the customization of user activities should be able to sequence these activities according to the needs of the business process. This allows functional procedures to be combined with events, alerts, and actions in order to build custom activities that can be selected from menus and mapped to steps in a business process workflow.

(ix) Infrastructure Integration

This allows a package to integrate more closely with external software through e-mail or database gateways. Also useful is support for cross-application communication channels such as Microsoft's dynamic data exchange (DDE), or the more sophisticated object-linking-and-embedding (OLE). These features make accounting part of a compound application environment in which the boundary between accounting, decision-support, and office-automation software becomes blurred.

(x) Self Maintenance

The customization features should allow easy documentation of the new enhancements to assist maintenance. The new features should be able to be rolled back if required. The features should be upgrade sensitive; that is, a new core software upgrade should not overwrite or ignore the customized features added by the user when the application upgrade is installed.

The shift to client/server accounting has encouraged vendors to deliver customization capabilities that are getting deeper in scope, are easier to use through graphical interfaces, and provide immediate results without programming and recompilation. From a user's perspective these new products render the need to buy or maintain source code obsolete. Instead the market is moving towards a component-based accounting paradigm allowing business accounting products adaptable to the needs of even small-niche or specialized vertical markets. Rolling your own accounting software is close to becoming a reality.

(e) Adaptable Accounting Checklist

Use the following checklist to help determine how sophisticated the adaptability of a client/server accounting package really is:

Adaptable Interface

- ☐ Screen field labels may be edited.
- ☐ Screen fields may be added or modified.
- ☐ Screen fields may be hidden or deleted.

Adaptable Database

- ☐ New tables may be added to the database.
- ☐ New data-entry or query forms may be linked to tables.
- ☐ New forms may be loaded from menus or buttons.

Adaptable Scripts

- ☐ Script processes may be defined using internal language.
- ☐ Scripts may be attached to menus or buttons.
- ☐ Scripts may call external software functions.

Adaptable Events

- ☐ New field events may be defined.
- ☐ New form events may be defined.
- ☐ New system events may be defined.

Adaptable Usability

- ☐ System messages may be edited.
- ☐ System hypertext help may be edited.
- ☐ New help popups may be defined.

Adaptable Processes

- ☐ Process workflows may be remodeled.
- ☐ Transaction logic may be client- or server-based.
- ☐ Transaction processes may be accessed from other applications.

7.9 COOPERATIVE ACCOUNTING

Cooperative accounting recognizes that accounting is just another desktop application like word processing or worksheet processing. For many years, accounting has been treated as if it were an information island—isolated from the rest of the organization and only accessible to accounting specialists. This has often been a reflection of the reality of arcane accounting-application designs, and closed proprietary accounting databases. The information island scenario has also reflected a protective attitude toward accounting data, which has been treated like a diamond ring in a jeweler's case rather than a diamond cutting edge to a drill used to mine for gold.

Client/server accounting applications encourage system managers to view the accounting system and its data as an information asset rather than an information island. The foundation for this is the use of relational databases that open up the accounting data to desktop application access through standards such as SQL or ODBC. This gives the accounting system the capability to cooperate with literally hundreds of inexpensive desktop query and reporting tools that add significant value to the decision support potential of the accounting data.

Client/server accounting applications are often designed to cooperate closely with specific desktop productivity tools such as the Microsoft Office suite of applications, or a worksheet tool such as Lotus 1-2-3. Indeed many accounting vendors are currently working with Microsoft to certify their applications through the Office-Compatible-logo authorization process. While it was possible to cooperate with similar applications in the past through exporting data from the source accounting system and importing it to the target productivity application, client/server accounting has raised this cooperation to new levels of sophistication and ease of use.

In many cases this cooperation is simply a mouse click away. Often, client/server accounting applications running under the Microsoft Windows GUI have toolbars with buttons that provide automatic transfer of correctly formatted data into other Microsoft applications such as Microsoft Word, Microsoft Excel, and Microsoft Access. Usually this data transfer is carried out after the user has queried the accounting system and displayed either the results of a query such as a list of transactions on an account, or a formatted report such as an aged receivables report. In some applications data may also be transferred into the accounting system in the same fashion.

Table 7.2 discusses some examples of cooperation between a client/server accounting system and applications in the Microsoft Office suite.

Client/server accounting applications not only make cooperation with other applications more sophisticated and easier but also allow other applications literally to be embedded into the accounting modules. This is done using technology such as Microsoft's OLE 2.0 programming interfaces. Through OLE, an accounting system can embed an object that was created and is maintained by another software application. When a user focuses on the embedded object, usually by clicking on a thumbnail icon, the application that created the object is loaded in a new window within the accounting application so the user can take advantage of a whole new set of application facilities to manipulate the object or its data.

An example of such an embedded object might be a worksheet of budget figures that is embedded in the budget entry form in the accounting system. To change the budget figures, the user clicks on the worksheet, which in turn instantiates itself by loading the worksheet application in which it was created so the user can work on the numbers. Once the numbers are changed the data is saved, the worksheet application is unloaded, and the control is returned to the accounting system.

Table 7.2. Cooperation with Microsoft Office.

Product (Application)	*Cooperative Activity*
Word	Report Publishing Having produced a formatted financial statement in the accounting system, the report can be transferred directly into Word in order to publish the report using Word's extensive formatting tools. Dunning Letters A query to retrieve customer address and balance information from accounting database can be transferred directly into a Word mailmerge file for merging with a dunning letter already created in Word and printing.
Excel	Financial Ratio Management Balance-sheet and income-statement reports may be transferred directly into Excel worksheets and used as the source data for other worksheets that automatically calculate, display, and chart financial ratios showing the relative health of your business to industry norms. Budget Entry Budgets may be managed in multiple Excel worksheets then transferred directly from the worksheets to the budget-entry forms used by the accounting system, instead of being rekeyed.
Access	Customer Information Updates Field sales reps may have a personal-contact management database built in Access for use on their laptops. A query from the accounting database extracting up-to-date customer balances can be directly transferred into a snapshot Access database and copied to the rep's laptop. Statistical Information Input Marketing may manage statistical data on the company-performance and comparative-performance data on industry peers in an Access database. This information can be directly imported into statistical accounts in the General ledger for use in financial statement reporting that includes statistical data.

Another example of an embedded object is a document thumbnail displayed when transaction data, such as a vendor invoice, is displayed in the accounting system. The thumbnail is a miniature graphical representation of the original invoice document that was scanned into a document management system and tagged to the accounting transaction. When the user clicks on the thumbnail, the document is displayed and the document-management system loaded. The user may then view, annotate, or print the document before closing the embedded application and returning to the accounting system.

Another aspect of cooperative accounting is the passing of data or formal transactions between multivendor accounting systems. For example, this may be required when you are using one vendor's manufacturing package and another's financial package. Receipt of inventory into finished goods may be managed by the manufacturing packages, and require the generation of a journal in the financial system's general ledger module. Anything that eases or automates the transfer of data between systems is going to reduce the complexity of multivendor system management. Some vendors are attacking this problem through membership of an association—the Open Applications Group (OAG), which is dedicated to defining standards for multivendor interapplication transaction management. The OAG is defining business-transaction documents that can be used as a standard means of passing transactions between applications—similar in many ways to the concept of electronic data interchange (EDI).

Whether the client/server accounting system offers one-click data transfer to and from external applications, the direct embedding of other applications, or support for the OAG's transaction-document-interface objects, this type of cooperative processing adds value to the accounting system and leverages more value from other software application investments, while building on the skills that users may already have in using those applications.

Workflow management systems are also rapidly developing the transaction choreography sophistication required to pass accounting transactions across multi-vendor applications and facilitate interapplication cooperation.

(a) Cooperative Accounting Checklist

Use the following checklist to help determine the relative sophistication of the cooperative accounting offered by a client/server accounting package:

Cooperative Functions

- ☐ One-click toolbar-button data export to other desktop applications
- ☐ One-click toolbar-button data import to other desktop applications
- ☐ Support for Microsoft OLE 2.0 applications as both a client and a server
- ☐ Microsoft Office Compatible logo demonstrating close compatibility in look, feel, and function with the Office-desktop applications suite
- ☐ A vendor being an active member of the OAG

7.10 EXTENSIBLE ACCOUNTING

Extensible accounting means the ability to extend both the functionality of accounting applications and their interaction with other nonaccounting users and applications—to expand the information domain and the application reach of the accounting system outside of the normal accounting modules and users. There are at least five technologies that are helping to deliver extensible accounting:

1. Electronic messaging
2. The Internet
3. Document management
4. Workflow
5. Software components

(a) Electronic messaging

Electronic messaging includes the delivery of digitized messages and software data file attachments via electronic messaging infrastructures such as electronic mail and the fax. Despite the rapid success of the fax as an electronic messaging system in the 1980s and 1990s, and the continued dominance of the telephone as the primary business communication tool, electronic mail is quickly overtaking fax and rivaling the telephone as a messaging medium. Electronic mail provides an ideal mechanism for extending the reach of accounting systems and is being used in client/server accounting applications to:

- Distribute digital reports and report packs to management
- Notify accounting and nonaccounting staff of exception events
- Send to-do items to participants in process workflows
- Replicate snapshots of accounting data to remote or field users

(b) The Internet

The Internet and its sibling, the internal corporate intranet, can also be used for all the same purposes as electronic mail. However, the Internet can also be utilized to realize the concept of the extended enterprise that reaches out to an audience including internal users, external customers, vendors, outsource service providers, press, analysts, and shareholders. In conjunction with an accounting system, the Internet can be used to:

- Advertise products and services and allow on-line order taking
- Disseminate financial information to any Internet user authorized to receive it
- Inform suppliers of procurement needs without paper orders
- Allow staff to submit budgets or travel and expense timesheets remotely
- Allow staff to requisition items remotely

- Allow staff to manage their salary and benefit packages remotely
- Allow staff to query accounting systems using low-cost desktop browser software

(c) Document Management

Document management is the digitizing of paper documents in order to route and manage them electronically. Because accounting departments can be inundated with paper orders, invoices, checks, and so forth, document management can deliver real benefits in terms of more efficient and lower-cost business processes. By scanning these documents into a digital document repository and tagging them to specific accounting transactions, the information domain of the accounting system is extended because users can have access to the original source documents associated with the accounting transactions. This provides the ultimate audit trail as well as eliminating a great deal of paper and paper-storage requirements from the accounting department.

(d) Workflow

Workflow, which is the automation of business processes through software, can play a major role in expanding the domain and extending the reach of client/server accounting applications. Workflow management software is like a choreographer of software processes, managing the linking of tasks within the accounting and external applications. Workflow can allow accounting business processes to be:

- Initiated in other applications and conclude in the accounting software
- Initiated in accounting, routed through other applications, and concluded in accounting
- Initiated in accounting and concluded in other applications

Workflow can take advantage of e-mail, the Internet, and document management as part of the automation of specific business processes. By initiating processes in nonaccounting applications such as worksheets or groupware like Lotus Notes, by concluding business processes in the same applications, or by disseminating data via e-mail, workflow expands the accounting domain and extends the reach of the accounting system to other nonaccounting-system users. By combining accounting application activities and tasks with activities and tasks in other business-management applications, workflow allows system managers to build process-centric virtual applications that transcend the boundaries of traditional functional departments within an organization.

(e) Software Components

Software components are discrete software applications designed to provide a specific, usually specialized, piece of functionality for use within larger generic business applications. The OLE objects discussed briefly in section 7.9 use technology that is designed to assist the development and deployment of software components. Accounting systems that are compliant with technology such as OLE or other component specifications such as the common-object-request-broker architecture (CORBA) can be extended through the use of specialized add-in components such as:

- Report writers for financial and audit reporting
- Charting and graphing software for visualizing balances and trends
- Image managers to enable inventory or employee catalogues
- Telephonic access tools for dialing customers or vendors directly

Usually, these software components are not sourced from the accounting software vendors but from a nonaccounting-oriented third party that develops component software for specialized uses. As the vendors producing software components increase and component sophistication matures, accounting applications will be expanded and extended into more innovative new areas.

(f) Extensible Accounting Checklist

Use the following checklist to help determine the relative sophistication of the extensible accounting offered by a client/server accounting package:

Extensibility Functions

- ☐ Support for messaging systems such as Microsoft MAPI, Lotus VIM, or Novell MHS
- ☐ Support for access to accounting data via desktop Web browsers such as Netscape Navigator, Mosiac, or Microsoft Internet Explorer
- ☐ Support for document- and image-management applications through OLE using packages such as Watermark Enterprise or Wang ImageVue
- ☐ Support for workflow management either internally or via a third party package such as FileNet Visual Workflo or Lotus Notes
- ☐ Support for integration of OLE 2.0 compliant software components and use of CORBA compliant business objects

7.11 CONCLUSION

There are a great many new styles of accounting and expectations from accounting software. This is why client/server accounting is fundamentally different from traditional accounting software and why much accounting software in use today is functionally and technologically obsolete. Consequently it is no surprise that new client/server accounting applications have many new and different design features from their predecessors, which is the topic of the next chapter.

CHAPTER EIGHT

Client/Server Accounting Software Design

8.1 INTRODUCTION

The shift to client/server computing is having a significant impact on the design of accounting applications. Many of the accounting packages released during the early 1990s are fundamentally different in design from previous generations of accounting software. Some of the most recently released packages built using object-oriented development technologies are different yet again from the first generation of client/server accounting packages in both their underlying design and deployment options. The purpose of this section is to introduce and discuss some of the new design characteristics of client/server accounting software and to establish some points of differentiation between first and second generation client/server accounting systems. The design criteria discussed are:

- More use by vendors of commercial standards in their package development
- More use by vendors of object-oriented software development techniques

- Partitioning of accounting software applications for scaleability
- Recognition of the importance of rule- and model-driven software design
- Recognition of the importance of isolating business events and logic
- Enabling applications for electronic mail, workflow, and decision support
- Providing ways to integrate applications with telephone systems or the Internet
- Allowing accounting applications to manage document and image data

8.2 COMMERCIAL STANDARDS AND NONPROPRIETARY TOOLS

Accounting software vendors are benefiting from the emergence of commercial standards and more robust development tools in information technology generally. While a commercial standard, such as Microsoft's Windows GUI, is not a true open standard (because the code behind Windows is not freely available in the public domain) it represents a standard to ordinary users in terms of real-world business computing. Because Microsoft Corporation is so influential in this area, Table 8.1 shows a selective comparison between true standards and commercial standards owned by Microsoft.

Table 8.1. Microsoft Commercial Standards.

Technology	*True Open Standard*	*Microsoft Commercial Standard*
Operating System	UNIX	NT
Graphical User Interface	OSG/Motif, X-Windows	Windows 3.1, 95
Database Access	ANSI SQL	ODBC
Programming Language	COBOL, C	Visual Basic
Object Technology	CORBA	OLE Active X

In the past, accounting software developers had to literally invent and build their own standards for technology as diverse as user interfaces, printer connectivity drivers, or file management systems. To some extent they were helped by the tools, for instance screen formatters or file systems, associated with specific proprietary operating systems. But if they wanted to be able to supply their packages on more than one platform they had to build their own portable software tools. The result was a great deal of repetitive effort by each vendor, a lack of standards generally in accounting applications, and packages that often had at least one area of their technological foundation that was of inferior quality.

Client/server accounting applications have moved rapidly away from this model toward a business model that embraces open and commercial standards wherever possible and minimizes the amount of invented-here programming required. Simply running their accounting software under the Microsoft Windows GUI, for example, allows vendors to take advantage of:

- Windows-consistent look and feel
- Windows memory management
- Windows fonts and printer management
- Windows visual-help systems
- Windows multiple-document interface (MDI)
- Windows cut-and-paste transfer of textual data
- Windows drag-and-drop manipulation of data

Similarly, by utilizing any RDBMS for the accounting database, a vendor can take advantage of another set of useful functionality, including:

- Transaction rollback to undo incomplete or failed transaction postings
- A password-driven security system and table views for restricting access to the data

- The availability of event-driven triggers for responding to exception conditions
- Powerful stored-procedure programs for managing database activities
- Replication capabilities to automatically copy data between databases
- Parallel processing support for improving overall system performance

These and other free functional benefits come with the GUI or the relational database, and significantly reduce the amount of effort on the part of the vendor to manage much of the underlying plumbing of the user interface or database management. By utilizing ANSI SQL in their programs, vendors can offer a choice of databases for their accounting applications with only minor changes to accommodate differences between the SQL variants used by leading commercial database packages. By utilizing fourth-generation languages for building the bulk of their applications, vendors can reduce the time to market for new modules and accelerate the enhancement of existing modules, albeit with a performance penalty over traditional programming languages in many cases.

The success of Microsoft products commercially means that most accounting vendors have aligned themselves marginally, mainly, or completely with certain Microsoft products. Some vendors are in danger of becoming Microsoft captives in the same way that vendors were IBM captives in the past. Examples of Microsoft's increasing influence in the area of client/server accounting software design and deployment are many and include:

- Microsoft Windows is the universal standard client GUI for client/server accounting systems.
- Microsoft MAPI is the most popular e-mail protocol used to e-mail enable client/server accounting applications.
- Microsoft Office is the most popular desktop productivity suite to which accounting applications can transfer data.

- Microsoft OLE is the most popular component and application integration technology used by client/server accounting applications.
- Microsoft NT is quickly catching UNIX as the server operating system offered by most client/server accounting vendors.
- Microsoft SQL Server is quickly catching Oracle or Sybase as the RDBMS supported by most client/server accounting vendors.
- A handful of client/server accounting applications are wholly written using Microsoft's Visual Basic language or Access or FoxPro database development tools.

Clearly Microsoft is fast becoming the most influential partner in the industry for accounting vendors, displacing what used to be IBM's role. This role is only likely to be strengthened as Microsoft improves the marketing of its new BackOffice suite of server applications including the NT operating systems, SQL Server RDBMS, Exchange Server for message management, and Internet Information Server for electronic commerce.

From the accounting-system manager's perspective, whatever their view of Microsoft or its products, open, or commercial standards, there are real advantages to using accounting software that makes use of standards or commercially popular tools including:

- A consistency of look, feel, and functionality with other business applications that reduces learning curves and increases productivity
- A wider choice of add-in or add-on capabilities because the same standards are supported by application vendors other than simply accounting application vendors
- An expectation that vendors can get products to market and improve products faster through use of standards
- An expectation that more emphasis can be put on enhancing functionality because vendors do not have to be concerned with other nonfunctional programming tasks managed by the standards

- An expectation that functional benefits can be derived from enhancements made to the underlying standard or tools to add value to the accounting application

8.3 OBJECT ORIENTATION

While the client/server accounting vendors are making more and more use of commercial standards and tools in their applications, some are also exploring object-oriented (OO) design and deployment as a means of building the next generation of component-driven accounting applications. A true OO accounting application is fundamentally different from traditional accounting applications. While it is difficult for a user to tell the difference between an OO and a non-OO accounting system, from the developer's perspective they are as different as chalk and cheese. Designing an accounting system from an OO perspective is a wholly different approach, so a basic understanding of OO concepts is required to understand why.

An excellent introduction to OO technology for business managers is David A. Taylor, *Object Oriented Technology: A Manager's Guide*, (Reading: Addison-Wesley, 1991) in which Taylor explains the three essential mechanisms of OO technology: objects, messages, and classes. An object is a package of data attributes and procedures for working on that data. The procedures are called methods and an object's data can only be accessed via these methods. Objects communicate with one another using messages. A message is a request passed by a sending object to a receiving object specifying a method to be used to carry out an action. Many objects can use the same methods but the way the method responds to the message may differ—this is called polymorphism—whereby a common method, such as printing an object, can respond in many different ways depending on the object using it. Objects are instances of a specific class or collection of similar objects. A class has one or more common ancestor object(s) whose data and methods can be used as a template for creating specialized descendent objects.

Using a simplified example of an account class helps to put these concepts into practice. A common ancestor object called account could be defined with its own collection of data elements and methods that might include:

Data Elements	*Methods*	*Description*
AccountCode	CheckDuplicateCode	A unique code and method to prevent the creation of a duplicate code
AccountName	GetName	An account name and method to provide the name of the account to other objects
AccountType	ValidateType	An account-type identifier and method to ensure that the account type is valid
AccountBalance	GetBalance	An account current balance and method to provide the balance figure to other objects
	PrintAccount	A generic method to printing the account code, name, and balance sorted by account code

Using this account ancestor object we can inherit all the data elements and methods into a new descendent object within the same class, called customer. But because customer is a specialized instance of account class object, it has some new data and methods and a different response to the PrintAccount method, for example:

Data Elements	*Methods*	*Description*
CustomerTaxID	GetTaxID	A tax-related number and method to provide the tax ID to other objects
CustomerAddress	GetAddress	A customer address and method to provide the address to other objects
CustomerOverdue	GetOverdue	The customer's overdue balance and method to provide the balance figure to other objects
	PrintAccount	Through polymorphism, the response to the print method when used for a customer is to print the account code, name, tax ID, and overdue balance sorted by overdue balance

Already you can see how the account class can be expanded from the base account object to a whole series of more specialized objects in the form of an inheritance tree, as shown in Figure 8.1. At each level of the tree more specialized data elements are added or specific methods introduced to cope with the demands of a more specific instance of the ancestor object. At each level the object inherits all or some of the data elements and methods of its ancestor object(s).

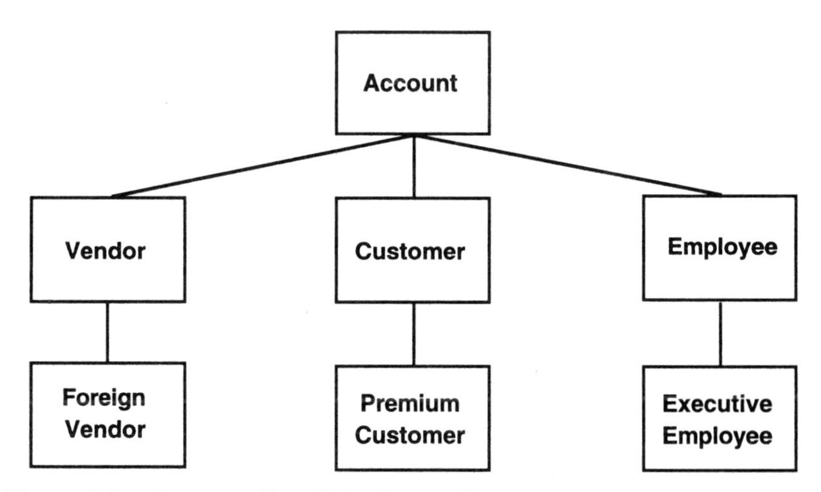

Figure 8.1. Account Class Inheritance Tree.

Accounting systems are particularly suited for the application of OO design techniques because so many aspects of an accounting system are essentially a hierarchy of specialization, for example:

Type	*Example*	*Variants*
Structure	Account	GL account, vendor, customer, employee
Transaction	Order	Requisition, purchase order, sales order
Query	Balance	Inception to date, year to date, overdue
Report	Audit trail	Debits and credits, receipts, payments

Instead of the accounting system being represented by a collection of linked database tables, database queries, program code, date entry, and query forms, it becomes a massive overlapping, interlocking, and interdependent hierarchy of object classes sharing a common core of procedural methods. Instead of the accounting system being represented by a massive block of program source code, it is represented by a roadmap that can be viewed from a macro- or microperspective and easily navigated by the developers working on specific enhancements.

By designing an accounting system using OO techniques, vendors are laying the groundwork for highly flexible accounting systems that are based on best-practice frameworks of class libraries and can be deployed in pieces or as a whole. Already vendors are working on building these frameworks for use in specific vertical industries such as healthcare or construction. Customers can then take these core frameworks and build their own more specialized objects and classes on top of these industry frameworks. Clearly this will completely change the whole basis for user customization of accounting software.

There are three key benefits to the use of OO design in accounting software. The developer benefits from the reusability of common ancestor objects and the polymorphic potential of common methods. While the initial effort to redesign accounting software using OO techniques is huge, it is when the reusability of classes, objects, and methods kicks in that the effort to broaden and deepen the application functionality becomes ever easier. The user benefits from the consistency of look, feel, and function delivered by systems built from common objects. There will no longer be obvious differences between accounting modules and functions resulting from their programming by different development teams because everything essentially inherits its behavior from something else. Both developer and user benefit from the ability of the developer to supply class libraries and objects as foundations or frameworks that can be used to specialize the system even further to meet the needs of specific businesses not addressed by the vendor.

8.4 PARTITIONED APPLICATIONS

The client/server architecture has focused more attention on the way that applications are constructed to take advantage of the distributed nature of the architecture. Breaking down an application into discrete layers allows some flexibility in the way an application can be deployed in order to make best use of the hardware resources available. The Gartner Group was one of the first industry analysts to focus on this aspect of client/server application design and Gartner has gradually refined their models of application design to illustrate various ways an application can be partitioned and deployed singly or combined on different physical hardware devices.

To understand partitioning it helps to identify the five layers that make up a typical accounting application:

Layer	*Description*
Presentation	The functionality that delivers what the user actually sees on the screen when they use a data-entry, query, or request form.
Validation	The functionality that is used to validate that the data the user enters into screen forms is correct and handles informing the user of errors.
Processes	The code, stored procedures, or triggers that carry out major transaction-related processes such as posting journals, running currency revaluations, creating reports, printing multiple documents, or batch-importing transactions.
Business Logic	The codification of the business rules that may be utilized by the program validation or process functions in order to reflect the specific needs of the business using the application.
Data Management	The functionality that organizes and manages the accounting data in a structured, reliable, and secure manner.

Traditional host-centric accounting systems, in which all the resources are centralized on the host and dumb terminals are used on the desktop, are partitioned as in Figure 8.2. This type of partitioning is sometimes called distributed presentation.

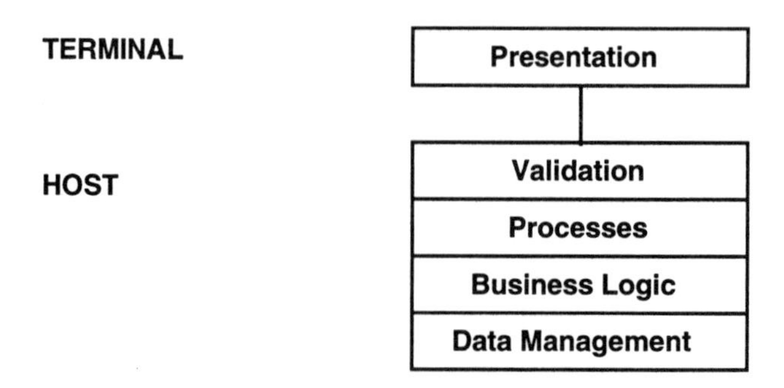

Figure 8.2. Host Application Partitioning (Terminal)

More advanced host-centric accounting systems, in which all the resources are centralized on the host and intelligent workstations or personal computers are used on the desktop, are partitioned as in Figure 8.3.

So-called two-tier client/server accounting systems can be partitioned in one of two ways: with a thin or thick client desktop computer connecting to a more powerful server computer. A thin client deployment is essentially similar to the workstation shown in Figure 8.3. In some cases, early versions of so-called client/server accounting software were simply this type of host-system architecture conveniently renamed for marketing purposes. A thick-client deployment does at least break the host-centric mold but requires a pumped-up desktop client with a fast processor, plenty of local memory, and disk resources to cope with the extra processing load being handled at the

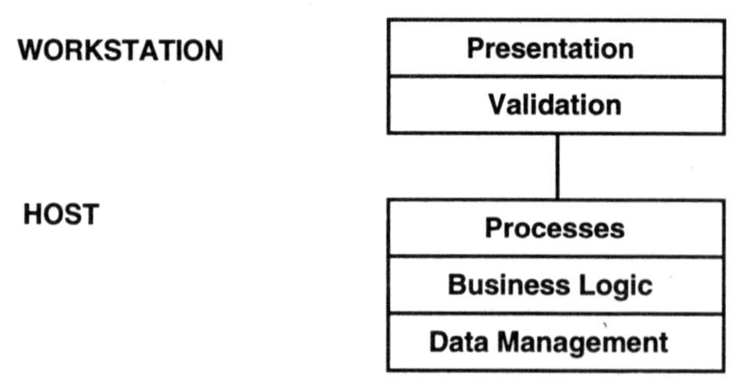

Figure 8.3. Host-Application Partitioning (Workstation).

desktop machine. Note that in a two-tier architecture, the system scaleability is isolated to one server machine, which may prove a limitation in complex transaction or high volume transaction businesses. The two-tier client server deployments are shown in Figure 8.4.

So-called three-tier client/server accounting applications can be deployed in a number of different ways, as shown in Figure 8.5. Three-tier client/server provides both more flexibility in system deployment options and more scaleability to cope with growth in transaction complexity or volume. This is because the applications have been designed and partitioned with more granularity, a burden for the developer but a benefit for the user. The essential difference

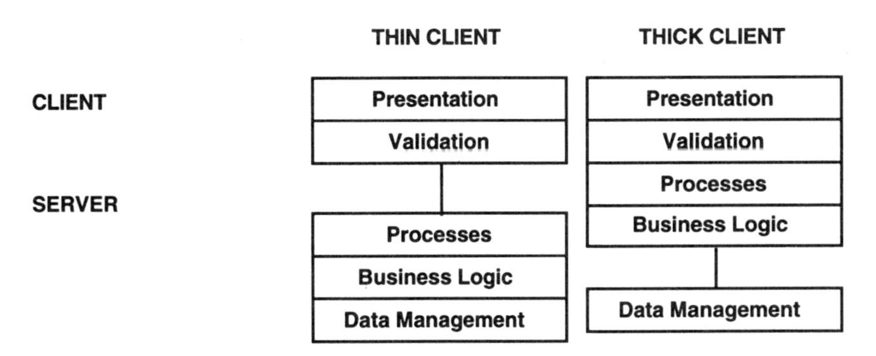

Figure 8.4. Two-Tier Client/Server Partitioning.

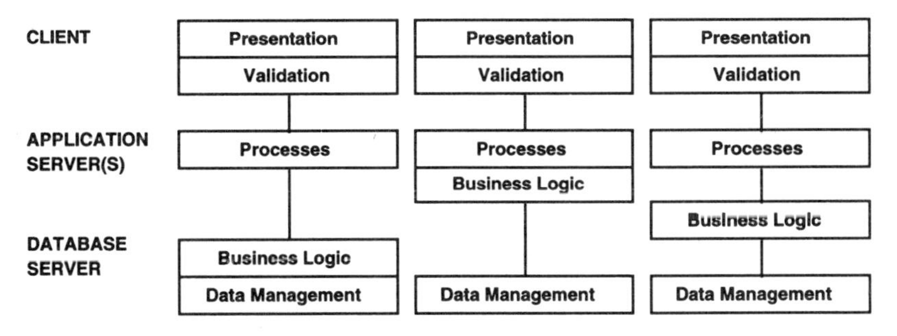

Figure 8.5. Three-Tier Client/Server Partitioning.

in three-tier client/server is the introduction of a third- or middle-application tier that can be physically deployed on one or more hardware servers. The business logic and/or the processes can be located on this middle tier, isolating them from the rest of the application and allowing their hardware resources to be scaled separately. In this configuration you are really using a client/server/server architecture as outlined in Table 8.2.

Because application and database servers can be deployed either as part of local-area, wide-area, or Internet networks, three-tier client/server affords a more flexible deployment option for client/server accounting systems. Because the process and business logic services can also be located on their own dedicated resources, three-tier client/server also offers better scaleability for a client/server accounting system. However, the best flexibility and scaleability are offered by n-tier client/server systems that are not limited to either two- or three-tier architectures, but can deploy the middle tier across multiple server resources. Organizations that anticipate rapid growth or transaction peaks and troughs should avoid two-tier client/server applications and opt instead for three- or n-tier applications.

8.5 EXPOSING METADATA

A great deal of the value in an accounting system is not only stored in the data itself but also in the data about the data, so-called metadata.

Table 8.2. Client/Server/Server.

Tier	*Description*
Client	A desktop PC or workstation running presentation and validation services
Application Server	A server providing business logic and/or business process services
Database Server	A server providing data management or data management and business logic services

Metadata is information about the data that the accounting application needs to know and use in order to:

- Prevent invalid data being stored in the database
- Present and format data when displayed by the user interface
- Determine other properties and behavior of the data

Now all this metadata can be hidden away someplace in the application source code or it can be stored in a structured way in tables in the database, just like the data itself. When metadata is stored in this way, it is usually referred to as a data dictionary because it provides a tool to understand more about the meaning and context of the data itself through its metadata. Like the data itself, this data dictionary can be exposed to users or other applications to provide a richer context for interacting with the accounting data.

The accounting application is then designed to go through the data dictionary for carrying out certain tasks such as displaying a data-entry form or validating data being imported into the system from an external application. The data dictionary may store metadata for every column within every table utilized by the accounting system and may include other information about the tables themselves or their relationships with other tables. In this sense it provides a kind of road map of the whole data structure of the application. Each column in a table may have metadata that describes a whole range of information about that data. Using the column account-code and in table accounts, one might expect the data dictionary to contain information about the data stored in the account-code column, as seen in Table 8.3. These are just some of the metadata items that could be required to be defined for each data item.

Isolating this information in this way makes the metadata easy to change without having to change anything about the way the application works, and without having to go into the application code and make laborious source-code changes. Then if the data dictionary is exposed to application system managers, it provides a very powerful customization tool that requires little or no actual code changes to effect many useful system look and feel changes from an operator

Table 8.3. Account Code Metadata.

Metadata	*Description*	*Example*
Name	The logical name of the column in the database table	Account Code
Label	The label for the data when it is displayed in a form on your screen	Account Code
Visible	Is this data usually visible on the screen or should it normally be hidden from view?	Visible
Type	The type of data that is allowed to be used to represent this data	Numeric
Length	The maximum length of the data that is allowed for this code	10 positions
Decimals	If the data is numeric then what precision of decimals is permitted?	0
Format	The way the data should be formatted when presented on screen to a user	999–999–9999
Prompt	The short prompt that should be displayed when a user is about to enter a new code	"Enter a 10-digit account code using numbers only."
Error	The message that should display if the user enters an incorrect code	"This code is invalid—try entering a new code"
Help	A block of text that is displayed by the help system if the user requests help on this data item	Appropriate help text

perspective. By changing metadata properties in a data dictionary you can simply and quickly:

- Customize screen labels to use your own specific business terminology
- Increase or decrease the length of data-entry items to suit coding needs
- Hide specific data items on specific data-entry forms because they either display sensitive information or are not used by your operators

- Edit prompts, help text, and messages to make them easier to understand, more helpful to your users, or reflect jargon understood by your business users
- Change the colors and display formats of data to suit local preferences

Isolating this type of metadata also makes it much easier for the vendor to deliver multilingual versions of its applications because the different-language versions simply access the data through different data dictionaries—one for each operating language. This also allows applications to operate in multilingual deployments so that one system may support many operators working with different language versions of the product. In fact the core application is the same, but multiple data dictionaries are being used by the application—one for each language variant.

The availability of a data dictionary does not just benefit application users, it is also useful for integrating accounting applications with other systems particularly when there is a need to feed data in or out of the accounting system. Other systems can also make use of the data dictionary metadata to:

- Ensure that correctly formatted data is being passed to the accounting system
- Display the same labels, prompts, and help text to users of nonaccounting applications that are viewing or entering the accounting data
- Help with managing batch processes or workflows that require passing of data to and from the accounting system and other complementary applications

Obviously there is a fine line between a data dictionary that delivers real added value, and a complex data dictionary that creates real processing overhead for the application and therefore negatively impacts performance. But in general, an application that has been designed around a data dictionary concept and exposes this dictionary to systems managers is likely to be more easily customized than an application without a data dictionary. It is also likely to be a better bet for deployment in a multilingual or specialized business in which access to the textual context of the data can be helpful. Many modern application-development languages and fourth-generation languages use a dictionary-driven approach to building their application data entry and query forms, so client/server accounting systems built using these types of tools usually provide a data dictionary for users.

Many vendors are exposing their metadata to allow users to integrate decision-support tools such as query, reporting, OLAP, or EIS tools more closely with the accounting data. Instead of working directly against the accounting data and requiring the tool users to build their own accounting metadata in the decision-support tool, these tools can work through the accounting metadata in the accounting system. This reduces the burden on the decision-support tool and its users, while also ensuring that consistent information can be delivered across all decision-support front ends because they all access the accounting data through the same metadata layer.

A data dictionary containing metadata is a rich repository of information about an accounting database, and even if it is not used for customization purposes it provides a useful and detailed description of certain aspects of the application for use by other applications and for understanding the system design.

8.6 EVENT-, RULE-, AND MESSAGE-DRIVEN MODELS

Designers of client/server accounting applications have begun to recognize the importance of identifying and isolating business events, the rules that determine how an application should respond to a specific event within a specific business context, and the messages generated as a result. By isolating these events, rules, and messages the application developer is introducing another type of granularity into their accounting system that increases its adaptability to different business scenarios. By exposing these events, rules, and messages so they can be customized when deployed, vendors are allowing users to custom fit these events, rules, and messages to their own functional tasks and processes. The isolation of business events, rules, and messages also fits into the object-oriented-application design approach because rules and events can often be mapped directly to an object's behavioral methods.

Using the 80/20 rule, probably 80 percent of business events are extensions of three events managed by an application database: the insertion, updating, or deletion of data. Each time one of these events takes place in an application, it may also be classed as a business event depending on the data being managed by the event. Each variation of business event may have specific rules associated with it that determine the action messages generated by the application depending on certain conditions. This can be represented as a looping relationship as in Figure 8.6. The rules associated with an event are often more or less complex versions of the IF...THEN...ELSE construct that is a foundation of basic programming logic.

A simplified example of common business events in a general ledger (GL) is the maintenance of chart-of-account codes as outlined in Table 8.4. Each time an account is inserted, updated, or deleted, the accounting application recognizes these as separate business

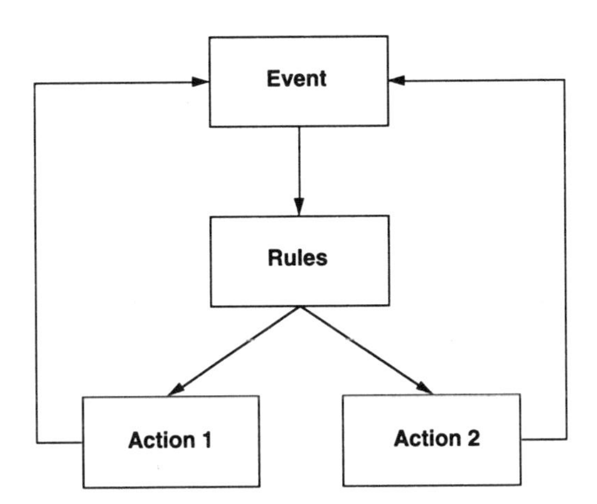

Figure 8.6. An Example Business Event Loop.

Table 8.4. GL Account Business Events.

Database Event	*Business Event*	*Rule*	*Action*
Insert	InsertAccount	ValidateCode	IF account code already used THEN reject insert and inform user with error message. ELSE if account code is unique accept insert and inform user with success message.
Update	UpdateAccount	ChangeCode	IF account code updated by user THEN reject update and inform user with error message. ELSE if account code is unchanged accept update and inform user with success message.
Delete	DeleteAccount	DeleteCode	IF transactions exist on ledger for account code deleted THEN reject delete and inform user with error message. ELSE if no transactions exist prompt user to confirm delete through dialog box and delete account.
Insert, Update, or Delete	AuditEvent	RecordAudit	IF system flag set to force all database events to be audited THEN insert record into system–audit table recording type of event, user ID, and date/time of event. ELSE do nothing.

events, applies specific rules, and takes action based on the result of applying the rule(s).

In practice the insert of an account, for example, can generate many more business events than those outlined in Table 8.4 and be subject to more complex rules. In an accounting system it is typically the insertion, updating, and deletion of transactions (such as orders, invoices, or checks) that generate both the most business events and the most complex rules. The point is that these rules are identified and isolated from the general program logic and simply called or invoked when required. This makes them easier to edit and amend by adding more or less complexity to comply with the requirements of different business scenarios. Inserting or deleting an account in a general ledger may require less sophistication in one business than another. It may also require less business-event and rule sophistication than inserting a new customer account for example.

The insertion of a new customer account is a good example of where isolating the business event allows the system designers to create a collaboration scenario that crosses functional boundaries between staff in an organization. In this case the event is used as a trigger for a sequence of notifications that reach out to a number of people unconnected with the actual insertion of the customer data. Instead of forcing the data-entry operator to hold up creating the customer account in order to call or fax participants for their essential input information, the system takes over and automates this chore using some form of electronic messaging to manage what is essentially an event driven workflow. Table 8.5 shows how inserting a new customer could prompt various notifications to take place.

Notifications are messages generated as a result of a specific business event taking place and firing a particular rule based condition. Notifications can be viewed as comprising five types:

1. Display Messages
   - Simple informational messages such as, "Your new account inserted successfully and is ready for use," which display to the user immediately responsible for the data being managed at that point in time

Table 8.5. New Customer Account Notifications.

Event	*Rule*	*Notification*
InsertCustomer	SetCredit	Send e-mail to credit controller with relevant customer and order data to allow a credit check to be performed and a credit limit set on the customer record.
	AllocateRep	Send e-mail to sales manager with relevant customer and order data to allow manager to allocate new customer an appropriate salesperson.
	WelcomeCustomer	Generate a form letter that welcomes the customer and send e-mail to marketing to send letter with standard information packet.
	ThankSource	Send e-mail to line of business manager with contact data of source of customer contact so source can be called and thanked for business.

- Simple alert messages sent by e-mail such as "Your available cash balance has dropped below $100,000," which warn specific types of user that an exception event has occurred

2. Electronic Messages with Attachments

   A message sent by e-mail in which specific information is packaged with the message as an attachment to allow the recipient to take action outside of the system. For example to supply the credit-control manager with new customer information to allow a credit check call to be made.

3. Electronic Messages with Actionable Attachments

   A message sent by e-mail with an attachment of package information that allows the recipient to action the item. For example a request to approve an invoice that presents the approver with the invoice data, a checkbox to confirm the invoice as approved, and a button to click to update the system with the new invoice status.

4. Electronic Data Transfer Messages on an Intra- or Interapplication Basis

   This is a specialized type of message that is not visible to users but transfers data between tables or screens within applications. This allows a business event to pass data around and between applications. For example the purchase-requisition data-entry form could have an insert event that passes data to the purchase-requisition-approval form, which is then sent to an approver for actioning.

5. Data-Generating Messages

   This is a business event that causes data to be inserted, updated, or deleted from tables within the same application database or other application databases. This is often used to create simple audit records of user activity in a system, to cascade deletions so that a delete in one table forces a delete in other connected tables, or to replicate data from one database into another database, which might be required by an intercompany transaction.

An effective notification system can deliver so much added value to an accounting application that it can only be a few years before every system ships with some form of notification system built-in. However, sophisticated notification systems depend on the accounting application being designed around the business event, rule, and message paradigm. To date, only a handful of client/server vendors have restructured their systems around this paradigm but this is likely to change as more vendors and users recognize the power and potential of business event-, rule-, and message-driven systems.

8.7 BUSINESS INTELLIGENCE

Many surveys undertaken over the last five years have highlighted that financial system managers are often dissatisfied with their accounting applications. They are especially dissatisfied with the ability of their systems to provide useful management and decision-support information because of inadequate or difficult to use reporting and analysis functionality. Part of the reason for this is that accounting systems have focused for too long on managing transaction processing rather than delivering business intelligence.

The accurate and secure entry of transactions along with rock-solid audit trails for those transactions is of course fundamental to all accounting systems. So are the checks-and-balances-type reporting that systems must produce to support the transaction-processing function. But transaction capture should not be the true purpose of an accounting system. Rather the system should be viewed as an information asset whose true worth is to act as a real-time, business-management system. In the following sections, three approaches to the deployment of business intelligence software are discussed using executive information systems (EIS), On-Line Analytical Processing (OLAP), and data warehouse systems as examples. Each of these deployment options may be used alone or in combination with each other to deliver business intelligence from the foundation accounting system, as shown in Figure 8.7.

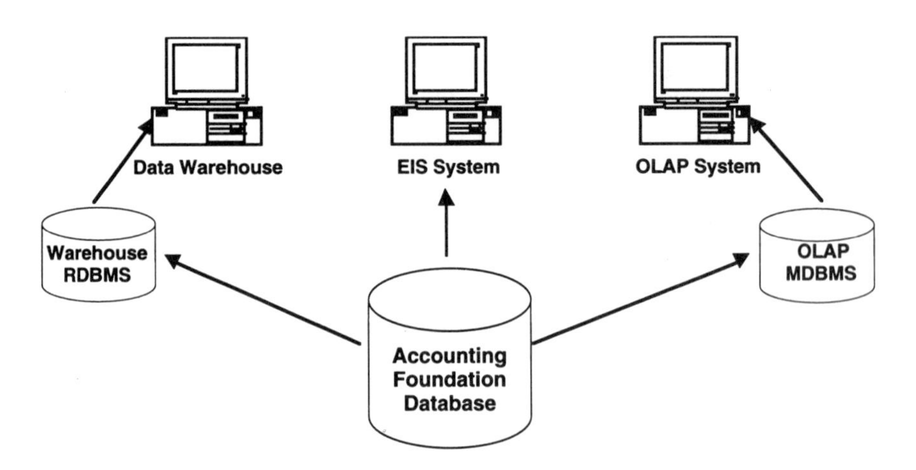

Figure 8.7. Three Deployments of Business Intelligence Systems.

(a) Business Intelligence Using EIS

Executive information systems (EIS) are not new, having been around on mainframes for two decades during which they were often termed decision support systems (DSS). This was a software market dominated by companies such as Comshare and Pilot Software delivering costly systems to large, mainframe-based, enterprise customers. What is new about EIS is that the systems have moved on to low-cost desktop platforms and can now be justified by most businesses as cost-effective additions to any accounting system.

A common rationale for an EIS was to enable a business to track critical success factors (CSFs) or key performance indicators (KPIs). These were internally defined metrics that business managers could use to monitor their business and compare it to peer businesses. The classic financial ratios produced by financial report writers are essentially internal KPIs.

An EIS typically managed highly summarized information, presented in fixed, on-screen formats to senior management users for whom the EIS presented a kind of business management console or dashboard. While the EIS could do a good job at visually presenting business intelligence, it suffered from drawbacks such as:

- No ability to vary the presentation or content of the information without programming
- No ability to investigate the data by drilling down, or unpeeling the onion
- Presentations were predefined so ad hoc analysis was limited or nonexistent
- The EIS was a snapshot of data usually removed from the source data more than once
- The EIS put an administrative burden on IS to collect, reformat, and aggregate the data

Consequently EIS systems, while useful, are limited business intelligence tools.

The term briefing book often referred to the presentation style used by many EIS systems. Data was gathered into an on-screen briefing book that the user could page through to view the contents. Today's briefing book is a little more sophisticated, acting as an intelligent container for objects that might be financial reports, document images, tables, charts, and pictures.

These modern briefing books are powered by Microsoft's OLE technology that allows a discrete application object such as a report or a chart to be dragged and dropped onto the container briefing book's workspace. The briefing book can be separated into pages that are identified by tabs. Clicking a tab with the mouse opens the page and displays the report or chart. Some briefing books simply redisplay the data snapshot taken at the time they were compiled. Others will dynamically requery the database to update the briefing book's contents each time it is opened. Briefing books can now be distributed to users via e-mail so that an analyst can compile the book, then publish it electronically to a distribution list of subscriber users. The briefing book is attached to an e-mail message and can be retrieved and viewed on the manager's local machine. This extends the reach of EIS to remote users and road warriors.

(b) Business Intelligence Using OLAP

In a 1993 white paper (*Providing OLAP to User Analysts*, E. F. Codd & Associates, 1993) the authors and their sponsor, Arbor Software, coined the term On-Line Analytical Processing (OLAP). Intended to contrast with the term OLTP, this paper discussed a new architecture for decision-support systems called OLAP and suggested 12 defining rules for OLAP applications. While the 12 rules of OLAP are useful, OLAP as delivered by commercial applications is fundamentally about:

- The use of a multidimensional database engine for data management
- The ability to import and convert data from heterogeneous file and database systems

- The provision of graphical query and reporting tools allowing ad hoc data analysis

By utilizing a multidimensional, rather than relational database engine, OLAP applications used a foundation that delivered a means to analyze summarized information flexibly and above all quickly. In a multidimensional database a value can be stored for the intersection of every combination of dimension managed by the database. It is therefore relatively easy for an application to zero in on a specific matrix of values very quickly and to react to ad hoc user changes in the dimensional set requested in order to provide a new view of the data.

OLAP may be client- or server-based. Client-based OLAP locates the multidimensional database and query processing locally on a client workstation and is often memory-dependent. This may be appropriate when there is a small community of OLAP users in an organization and a single source for the data. An example of a client-based OLAP application is Applix TM/1.

Server-based OLAP locates the multidimensional database and query processing primarily on the server and is often disk-dependent. This is appropriate if the source data needs to be collected from heterogeneous source databases and there is a large community of OLAP users. An example of a server based OLAP application is Arbor Software's Essbase. Some OLAP applications, such as PowerPlay from Cognos, may be deployed as an OLAP client application or as the front end to an OLAP server application.

From a business intelligence perspective, OLAP delivers a rich set of functionality including:

- Multidimensional retrieval criteria that can be varied on an ad hoc basis
- Easy point and click rotation of data axis to recast matrix reports
- Drilldown to uncover detail balances from summary balances
- Concertina functions to collapse and expand views of the data
- Drillthrough to reach out to transaction data in the original source database

OLAP is often used as the front end to a data warehouse or datamart but is becoming an essential standard component of client/server accounting systems either as a built-in module or through integration of third party OLAP technology.

(c) Business Intelligence Using Data Warehouses

Data warehouses are an attempt to get clean, unified data that has been optimized for query intensive activities into a single database. The data may come from internal or external systems and data warehouses; or their datamart may be deployed at various levels within a distributed enterprise.

The warehouse can then be surrounded with specialized query and reporting tools that treat the warehouse as a hub application for decision support and business intelligence. Although the concept of data warehouses has been around for some time, the deployment of data warehouses has recently become popular for these reasons:

- Users of older mainframe and mini business management software—so called legacy systems—are using warehouses as a means to clean, aggregate, and consolidate their legacy system data. The warehouse then provides a platform for using low-cost, desktop, graphical query and reporting tools against the data in order to extract better value from it.
- Users that have moved a subset of their business management applications to client/server platforms use a warehouse as a means to combine information from these new platforms with data from existing legacy systems that, for one reason or another, are not yet ready to convert to the new platforms.

However, for many businesses the setup and administration costs of setting up and maintaining a data warehouse may outweigh the value of this additional technology infrastructure. The need for a data warehouse may be marginal if the line of business software itself provided the business intelligence functionality needed, without having to export or stage data into the data warehouse.

An alternative or adjunct to the data warehouse is the datamart. A datamart is a smaller scale information-delivery initiative that is designed to service a specific functional need, such as sales and marketing analysis, or a specific user group, such as executive management. These datamarts may be set up as separately managed databases fed from one or more source transaction systems or they may be fed from the main data warehouse. In the latter case, they are at least two steps away from the operational data, which may limit their timeliness or effectiveness. Datamarts may also be used as a stepping stone to the main corporate data warehouse. The various architectures for datamarts are shown in Figure 8.8.

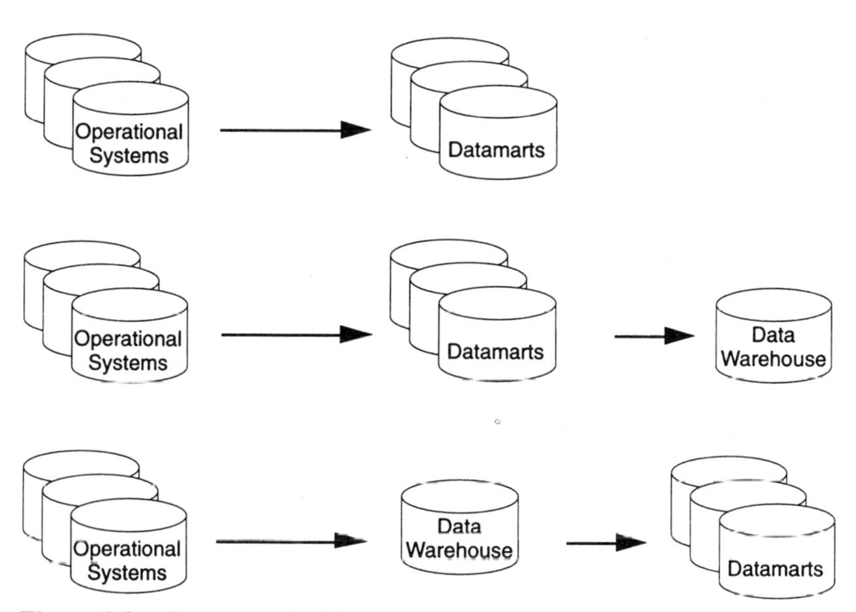

Figure 8.8. Datamart Architectures.

(d) Practical Business Intelligence Features

Business intelligence demands that software uses certain features to provide the functionality required to analyze data and pinpoint business intelligence. These features are finding their way into client/server accounting software either because they have been included in the core functionality, or because links have been built to third party packages to supply the functionality from an external application.

(i) Cross Tabulations

Cross tabulations (crosstabs) are the basis of most business intelligence systems. Crosstabs are matrix tables where the intersection of a row and a column provides a discrete piece of information. A worksheet is a two-dimensional crosstab. A financial statement report is another two-dimensional crosstab, but in which extensive conditional processing has taken place at both the row- and column-content levels.

Crosstabs in business intelligence systems are usually multidimensional: Apart from the essential row and column dimensions, the data can be viewed against one or more additional dimensions. For example, consider a typical sales crosstab using four data dimensions: salesperson, product, city, and month. Using each dimension as the row content, the cross tabulation could be constructed in one of three ways. For example if salesperson were selected as the row content these possibilities exist:

Row	***Column***	***View Dimensions***	
Salesperson	Month	Product	City
Salesperson	Product	Month	City
Salesperson	City	Month	Product

As any of the four dimensions can be used as the row content this gives twelve possible matrices. But in addition, each dimension may be filtered to show some (rather than all or one) of the valid codes or names within a dimension. Consequently just these four dimensions can drive an extensive number of different views of the data that make it more likely that the data will meet the varying criteria of a wider range of information users.

Crosstabs usually provide a standard range of SQL aggregate functions to report numeric values at the row/column intersection. Based on the example above these could include:

- a sum e.g. total sales dollars
- a count e.g. number of products actually sold
- an average e.g. average sale value of products sold
- maximum/minimum e.g. maximum or minimum sale value
- <, <=, >, >= e.g. total sales greater than targeted sales

More sophisticated crosstab functionality allows the building of rules to allow the system to automatically highlight exceptions, such as values above or below a certain threshold constant such as a budget estimate or a stock price floor. This is achieved by using color, visual icons, animation, or sound in order to differentiate the exception data in a crosstab view. Data ranking may also be offered to show the top- or bottom-ten ranked products or salespeople for example.

(ii) Data Rotation

Once the fundamental data dimensions of a crosstab have been defined you can see that a common requirement would be to rotate or pivot the data dimensions. Essentially this means reselecting the dimensions used for either the row or column content (or both). This is usually achieved using the drag-and-drop functionality of a graphical user interface (GUI). Using the mouse, an icon representing a valid crosstab dimension can simply be dragged onto the row or column area of an on-screen crosstab panel and the crosstab automatically recomputed to reflect the new dimensional view.

The key here is that this can be done on the fly and that the system is able to respond quickly enough to keep the analyst's attention. This is a primary attraction of all OLAP systems and the worksheet pivoting functions found in desktop worksheet products such as Microsoft Excel.

(iii) Data Drilling

Data drilling is the term used for navigating data from summary to detail levels, in other words uncovering more information about an item. In accounting systems it is used as an investigative tool to answer questions that result from viewing data at the big-picture balance level. It allows a manager to begin managing data at a macro level but to choose to manage certain data at a micro level if circumstances warrant.

Drilldown. Crosstabs and other report formats are always aggregations of a set of transactional data that meets the dimension and filter criteria selected by the user. In other words to arrive at the crosstab, the system had to retrieve, select, and aggregate the transactions from which the crosstab was derived. These transactions may be stored temporarily, or the crosstab may hold a unique reference (a key) to allow it to access the set of transactions used to derive a particular value.

In any case crosstabs and reports in business intelligence tools generally provide a drilldown function. Drilldown allows a user to highlight a row or column value in a crosstab or report and click on the row or a button to navigate to the next level of detail.

There are two common types of drilldown: balance-driven and document-driven. Both are used primarily as means to investigate the data to look for discrepancies; unpeeling the onion is an analogy frequently used.

This is an example of balance drilldown against a general ledger income account that uncovers some unusual bank charges in period 12:

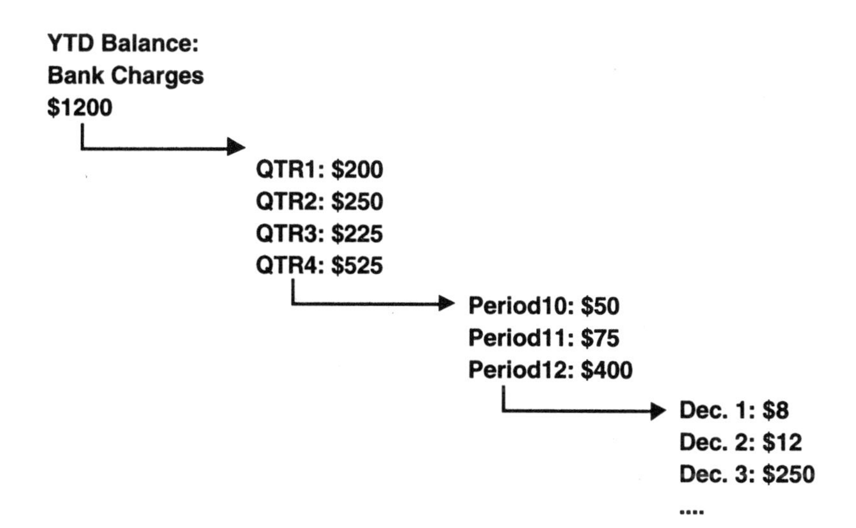

This is an example of a document drilldown that uncovers the origin of a certain check payment:

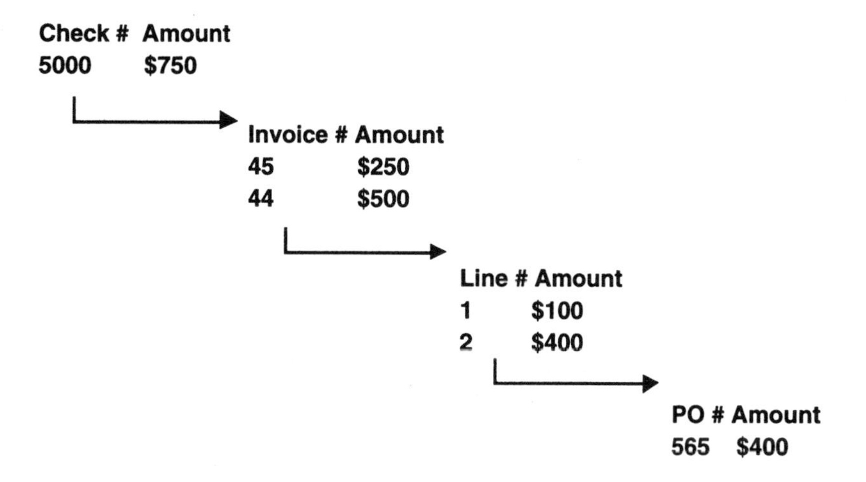

Drillthrough. The only difference between drilldown and drillthrough is that in the document drilldown example above all the data may have come from within the same physical database. Alternatively the purchase-order data may have been sourced from an external system requiring the drilldown to drill through or across to the supporting system in order to complete the data navigation.

Expand and Collapse (Concertina). Concertina viewing is a variation on the drilldown theme. Whereas drilldown is used to navigate the user down a specific path from summary to detail, concertina viewing is used to expand or collapse a current view of the data in order to toggle to the next level of detail within the current report format. You may concertina a row or a column, for example in the table below the YTD balance column can be expanded across to show the balances by quarter:

Expanded Column

Row	Column YTD	Qtr. 1	Qtr. 2	Qtr. 3
Dept. 1	$1000	$500	$200	$300
Dept. 2	$1500	$650	$350	$500

In the example below the Due 90 Days balance row can be expanded downwards to show the overdue invoices:

Expanded Row

Row	Column Due 90 Days	Invoice #	Due Date	Amount
Dept. 1	$1000			
		55	1/1/95	$450
		86	2/1/95	$250
		88	3/1/95	$300
Dept. 2	$1500			

Visual Hotspots. Hotspots are used to allow another form of drilldown, this time from visual screen objects such as charts or maps. In a chart the hotspot is an area of the chart on which the user can click with the mouse to display more detail. Usually these hotspots are on the bars, lines, or pie sections that comprise a business chart. State, county, or city names may be used as hotspots on a map to allow the users to see the sales figures attributable to a geographic territory on the map.

(iv) Contextual Linking

Contextual linking is simply the ability to make a collection of objects such as a table list, a summary report, and a chart dependent on each other. Changing a value in the table list for example can be immediately reflected in the report and the chart. This allows a highly visual and immediate way to "what if" the information presented in order to perform ad hoc analysis and see the information presented in different formats.

Contextual linking is also useful for impact analysis. For example, to assist in currency hedging decisions it can be helpful to vary forward exchange rates for currencies in which exposure exists. A business intelligence system could display a screen with two panels: one to display projected forward currency exchange rates and another to display a chart of existing exposure by currency. Varying a forward exchange rate in one panel would force the chart to refresh and show the impact of the rate change on future exposures. This type of what-if analysis depends on the existence of a business-intelligence relationship between the two data panels.

(v) Catalogs and Rule Repositories

There is a great deal of data stored in databases that is not necessarily formatted or labeled the way a business person would expect. A catalog is a term for a metadata layer that allows business intelligence systems administrators to provide some more meaningful labels and formats for the underlying database data. When data is retrieved into the business intelligence system from the database it is reformatted by the catalog to make it easier to understand on-screen.

A rule repository is used to manage the business rules that determine the access security to the data and the business rules used by the business intelligence system in order to manage tasks such as exception reporting. These rules may then be modified to suit new business conditions so that the business intelligence system is able to reflect the dynamic of the business itself. Rule repositories are used to store price floors and ceilings, break-even points, operating ratio formulas, and the like.

Accounting systems are often an underutilized information asset in many businesses. Business intelligence software is a means of unlocking the value of accounting systems and extending the reach of the information to users beyond the accounting department itself. Whether the accounting data is accessible through integration with third-party EIS, OLAP, or data warehouse systems or from within the accounting system is less important than recognizing that business intelligence can only be effectively delivered through query and reporting tools optimized for decision support.

8.8 E-MAIL ENABLED

Client/server accounting applications have benefitted from the availability of other corporate infrastructure components being available to them. E-mail is one of the most important infrastructure components that an accounting system can take advantage of. E-mail enabling of an accounting system means that the accounting application can pass data to or accept data from an electronic messaging such as Microsoft's mail application programming interface (MAPI) or Lotus vendor independent messaging (VIM) or other messaging protocols. This means that wherever there used to be an option to print data in an application, there can now be an option to send data. But often e-mail enabling has added new functionality that is simply not available from a non-e-mail-enabled system.

At this time, an electronic message can consist of three components:

- Some information about the message itself contained in the message header area. This could include who sent the message, from where, and when or how it was routed for example.

- The textual content of the message itself that tells the recipient what the message is about.
- An attachment that may be a document file from a wordprocessing system, a report format from an accounting system or a worksheet from a spreadsheet application.

An accounting system can either create or respond to electronic messages. Currently many vendors have e-mail enabled their accounting system primarily to create and send electronic messages. As discussed in section 8.5, electronic messages are the means of communicating notifications that result from the occurrence of a business event. However electronic messages can also be used as a mechanism to extend the reach of the accounting systems and add value to its functionality:

- Instead of printing paper financial statements and other accounting reports, the report data can be stored to files and sent as an attachment to an e-mail message that can be forwarded to multiple recipients both inside and outside a company.
- Instead of manually compiling to-do lists and schedule appointments, the accounting system can create these automatically to-do or tickler items in electronic schedulers.
- Instead of remembering to carry out specific tasks in a process, the system can push these tasks to the electronic in box of specified users through e-mail.
- Instead of printing and mailing or faxing paper documents to trading partners, e-mail can be used to communicate orders to vendors or acknowledgments to customers.

E-mail and the Internet already have the potential to replace electronic data interchange (EDI) systems that have been the preserve of the world's largest businesses and depend, on special value-added networks (VANs) to function. Once the security of e-mail is strengthened to commercially acceptable standards then the document formats that are currently processed by EDI systems can be sent via e-mail. These documents become message attachments with special headers for decoding or parsing the data contained in the attachment message. This methodology is already being introduced by vendors who are using Internet e-mail to transfer orders from Internet document forms directly into accounting systems. This use of e-mail is discussed more fully in section 8.11.

With an e-mail enabled accounting system it is hard to see justification for printing anything at all, because all output can be stored in digital format and viewed by any user connected to the corporate e-mail system. This is a major advantage, because accounting is a function that is responsible for generating a great deal of the corporate paper that fills filing cabinets in offices all over the world. Because e-mail depends on electronic information and communications network, rather than paper, printers, and fax machines, it is immediate in timeliness, worldwide in scope, void of both consumption of materials and the devices to output the paper. E-mail enabled accounting is a major step not just towards the paperless office and the printerless network but also towards a more efficient and timely distribution of accounting data inside and outside a company.

8.9 DOCUMENT AND IMAGE ENABLED

Accounting vendors are responding to user demands for handling more complex forms of data such as documents, images, and voice data. This recognizes that accounting systems are not just involved with data comprised solely of text and numbers. As a result more client/server accounting applications support document and image data than previous generations of accounting software and it looks likely that this will become a standard part of all accounting systems by the end of the 1990s.

(a) Document Management

While electronic commerce may eventually do away with paper documents entirely, many accounting transactions still begin their lifecycle as paper documents. Also many accounting systems actually create paper documents that have to be printed, folded, and mailed before they can reach their intended recipient. This can be called document reception and document transmission.

(i) Document Reception

Most of the electronic transactions created in an accounting system originate from data on documents received by a business, such as orders, invoices, packing slips, and checks. After transactions are created, either from source documents, or the vouchers created from them, they were typically stored in voluminous files in vast file cabinets, or on microfiche. The process is similar to that shown in Figure 8.9. Unfortunately this creates a situation in which the original source document for the transaction has not been systematized along with the electronic transaction created from it.

This paradigm is changing to one in which documents either never exist in paper format because they reach the accounting system through electronic commerce using electronic data interchange (EDI) or the Internet, or documents are immediately scanned and digitized as soon as they are received, as shown in Figure 8.10. Creating a digital version of the document is the essential first step to all forms of document reception management.

In the scenarios depicted in Figure 8.10, not only is the number of steps required to process a document-based transaction reduced, but also the document essentially becomes an integral part of the transaction through tagging. Tagging is simply the creation of an electronic link, usually based on a unique transaction ID, that links the accounting voucher to the file containing the document data. Once this is done the document can always be accessed from anywhere in

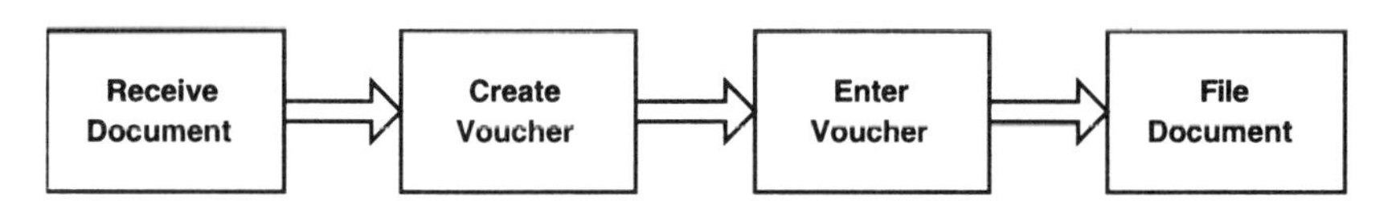

Figure 8.9. Traditional Accounting Document Management.

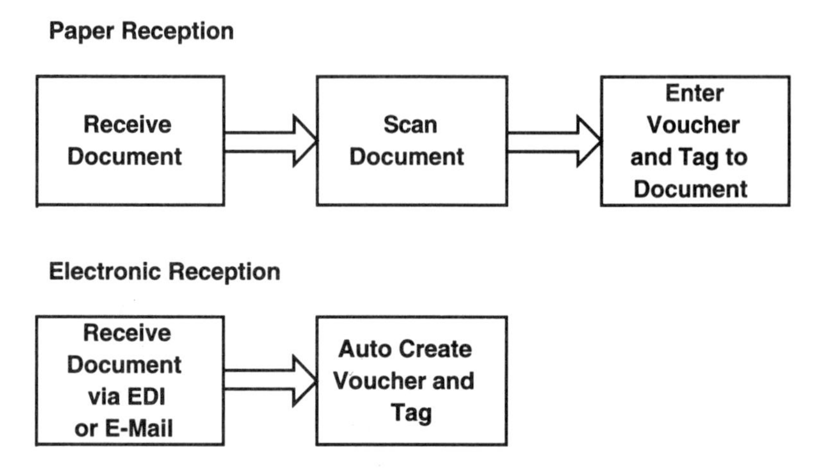

Figure 8.10. New Accounting Document Management.

the accounting system where the transaction record is edited, viewed, or reported. Access to documents is usually provided via clicking on a toolbar button or a thumbnail of the document, which is displayed alongside the transaction.

Furthermore the document itself can be edited by appending notes and comments, or annotating the document itself. This is because documents are often managed by external applications designed to provide a range of tools for managing and editing documents. These applications are seamlessly integrated with the accounting software, so when a document is being managed it is actually being managed by another application and is often physically stored in a separate database from the regular accounting data.

While scanning the document and tagging it to a transaction delivers many benefits it still requires the user to create manually an electronic transaction. When the document is initially received electronically, via EDI or e-mail, this step can be eliminated. This is because if the document data is received electronically in a structured format, the accounting system can parse the data contained in this message and automatically create an accounting entry without user intervention. Of course some intelligence is required to detect conditions of exception, such as receiving an order from a new customer or booking an invoice from a new vendor. The beauty of this type of situation is that the system can manage these exceptions by putting the transactions on hold and notifying the appropriate users via e-mail of the exception event's circumstances. Once appropriate action is taken the transaction can be rejected, or taken off hold and posted to the accounting database. Once this type of transaction processing becomes the norm it will change the face of accounting departments.

(ii) Document Transmission

Just as the aim is not to receive and process paper documents so the aim is also not to create and transmit paper documents. Sending orders and invoices by EDI or electronic mail, or payments via electronic funds transfer (EFT) systems such as the United Kingdom's Bankers' Automated Clearing House (BACS) should be the aim of all businesses. Client/server accounting systems are supporting this direction by providing e-mail and Internet connectivity and the ability to process payments not as paper checks but as files of electronic payment transactions that can be submitted directly to bank clearing systems. This type of functionality may only be visible through the location of a send option next to the print option on an application menu or toolbar or data entry form.

(b) Image and Voice Management

While image and voice data may not add as many benefits to an accounting system as document management, the availability of image and voice data certainly adds value. Images can be used to great effect in applications such as:

- Inventory—to show pictures of products on inventory records or cards or to show diagrams of assemblies in bill of material applications
- Human Resources—to show photographs of employees or certificates associated with their application for employment

- Warehousing—to show warehouse maps that depict and locate the stock situation in specific warehouse bins or racks
- Reporting Structures—to use images to help visualize organizational reporting structures or trees to make them more understandable to users maintaining the hierarchies

Voice data on the other hand can be used as an alternative or adjunct to textual note data, which can be added to explain information about specific transactions. When an accounting transaction is viewed, a voice-note icon can be clicked and a spoken message delivered to give some insight into the transaction data. Like the document data discussed above, this voice note is tagged to the transaction and can follow it to any destination.

Improved document management and the availability of image and voice data from accounting systems is here now and is certain to become a standard part of all accounting software functionality.

8.10 TELEPHONY ENABLED

Telephony is the merging of telephonic communications with computers. The primary way in which telephony impacts accounting systems is in its ability to extend the options for both submitting queries to the accounting system and transmitting messages from the accounting system. With appropriate security, there is no reason a touchtone phone cannot be used to query account balances, run reports, initiate workflow routings, or access messages created in an accounting system. Clearly this functionality not only extends the reach of an accounting system to any user with a telephone, it adds value by making accounting data more accessible and does so without any additional infrastructure costs.

Telephony enabling is another technology that supports the concept of the extended enterprise in which certain key customers and vendors become trusted partners in the business. Consequently, representatives of both can be given access to specific types of accounting system inquiry, such as the balance of their accounts, or the status of sales or purchase orders via a simple touchtone telephone inquiry. Telephony is already being exploited effectively in human resource applications in which employees and prospective employees are given telephonic access to:

- Information about the company, its hiring policies, and its benefit plans
- New job opportunities at the company
- The status of job applications at a given point in time
- Balances on pension, 401(K), or other benefit plans run by the employer
- The ability to select or change benefits in cafeteria schemes

As far as client/server accounting systems are concerned, the touchtone phone is becoming just another client that provides access to accounting data to a very wide audience for little or no additional cost to the system management infrastructure.

8.11 WORKFLOW ENABLED

As business process reengineering (BPR) coupled with various forms of quality initiatives took off worldwide as a means for corporate revitalization, so did the demand for software tools to assist in this effort. These software tools are generally labeled workflow management systems. Consequently the term workflow has become associated with all sorts of software applications from simple graphical flow charting tools to sophisticated document management systems. Workflow can be defined simply as the automation of business processes through software. A glossary of common workflow terms is provided in Table 8.6. The rapid ascent of workflow took many accounting application vendors by surprise. This is odd because accounting processes are often the obvious target for reengineering in many corporations, because these processes are both well-defined and usually easy to find fault in. Common accounting processes that

Table 8.6. A Workflow Glossary.

Term	*Description*
Agent	A piece of software code programmed to react to certain system events without human intervention
Action	The response of a user or a software agent that moves a workflow item forward in a process
Conclusion	An event that signifies the conclusion of a workflow, process, or task
Event	A system or database event (such as an insert, update, or delete) that is trapped by a workflow application and triggers a response
Initiation	An event that triggers the start of a workflow, process, or task
Item	A workflow item such as a transaction, form, document, or message that is subject to routes, rules, and roles
Notification	A message sent either to a system user or a system agent to inform or alert or trigger a response
Process	A series of logically linked tasks
Role	A skillset or organizational position required to perform a specific task
Route	A transfer of information from a sending role to a receiving role dependent on a specific set of rules
Rule	A conditional parameter that determines the action to be taken by a workflow transaction
State	The current status of a workflow item relative to the process of which it is a part
Task	A finite set of actions with a defined initiation and conclusion that can usually be timed (also known as an activity)
Workflow	A definable routing of an item through one or more processes from start to finish in which each event impacting the item and the consequences of those events are fully defined

have proven popular for reengineering using workflow technology include:

- Procurement
- Payment processing

- Collections management
- Employee travel and expense management
- Month-end reporting

Workflow as a means for reengineering accounting processes actually exploits the synergies between a number of technologies and application design approaches already discussed, including:

- Event-, rule-, and message-driven application designs
- E-mail connectivity
- Document management technology
- Telephony and Internet connectivity

(a) Message-Based Workflow

Perhaps the simplest form of workflow being implemented in applications is message-based workflow. By utilizing e-mail systems, such as Microsoft Mail or Lotus cc:Mail, accounting systems can automatically generate messages or create attachments, and route them to any e-mail-connected user. This type of workflow is often initiated automatically through the intervention of software agents or triggers working against the accounting database.

Examples of messages that can be sent include:

- Informational (e.g. "Your report is printed on Printer 1 and ready for collection.")
- Reminder (e.g. "Your intray now has 5 journals awaiting approval.")
- Alert (e.g. " You have overrun the departmental budget for travel this period.")

Examples of attachments that can be sent include:

- Audit trails, financial statements, and other reports in electronic formats

- Charts or worksheets resulting from running queries against the accounting data
- Briefing books containing reports, charts, and other data for executive review

In message-based workflow, the messages and attachments are usually used to view data rather than allow the user to take any specific action. Nevertheless, even this simplistic form of workflow can significantly minimize organizational paperflows, reduce human forgetfulness, alert managers to exception conditions, and extend the reach of the accounting system beyond the confines of the accounting department.

(b) Form-Based Workflow

The next level of workflow sophistication is form- or document-based workflow. In this scenario a business form or document, such as a purchase requisition, vendor invoice, or employee T&E worksheet, is captured electronically. Then the form is electronically routed, usually via an e-mail system, and depending on rules associated with the form, the data is actioned by a user who performs a specific organizational role such as a reviewer or approver.

Clearly the addition of routes, rules, and roles into the workflow paradigm adds both complexity to the software and sophistication to the workflow. Routes are usually based on organizational hierarchies such as reporting trees, organization charts, or territory structures that are often already defined and maintained in your accounting software.

Rules are conditions, usually based on an <If..Then..Else> construct, that determine how and to whom the form is routed. Examples of rules could include:

- If the purchase requisition value is less than $100 then flag the requisition as approved, else route requisition for approval to department manager.

- If the vendor invoice has a due date less than five days from today then alert the accounts payable manager to review invoice.
- If the T&E form total causes the employee's period budget to be exceeded then alert the department manager, else approve the T&E worksheet.

Roles are usually associated with workgroups of users who perform a discrete organizational function from an accounting perspective such as entry clerks, supervisors, and managers.

Form-based workflow is often implemented by combining the accounting system with another package such as an electronic forms manager like Symantec FormFlow, a groupware package like Lotus Notes or a worksheet like Microsoft Excel. The workflow may be initiated in the external package and eventually received into the accounting system. For example an employee T&E worksheet entered into Microsoft Excel is passed into the accounting system for posting as credit to the employee account and a debit to the various expenses accounts. Alternatively a transaction may be initiated in the accounting system, routed via the external package, and then received back into the accounting system. For example a purchase requisition may be raised in the accounting system, routed through Lotus Notes for approval, then returned to the accounting system in its new state as an open purchase order.

Form-based workflow in accounting systems usually focuses on document-driven processes that require documents to pass through various review, appending, revision, and approval stages before the transaction data is posted to the ledgers. Form-based workflow helps move businesses towards paperless accounting and the use of electronic inboxes that can be managed on screen in order to deliver more efficient transaction throughput.

(c) Collaborative Process-Based Workflow

While message- and form-based workflows both require the collaboration of an accounting system and another software package, and are process-based, neither of these forms of workflow are essentially very complex to implement or plan.

When the business process model demands that a number of applications and/or different parts of an organization must work together to carry out a specific business process, its workflow is best defined as process-based. In this scenario a transaction may be routed between applications and across organizational boundaries. Typically, a more complex set of route, rule, and role parameters are applied to the transaction that requires more depth in the workflow functionality of the software. In this case the workflow software effectively becomes a transaction management system that monitors what transactions are in workflows, what their current state is, who is available to process them, and audits their progress through the workflow. Often the workflow essentially becomes an application within an application, a virtual application that instantiates itself when the workflow starts and goes into hibernation when the workflow ends.

A purchasing process-based workflow may require that the workflow engine manages transactions that begin life in a purchase-requisition form in Lotus Notes and are then processed by the purchase, order, accounts-payable, fixed-asset, and general-ledger modules of an accounting system with a final e-mail notification to the requisitioner that the requested items are available for pickup. This relatively straightforward workflow still requires a single transaction to be managed by workflow across seven applications and user workgroups.

Process-based workflows require that the accounting software or its integrated-workflow engine offers more sophisticated functions such as:

- Graphical process modelers for building and visualizing workflows on screen
- Software to track the state and transfer time of workflow transactions
- Data-collection forms for defining primary and alternate routes, rules, and roles

- Workflow administration functions to audit, redirect, suspend, or terminate workflows
- The ability to receive transactions from and pass transactions to other systems

Process-based workflow systems allow organizations to map their business processes much more closely to their accounting software rather than the other way around. These systems also allow financial systems managers to use the functionality of the accounting software to build customized applications that are customized for the day to day responsibilities or function of their users. In this way workflow is releasing users from the straight jacket of general ledgers, accounts payable, and the like, by allowing them to construct applications around their business processes by using workflow as form of technological glue.

(d) Why is Workflow Important?

Workflow is an important addition to the functionality offered by an accounting system for any size or type of business. Firstly, workflow focuses the software designer's attention on business processes rather than software features. This means that software is being delivered with more functional granularity and with best-practice business models so that the application can be assembled more closely to the way your business works.

Second, workflow breaks down the barriers between applications and between accounting and other organizational users who need to utilize accounting data. It does this by pushing information out to the users who need to use it and by crossing application boundaries through using workflow to build process-based virtual applications.

Third, workflow reduces paperflows, increases information visibility, cuts the need for human intervention, and helps an organization to become exception driven. It does this by using electronic rather than paper distribution and by letting preprogrammed system rules and agents do jobs that humans easily forget, ignore, or simply should not be doing.

Finally, making use of the workflow functionality offered by your next accounting system demands that you have a clear handle on your business processes. In this way, workflow acts as a practical catalyst for beginning the reengineering effort that will certainly be required for you to take best advantage of workflow functionality. Utilizing workflow technology is one way you can truly add value to your business processes and begin the task of converting your accounting users from transaction processors to knowledge workers.

8.12 INTERNET ENABLED

The Internet is set to have an effect on the accounting software marketplace that is greater than that of the introduction of the IBM PC in the early 1980s. As the Internet matures as a platform for managing business transactions it will not only introduce a vast range of new vendors and products into the marketplace, but will also change the way in which accounting systems are built and used. The Internet offers the ultimate mechanism for extending the reach and domain of an accounting system. An Internet-enabled accounting application is automatically global in reach and independent of any specific hardware platform. By leveraging the existing Internet infrastructure, a global and essentially free communications network accessed by simple, low-cost, information browser tools, accounting systems gain many benefits at very little additional cost.

The Internet is particularly timely as a communication infrastructure for helping accounting systems cope with the demands of mobile computing road warriors and home-based telecommuters. To understand the potential impact of the Internet on accounting systems it helps to consider the basic functional purpose of an accounting system, namely:

- To receive transactions
- To process transactions

- To query and report transactions
- To feed transactions to other systems

The Internet provides a platform for changing the basis of all these functions, unlike traditional, closed accounting systems. In reality the applications that will provide this functionality will be intranet rather than Internet applications. An intranet is effectively an internal corporate application that runs on the back of the Internet but is protected from nonauthorized users by a firewall—a set of security routines that ensure that only authorized access is provided to an application hosted on an Internet-connected server. The firewall also manages the receipt and transmission of data into and from the application to users connected via the Internet.

(a) Internet-Enabled Transaction Reception

If you consider accounting systems as transaction receivers then it becomes clear that there are specific transaction types a system expects to receive and that there are organizational roles that are responsible for initiating those transactions. For example:

Transaction	*Role*
Travel and Expense Timesheet	Any employee
Purchase Requisitions/Orders	Any employee
Sales Quotations/Orders	Salespeople, telephone order takers
Budget Forecasts/Revisions	Department/Line of Business managers

From these examples it is clear that these roles are not typically associated with typical accounting system users, but nevertheless may be generating a significant number of transactions that end up in the accounting system. Also many of these roles are operating in a distributed and mobile mode; they are not necessarily local to the accounting department.

The Internet allows these people to participate directly in the accounting process by providing simple applets that allow them to submit transactions to the accounting system remotely—whether from home, the car, or a temporary business location. These applets are miniapplications that handle a specific transaction, such as travel and expense submission, from within standard Internet browser software. All that is required is for the accounting system vendor to break out this transaction type and embed the functionality into a small program that is linked into a standard Internet Web page. This type of functionality is easier to provide if the accounting system is built with the right level of granularity in its design.

(b) Internet-Enabled Transaction Processing

A great deal of the business value in accounting applications is in their transaction processing functionality. These are the batch processes that manage large numbers of transactions in order to carry out tasks such as:

- Posting transactions to the database
- Extracting transactions from the database
- Aggregating transaction data for use in financial reports
- Selecting and sorting data for satisfying user queries
- Batch printing of documents such as invoices or checks
- Business processing such as currency revaluations or translations

There is no reason these processes cannot also be initiated by users on the Internet, again by simple applets that submit a remote request to an accounting application to initiate a process and take some action when it is finished. A typical action would be to e-mail a report back to the initiating user or a group of users for decision support purposes when the process is finished. This type of remote request processing means there should never be a reason a decision should be delayed due to the absence of an accounting staff to run the process because it's after 4 P.M. on a Friday or the accounts payable clerk is off sick.

Probably the most compelling reason for using the Internet to process transactions is for receiving orders. An Internet storefront page is used to advertise goods and services and to accept orders from any Internet user. The user fills out a simple on-screen order form and their data is either transmitted by e-mail to the vendor or stored directly into an order database table.

Either method allows the vendor to receive the order electronically, then to confirm it via e-mail acknowledgment back to the customer, to transfer the order into their accounting order-entry system and eventually ship the goods without any human involvement. The audience for the storefront is global and the cost of processing the transaction minimal compared to the typical paper-driven, human-managed order process.

(c) Internet-Enabled Transaction Query/Reporting

The Internet is an ideal infrastructure for requesting queries or financial reports generated from an accounting system and for disseminating the results. This is because, as outlined in section (b), the Internet can be used to initiate a process such as running a financial statement and communicate the results via e-mail. Instead of printing a report, the accounting application generates a digital file that is attached to a simple e-mail message and routed back to the initiating user or user group that subscribes to the publication of the results of the process. This publish-and-subscribe concept of financial reporting across the Internet is more likely to transform accounting departments into paperless offices than the addition of any document management software. This is because the accounting system data is now available to any authorized user worldwide across the Internet and the report data only ever exists in digital formats.

The data may be published to users in one of four formats:

- Traditional, static report formats than can be scrolled and viewed and printed if necessary at the user location, wherever that might be.

- Hypertext-linked reports that enable the content to be navigated intelligently by the user.
- New data-rich report formats that behave just like static reports with the addition of built-in drilldown to navigate from summary report lines to more detailed ones. In this scenario what is transmitted to the user is not a report text file but a report database table that contains the base-level transactions that made up the report and structural logic to deliver the drilldown navigation. This type of delivery allows more investigative analysis of the report numbers to be carried out on the users' local laptop or PC.
- Data snapshots that are designed to be stored on a local database on the users' laptop or PC. These snapshots are appended to prior data and allow the users to build their own local view of specific accounting data and analyze the data locally in their own time. This type of delivery can be used to provide salespeople with the data to allow them to maintain their own receivables off the accounting system's line.

All the main database vendors have released local or personal versions of their database engines to cope with the increasing demand for databases that can be used in mobile computing environments. These versions allow the main accounting system to run the full-powered enterprise version of a database such as Oracle, Sybase, or Informix and the remote user to run a lite version on their laptop or home PC. The transfer of snapshot data can then be managed and synchronized by the replication functionality that the enterprise database offers for copying data to and from the remote database.

(d) Internet-Enabled Transaction Feeds

Many accounting systems, particularly in very large organizations, are collections of feeder systems that transfer data among themselves using complex batch processes. Examples of such batch processes are:

- Updating a local general ledger from a local accounts payable
- Updating a local general ledger from a remote payroll system
- Transmitting or receiving payments electronically to or from a bank clearing system
- Transmitting or receiving documents electronically to or from an EDI system

There is no reason the Internet, or more likely intranets, should not handle all these transaction feeds in the future. This of course assumes that the whole infrastructure is more secure and offers sufficient bandwidth to cope with what would be an enormous load generated by commercial transaction processing. Internet-hosted document and transaction management stands a good chance of killing off EDI as we know it and replacing it with an e-mail- and attachment-driven paradigm for communicating documents between businesses.

(e) Self-Service Accounting

Self-service accounting refers to the ability of data owners to service their own data in a third party's accounting system. For example, employees can manage their own benefit plans in the company human resource system by accessing the data through a web browser on their home PC. Similarly, customers and vendors can service and query their own account data and transactions in accounts receivable or accounts payable systems. Self-service accounting moves responsibility for the data to the data owners and frees up accounting staff from the burden of answering routine inquiries or maintaining address changes. The Internet and intranets are opening up accounting systems to self-service data management.

The Internet will have a profound effect on the design, deployment, and use of current and future accounting applications. It will demand granularity in the application design and more sophisticated workflow management to choreograph the transactions managed across the Internet or corporate intranets. Accounting systems will be deployed in a hub-and-spoke fashion in which the spokes will be a variety of accounting-specific applets managed by users from their local laptop, PC, or network PC (NC). Accounting systems will be used by a wider variety of people across functional or organizational boundaries. It will facilitate the cooperation of business partners, suppliers, customers, and outsource service providers in the accounting process of a corporation. The combination of granular accounting software, workflow management, and software agents with the Internet is what will make the concept of the extended enterprise an operating reality.

(f) Intranets, Extranets, and Indenets

An unsecured web server connected to the Internet is essentially available to access from any Internet browser. However, most users of web-enabled accounting software will be accessing their data via an intranet server. This is a web server that is protected by a security "firewall" to prevent and monitor unauthorized attempts to access critical corporate data. Essentially, an intranet is a private network that can be accessed via the Internet, but only to authorized users that are normally members of the same corporate entity.

An extranet is similar in concept to an intranet except that the extranet server usually would be controlled by an independent service provider and accessed by users from a group of businesses. This group of businesses would usually represent an extended enterprise of customers, suppliers, and outsource service providers using the extranet as a means for business transaction collaborations. In the short term, extranets are likely to become the future direction for today's EDI value-added networks (VANs).

Indenets are another potential direction that independent vendors of accounting software could take. In this case, the accounting software is not purchased by a business for in-house use, but rather it's run from the software vendor's own intranet and paid for on a usage or transaction volume basis. The accounting data may be on the indenet server or may be on the customer's own intranet servers. The point is that the software is maintained and operated by the vendor, and users are effectively "timesharing" the software across the Internet—a modern-day twist on the mainframe-based "bureau." A major benefit of indenets, of course, is that the vendor maintains the software inventory, not the customer, while the customer may also have full ownership and control of their own accounting data.

8.13 CONCLUSION

Client/server accounting software design is being influenced by the commercial acceptance of a wide range of new and complementary technologies like workflow and the Internet. These technologies can dramatically change the way users and other systems interact with the accounting system. They also extend the reach and functionality of accounting applications beyond their traditional confines of the finance department and pure financial management, transforming accounting into a much more influential business management tool.

PART FOUR

Reengineering Your Accounting System

CHAPTER 9 MAKING THE TRANSITION TO CLIENT/ SERVER ACCOUNTING

Making the transition to client/server accounting is not a clear-cut choice for many organizations currently using legacy applications. These organizations may need to consider a range of migration strategies other than switching to client/server accounting. Even if switching to client/server accounting is practicable, it is worth considering how to lay the foundation by preparing your people and technology for the change. The chapter also gives some hints on how to manage the software selection process.

CHAPTER 10 REENGINEERING ACCOUNTING TRANSACTION PROCESSING

This chapter focuses on ways of improving the way accounting transactions are processed through the use of client/server accounting and other complementary software applications. Typical transaction processing problems are introduced and then potential reengineering approaches and resources outlined.

CHAPTER 11 REENGINEERING ACCOUNTING DECISION SUPPORT

This chapter focuses on ways of improving the delivery of decision support information from accounting data, through the use of client/server accounting, and other complementary software applications. In the same manner as Chapter 10, typical decision support problems are introduced and then potential reengineering approaches and resources outlined.

CHAPTER NINE

Making the Transition to Client/Server Accounting

9.1 INTRODUCTION

Because almost every accounting software vendor is concentrating its development resources on delivering new client/server accounting packages, it may appear that wholesale conversion to client/server accounting is inevitable for most organizations. In practice the situation is not that simple. A large number of organizations are unable to switch to client/server accounting for one or a combination of the following reasons:

- Client/server accounting systems have not been proven to meet the high-volume transaction processing needs of the organization.
- Client/server accounting systems cannot offer the specific functional breadth or depth required by the organization.
- Client/server accounting systems would require replacement of a wide range of computing hardware that the organization cannot afford.
- The whole process of moving to a client/server accounting system is too costly in terms of time and money.

Many accounting departments may find the changeover to client/server accounting traumatic because the applications are not the familiar evolutionary or incremental system upgrades associated with legacy systems. In fact many accounting departments may not be at all accustomed to major application changes because many have been using the same incrementally upgraded software for over a decade. Client/server accounting applications can be a traumatic change because they actually bundle together a number of technology and functional changes, including:

- The use of graphical user interfaces at the desktop
- A process orientation towards the accounting tasks
- More use of automated technology as part of the accounting process
- A PC-based desktop and a network architecture
- Use of electronic messaging and digital reporting

Consequently, preparing your people for the switch to client/server accounting is as important as ensuring that the appropriate technology foundation is in place to leverage the full benefits of these powerful new applications.

9.2 DATA MIGRATION STRATEGIES

Many organizations have to consider migration strategies that allow them to make the transition to client/server gradually—concentrating on preservation rather than desecration of their current technology investment. These organizations are currently running centralized systems on mainframe or midrange hosts, so-called legacy or heritage systems. They have invested considerable time and money in the hardware, software, and people skills that deliver productive value from these heritage systems. This chapter outlines some of the potential migration strategies open to such host-based accounting system users.

(a) Data Staging

Many people currently running their accounting systems on mainframes are reluctant, unable, or unwilling to do anything that makes running their decades-old systems more difficult than it already is. These are the businesses in which considerable effort and money has been invested in host-based infrastructures that have dozens of interlocking and interfacing software applications that have been subjected to many years of customization. For these folks, reengineering is a distant dream and their aim is simply to provide desktop users an easier means to access and analyze accounting data that is locked away in their mainframe-based application silos.

Data staging is one way to provide users better access to the accounting data, as shown in Figure 9.1. Essentially data staging is the process of staging subsets of the data from the mainframe to another computing platform where it can be manipulated more easily, accessed directly from desktop tools, or pumped into specialized data warehouses or decision support servers. Data staging is a means of making accounting data more available without changing the accounting application itself. The staging of the data—the transfer of data out of the mainframe database to the staging area—is a batch

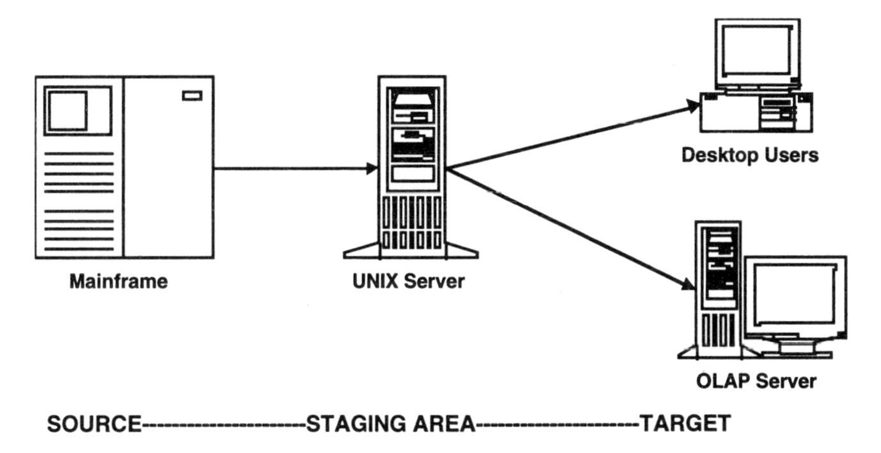

Figure 9.1. Data Staging—Making Data Available.

process that can be scheduled to run during processor lulls, such as off hours or weekends. Thus staged data is never live but may be as timely as the business need and batch processing availability can allow. The staged data is usually stored on a less expensive and easier to manage platform, such as a UNIX- or Microsoft-NT-based server, and in a database that is more accessible to desktop tools, such as any one of many leading relational databases.

Dun & Bradstreet Software's SmartStream client/server accounting suite started life as a means of staging data from their E- and M-series mainframe-based accounting software before it was expanded into a full suite of client/server applications. Subsets of the data could be staged onto UNIX-based computers running the Sybase RDBMS so the accounting information could be accessed more easily from the desktop and used more productively for decision support activities.

Data staging is a relatively low-cost means of making mainframe (or other host-based) data available without any major hardware architecture or software application changes. The data-staging process itself must be managed on a regular basis by the information systems department as must any subsequent staging that the data undergoes.

(b) Data Warehousing

Data warehousing, as a migration strategy for accounting data, is essentially a refinement of the data-staging strategy discussed above. Whereas data staging simply makes host-based data more accessible to other tools (one of which may be a data warehouse application) the data warehousing staging area is more specialized and comprises the data warehouse itself. A data warehouse is simply a facility for storing data from a variety of internal and external sources in a consistent and usually aggregated format to make it available for enterprise-wide and cross-functional decision support to a wide range of business analysts and managers. Data warehouses take feeds from many internal systems, as shown in Figure 9.2.

Because the data warehouse typically fulfills a more important enterprise role than a simple data-staging server, it may be a more costly and time-consuming effort to implement. For example, special programs may need to be developed or utilities purchased in order to clean and transform the data after it is extracted from the host system and before it reaches the data warehouse. Otherwise the data warehousing approach is similar to data staging in that its data is not live and it is also managed on a less expensive platform using a RDBMS.

A number of client/server accounting vendors such as The Dodge Group, KaPRE Software, and Timeline Inc. have repositioned their general ledger products to serve as financial data warehouses to provide a solution for this particular migration strategy.

(c) System Wrappers

Wrapping is a means of hiding the internals of a system with technology that makes it appear to be something else. Wrapping is often implemented as some form of metadata layer—data describing data—that can be set up and used by external applications to interact with

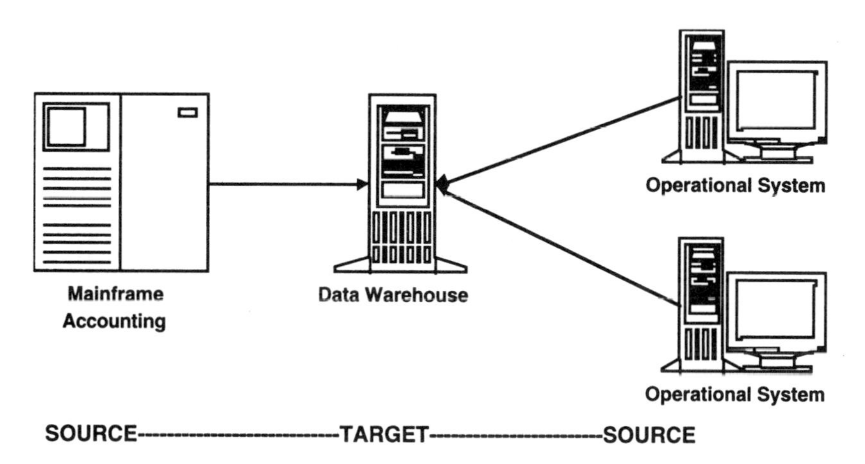

Figure 9.2. Data Warehousing—Making Data Available.

the accounting data. A wrapper can be used to manage the input and output of information from the accounting data by isolating the data from external applications and forcing these applications to work with the data through the appropriate wrapper technology.

The wrapper allows more flexibility in terms of how accounting transactions can be entered into and extracted from the system. This is because the transaction entry system or financial reporting system interacts with the wrapper technology rather than directly with the system or its data. As a result wrappers are also potential solutions when the main goal is to preserve the current accounting system applications and platforms while providing a means to reengineer the way in which transactions are entered or retrieved from the system. Transaction entry and retrieval can then be managed from graphical desktop tools through wrapper technology that resides on its own dedicated server acting as an intelligent gateway to the host-based accounting system. Decision support may be facilitated by using a Microsoft OLE wrapper to manage access to legacy accounting applications, as shown in Figure 9.3. Vendors such as FRx Software, KaPRE Software, and Timeline Inc. have software that can be used

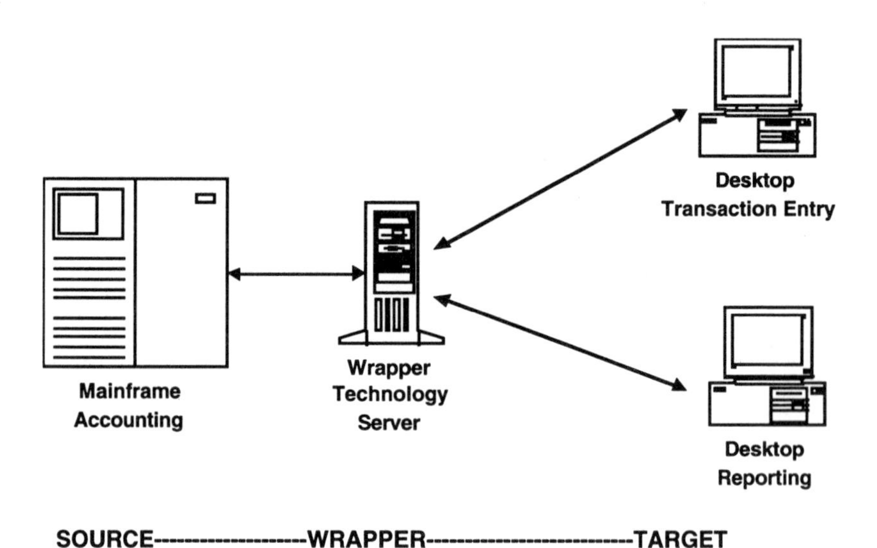

Figure 9.3. System Wrappers.

in this wrapper role on UNIX- and Microsoft-NT-based servers, which can be configured to connect to mainframe- or midrange-hosted legacy accounting software.

(d) The Host as Server

Both data staging and data warehousing essentially preserve the accounting system's original state, requiring no abandonment of the host asset system because the host is surrounded by staging areas or data warehouses in a hub-and-spoke configuration. As mainframe sales sagged in the early days of client/server, IBM, the mainframe market leader, has fought back by delivering technology that is designed to allow mainframe or midrange computers to act less as a host and more as a server, particularly as a database server. Consequently it is possible to run a mainframe as the database server for a client/server accounting system using IBM's DB2 RDBMS as the database engine, as shown in Figure 9.4. Vendors such as PeopleSoft and FlexiInternational can deliver this kind of solution while other vendors are delivering similar solutions for IBM's popular midrange AS/400 host system.

The point of this approach is that investments in hardware infra-

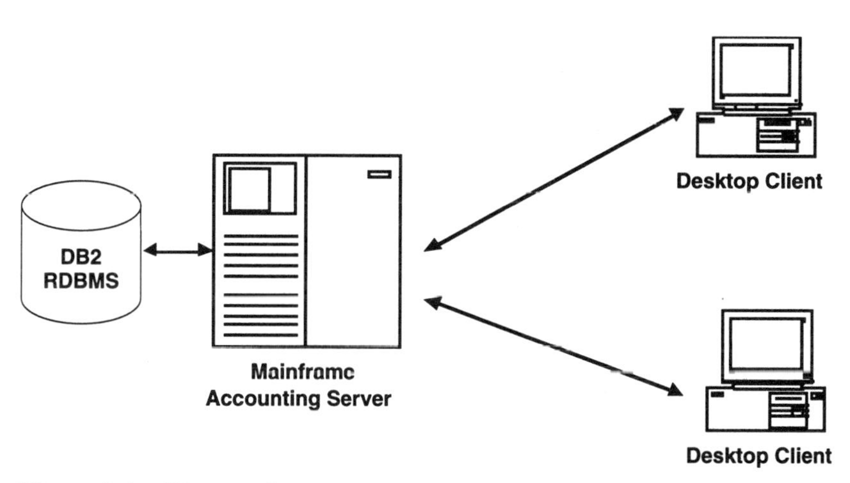

Figure 9.4. Host as Server.

structures, the tools, and the people to support them can be largely retained because the mainframe or mini can become a database server to a client/server accounting system. The database may be a version of IBM's powerful DB2 RDBMS, which is more accessible and easier to use than traditional mainframe and midrange network or navigational databases because DB2 is relational and accessible from the desktop through SQL. Although the accounting application itself must be scrapped and replaced with a new client/server package, at least the hardware and skills base are retained and significant benefit is gained from the use of a more contemporary and accessible application and database architecture.

(e) Front-Ending Legacy Systems

Many legacy accounting systems contain a great deal of business-specific, customized programming and links to other internal and external systems that have taken many years to build and improve. This effort relies on the host system remaining a transaction hub for the business. One problem with this situation is that decision support may suffer, which is why the data-staging and data-warehousing migration strategies may be necessary. Another problem is that the mainframe accounting software may not be able to offer the reengineering advantages such as workflow, document imaging, or e-mail.

In this case, it may be possible to front end the host system with a workflow or document-routing system that supplements and enhances the functionality of the existing legacy system, as shown in Figure 9.5. Examples of business areas in which this can be achieved are in distributed procurement or sales ordering. In essence the front-end system is a separate software application that manages the initiation, routing, and approval of procurement or sales-order transactions. This application may be entirely separate from the mainframe, run on its own discrete servers, provide modern graphical application software, and utilize other desktop tools such as productivity suite software or e-mail. Transactions such as purchase requisitions

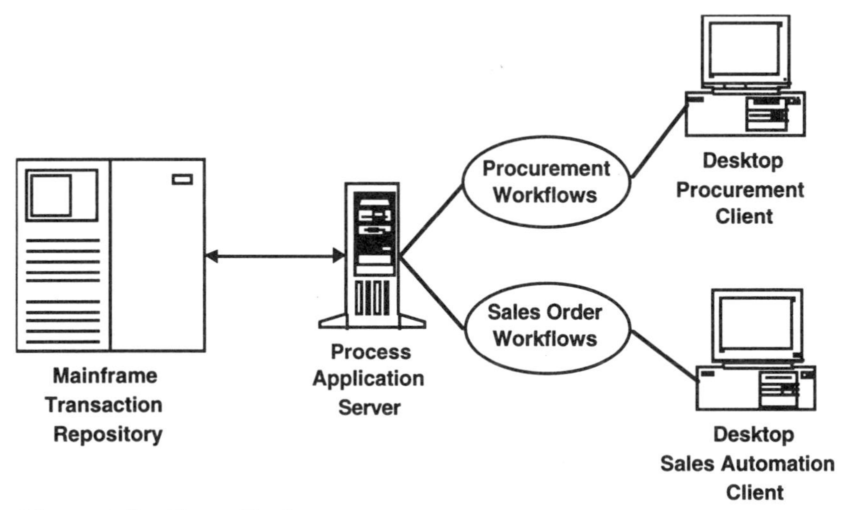

Figure 9.5. Front Ending.

or sales orders begin their life cycle in this front-end application but eventually complete their life cycle by being passed to the host accounting system as a qualified accounting transaction. The host is now performing a role that could be called a transaction repository.

While this front-end strategy does have the disadvantage of requiring the maintenance and synchronization of two systems instead of one, it can be one way of retaining an untouched host system while providing users with access to modern technology that enhances and leverages the information asset value of the host. This is also a good way to test the potential of these types of systems before converting wholesale to client/server technology and business processes and switching off the host.

(f) Client/Server Coexistence

In some cases it may be practicable to implement client/server accounting as a coexistence strategy, in other words alongside the host-based systems. This strategy may be practicable because:

- The host is overloaded and any application that can be moved from the host and rightsized to another platform is viewed as a positive.

- The application to be moved should never have been on the mainframe in the first place, and was deployed this way because the mainframe was there.
- The application is a low-transaction volume module or can stand alone functionally from the other legacy accounting systems such as a fixed-assets, payroll, or human-resource module.
- The module is being used more heavily for decision support and reporting than transaction entry, or depends largely on feeds for its transaction input, such as a general ledger or budgeting module.
- The application being removed allows a particular business unit, legal entity, or line of business to be spun off onto its own dedicated accounting system.

In these cases it may make sense to pursue a partial client/server migration strategy, as shown in Figure 9.6, in which the bulk of the accounting applications remain on the legacy system and only se-

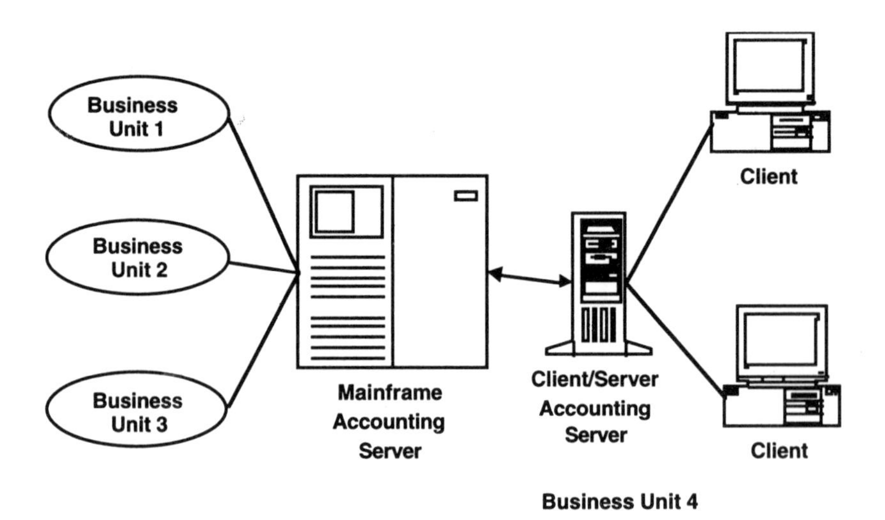

Figure 9.6. Partial Client/Server.

lected modules are moved to client/server platforms. This strategy also has the advantage of a try-before-you-buy approach, before implementing client/server accounting on an enterprise-wide basis.

9.3 PREPARING YOUR PEOPLE

Changing to client/server accounting can be difficult initially for some accounting staff and supervisors to get used to because the new systems usually have a direct impact on their day-to-day responsibilities as well as their overall role in the accounting departments. Clerks may be required to take on a wider technological skillset than simply punching the numeric keypad as the first step in their transformation into added-value knowledge workers. Supervisors may be required to make a transition from managers of the closing process or audit trail checkers to business analysts or human exception handlers.

Clearly accounting staff should be prepared for these changes through seminars and training courses that emphasize the positive aspects to these changes for their work environment and careers. Equally important are technology reality check sessions that explain how new technology such as workflow and e-mail may completely restructure the accounting processes to which they are accustomed and may eliminate many roles altogether.

(a) Graphical Accounting

While GUIs may be on millions of corporate desktops, there are still substantial numbers of desktops that support the old green-screen dumb terminal, particularly in accounting departments. Almost all client/server accounting systems will require these users to exchange their terminals for a desktop PC to run their GUI client applications. Despite the relative homogeneity of GUI applications, which contributes to the ease of use factor claimed for GUI applications, the initial transition from green screens to GUIs can be difficult and cause a short-term drop in productivity.

This productivity impact can be reduced by ensuring that accounting operators are given proper training in the GUI before the new system is installed. This seemingly obvious and simple step is often neglected. Somehow warp-speed numeric keypad operators are often the slowest to adapt to double clicking a mouse button. This GUI training should achieve two purposes: First it should ensure that the new application interface is already familiar so that operators can be productive from day one without having to learn a new interface and the new system functionality at the same time; Second it should make the operators feel excited and positive about the switch to the new system when they see how the new GUI can make their work easier or more interesting.

(b) Process Accounting

As workflow concepts make greater inroads into accounting systems, more and more applications are breaking down the walls between traditional ledger-based modules and focusing on the business process. This too can be a big change for operators used to their functional borders, responsibilities, and access to applications based on the module and the option rather than the process and the task. Operators may not be familiar with the concept of having work electronically pushed down to them and its impact their daily work routine.

Providing operators with basic business process training can be beneficial by making them aware of the business processes in which they in fact participate and how those processes are being automated by the new system functionality. This training provides users with a big picture of the new system's functions, highlighting these processes and explaining their new roles.

(c) Electronic Accounting

As accounting systems integrate more seamlessly with other technology it is a good idea to make sure that at least senior clerks and supervisors, if not all staff involved, have a basic understanding of the overlap or synergy between accounting applications and other technologies such as:

- Workflow management
- Document imaging
- E-mail
- EDI and EFT
- Intranets and the Internet

It is simply unrealistic to expect that the average accounting user has a grip on how these technologies will become part of their day-to-day life when many dedicated information technologists are themselves unable to grasp the full potential of these technologies. These are the technologies that are changing the face of accounting software and becoming a part of every accounting system. Without a basic understanding of these technologies, client/server accounting users may neither be as productive as they could be nor as able to realize the full potential of their new systems.

9.4 TECHNOLOGICAL INFRASTRUCTURES

To fully leverage a client/server accounting system, certain technology infrastructures need to be in place for the accounting application itself to function to its design potential. These infrastructures include:

- A robust network
- Database systems and expertise
- Properly configured desktop client computers
- Scaleable server computers
- Scanners
- Desktop productivity suites
- E-mail
- Internet or intranet connectivity

If these infrastructures are in place before the client/server accounting system is installed and appropriate accounting users are aware of their role relative to the accounting system, the system implementation will proceed more smoothly and efficiently.

(a) Network

Without a stable, reliable, and fast network infrastructure in place, there is little point in installing a client/server accouting system. An unstable or slow network can cause a wide range of frustrating and difficult to diagnose problems to plague any client/server application. It is also unlikely that a client/server accounting application can be managed without a network and database administrator available on a part-time or full-time basis. Also, because a client/server accounting application may significantly increase the volume of traffic on a network, part of the application pre-implementation planning should include reviewing whether to upgrade the network bandwidth or servers.

(b) Databases

Client/server accounting systems almost always require the use of a relational database management system to manage the accounting data. While the installation automation and ease of use of modern databases is far better than in the past, you will need a database administrator either on staff or easily accessible. The role of the database administrator is to manage the security and availability of the accounting data, to tune and maintain the database for optimum performance, and to help with troubleshooting. Client/server accounting systems depend on the underlying database not just to manage the data but also to manage business rules and major batch processes so more work is being controlled by the database engine than in previous file based accounting systems.

(c) Clients

Graphical user interfaces and sophisticated application functionality combined with on-line help and multitasking applications demand considerable resources from desktop client workstations. It is likely that you will need desktop PCs with hundreds of megabytes of free hard-disk capacity, local memory (RAM) of 16MB or more, and an Intel Pentium class processor or better to run most client/server accounting software effectively. Trying to shoehorn these applications into old Intel 286 or 386 class machines is not practical. You should factor in the cost of upgrading your existing desktop workstations or replacing your terminals with 486 class or better PCs when budgeting for client/server accounting systems.

(d) Servers

Client/server accounting systems may require one or more database- and/or applications-server computers typically with configurations that allow for multiprocessor support, multigigabyte disk space, and operating memory of at least 64MB and up. The processor, disk, and RAM scaleability of the server should be a critical part of its selection criteria. Client/server accounting applications can usually take advantage of as much server resources they can get. It is the power of the server and the network bandwidth that will largely determine overall performance of the accounting system when it comes to handling increasing transaction load. Even if the network server is in place, you will certainly need to add one or more database and application servers before installing the client/server accounting system. It is also important to budget for additional process servers in the future if you are purchasing a three-tier client/server application.

(e) Scanners

To utilize document management in a client/server accounting system, a budget has to be allocated for scanners and probably for image servers also. Low volume document management may require only a handful of desktop page scanners for use by specific users. High volume document management will require the purchase of one or more high-speed scanners designed to process batches of documents for conversion into document databases.

(f) Desktop Productivity Suites

Most client/server accounting software offers useful and seamless integration with desktop software suites containing wordprocessing, spreadsheet, presentation, and desktop-data analysis software. It makes sense to equip accounting desktops with these suites because they can be used increase the productivity of individual accounting users. These suites can also ensure that consistent enterprise application standards are being enforced to reduce duplication of effort, allow staff to function effectively across locations, and standardize the user business desktop enterprise wide.

(g) E-Mail

E-mail adds so much value to client/server accounting software in its role as a workflow routing tool, a report dissemination tool, and a business alert system that an accounting application without it in place prior to the installation of the software is of reduced value. Having the e-mail system in place should also mean that the concept of user workgroups and mail subscriber groups has been tackled so that these groups can be mapped onto or used by the accounting software.

(h) Internet/Intranet Access

Client/server accounting applications are already beginning to tap the value of the Internet and corporate intranets as a means of adding value to the accounting process. Your accounting system users should know how to use the Internet and how the technology can be applied to the accounting process. Internet accounts should be available for users to test this new functionality and understand the potential of this new communication infrastructure for changing the way that business processes can be managed through the use of new Internet applets.

9.5 THE SOFTWARE SELECTION PROCESS

When selecting a client/server accounting system, businesses are almost certainly making multiple decisions. For example the selection may include:

- A new database architecture to install on your network
- A new development environment for your IS folks to learn
- A new user interface for your accounting staff to use every day
- A vendor who may have been in business less than five years
- A system that has been field tested for less than a year or two
- Consulting partners who know as little about the system as your own people
- A whole new approach to managing your accounting processes

In the past, there was seldom this combination of circumstances associated with the selection of an accounting package. So now more than ever the vendor and package selection process should be even more rigorous because it is easier to make a mistake, and the consequences of a bad decision are potentially more expensive to fix. This section provides some basic pointers on how to ensure that your software selection process is as efficient as possible.

(a) Making Sense of the Market

The client/server accounting software market has really only existed since 1992. Early new-generation systems, such as the original Oracle

Financials released in 1988, were relational accounting products rather than true client/server accounting systems. But in the last three years, client/server accounting has become a crowded and confusing market as existing vendors have retooled their application suites for client/server, and over a dozen new vendors have taken advantage of the platform shift to release new products and suites onto the market. These new vendors include:

Vendor	*Founded*
PeopleSoft	1989
KaPRE Software	1992
Ramco Systems	1989
FlexiInternational Software	1991
SQL Financials	1991
Design Data Systems	1988
The Dodge Group	1991
Apprise Software	1992
Skylight Systems	1988

To date, the biggest success story among these new vendors is PeopleSoft. Founded in 1989, the company successfully went public in 1992 and reported over $200 million in revenues in fiscal 1995. However, no other new vendor has come anywhere close to emulating this success and some of those listed above will undoubtedly be taken over, as Dun & Bradstreet software was in 1996, or reach the end of their venture capital by the end of the decade.

Leading market analysts have attempted to identify accurate market share figures for this turbulent market sector. However, their rankings are open to dispute due to a variety of factors:

- Some client/server packages are not truly client/server in design.
- Rankings are often based on revenues rather than number of sites.
- Site figures often include pilot, evaluation, or even reseller sites.
- Vendors themselves are reluctant or unable to provide accurate revenue or user-base figures.

- Pre-client/server user bases are mysteriously converted to client/ server user bases.

Consequently circumspection is advised when faced with impressive claims of leadership positions and any claim of client/server user bases in the thousands of sites. Few if any vendors truly have over a thousand fully operational client/server accounting sites and most have just a few hundred or less in early 1996. This compares to the many thousands or even tens of thousands of sites that some vendors can legitimately claim for their more mature, non-client/server applications.

(b) The Software Selection Process

This section outlines just one variant of the software selection process for a client/server accounting systems. Every firm or consultant has their own spin on this process. There are three overlapping dimensions in any selection process (shown in Figure 9.7):

- Select solutions based as much on your assessment of the vendor as their products.
- Select solutions that allow you to map the product functionality

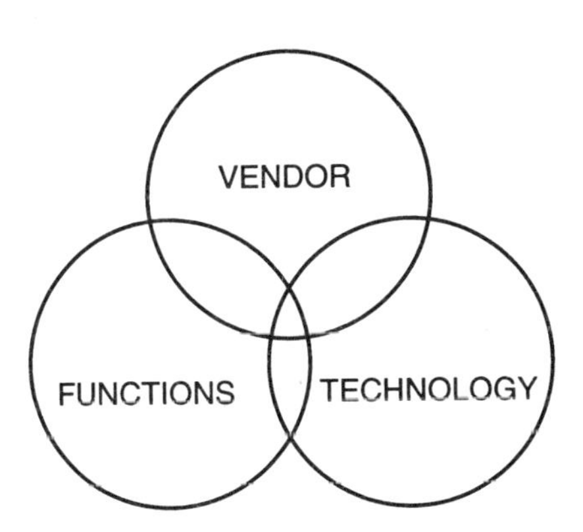

Figure 9.7. The Three Selection Dimensions.

to the way you want your business processes to function in the future.

- Select solutions that show a solid understanding of the potential of the underlying technology, and demonstrate technology vision either in the product itself or through partnerships with other complementary technology providers.

(i) Vendor Selection

Obviously in a new and turbulent software market sector, vendor selection becomes even more important than ever. The last thing any accounting system manager wants is for their vendor to go out of business leaving them with an unsupported financial system. How to evaluate a new vendor, especially a privately held, venture-capital backed vendor is more of an art than a science and depends on:

- Assessing the quality of the management team and the firms or individuals backing the company with venture capital
- Gathering independent opinions of the company's current and potential revenue potential going out five years
- Determining whether the technology and product vision is truly pragmatic given the company's resources and staffing
- Confirming that the staff really understands the function and potential of the technology it is marketing
- Checking the stature and opinions of the resellers and technology partners who are betting on the company succeeding
- Rigorously evaluating the installed site references provided by the vendor to ensure that their support and expertise are up to the task of implementing your system

(ii) Package Selection

Accounting software used to be selected on the basis of a detailed and voluminous request for proposal (RFP). These RFPs were often prepared by big-six-type accounting firms or large systems integrators. RFPs or death-by-checklist documents achieved little except generating fee income for the consulting firms, fostering a false comfort level for internal software evaluators, and forcing vendors to invent new ways to justify answering yes to questions that deserved a no. It was possible to make a whole business out of interpreting or translating RFPs that were often written with the knowledge of a specific vendor's system in mind.

While the detailed checklist element of an RFP may be useful as an appendix, completed and delivered as part of the final confirmation step before signing any software acquisition contract, an RFP should not be the first step in the software selection process. The first step should be a document of less than ten pages that is sent to vendors to invite their participation in your evaluation and summarizes your new system expectations in terms of:

- The business environment in which the system will operate
- The variety of technology platforms the new system must support
- The ease of integration required with other internal and external systems
- The business processes the system must support
- Mission-critical features or functions the application must provide
- Implementation support that the vendor must be capable of delivering
- Performance benchmarks the system must come close to achieving

While waiting for responses to this initial invitation to tender document, your internal project team should be preparing business scenarios against which they expect the vendors' software to be demonstrated. These business scenarios should be based on the 80/20 rule: Each scenario should represent 80 percent of a system operator's involvement with the business process that is being tested. At least one or more business scenarios should be defined for each module of the application suite being purchased. While the business scenario is the main attraction, a weighted shortlist of supporting features should also be defined to surround each business scenario. Typical business scenarios that need to be documented include:

- Transaction lifecycles
- Decision support inquiries and reports
- Month-end processing workflows
- System administration routines

Vendors should be given the opportunity to review and query these business scenarios before any formal product demonstration is undertaken. Almost certainly one or two will drop out at this point as demonstrating against business scenarios requires much more preparation than rolling out the same old canned product dog-and-pony shows. The audience for these business scenario demonstrations should not be the CFO but the people who will actually manage these business processes when the system is installed.

(iii) Focus on Differences

While the performance of the software in meeting the demands of the respective business scenarios is key to the evaluation decision process, when products are functionally close it helps to focus on differentiating factors such as:

- The underlying technology of the system including its database management system or application development system
- The eas of use and intuitiveness of the application's user-interface design
- The integration of the system with other complementary or value-added applications or technologies such as workflow, e-mail, or the Internet
- The integration of the application with your legacy systems that are to be maintained throughout the upgrade
- The quality of setup tools and inclusion of other user-friendly

functions such as cue cards, process wizards, on-line process flows, and help screens
- The range of technology, support, reselling, and implementation partnerships of the vendor with other third parties
- The availability of user references that are in a similar line of business and processing similar transaction volumes with similar numbers of users as your business

(iv) Conference Room Pilots

The purpose of the conference room pilot (CRP) is simply to set up the new system and use it in a manner that approximates how it would be used when implemented. The idea of a CRP is to look for success not failure, so try to ensure that as many of the vendor's recommendations regarding the operating environment for the software can be met as possible. A CRP is not a trivial exercise and will typically involve internal staff, external consultants, and vendor representatives for weeks rather than days. A CRP is nothing less than a mini-implementation and should be managed by an internal product champion, usually a manager from the first internal business unit or entity due to receive the system, who can ensure that the momentum of the pilot is kept going. After all, the system resulting from the CRP may be able to be transferred immediately to the first internal implementation site. The manager who will benefit from this effort should be the same person who oversees its inception.

A typical CRP for confirming whether a package is fit for purpose requires:

- Setup of clients, servers, peripherals, and network connections to run the new software
- A full installation of the applications to be tested during the CRP
- Populating the test applications with realistic structural data to reflect the volume and complexity of the application when in use
- Providing transaction input-data sets to reflect the type and volume of the most common transactions processed

- Benchmarking the system to understand the performance of the system in handling critical levels of transaction and user load
- Defining key reporting formats and testing the critical integration flows and feeds with other third-party or legacy systems
- Retesting the business scenarios used in the product evaluation phase but under the control of your own people rather than vendor consultants

A CRP is also an opportunity for your IS people to get a more detailed idea of:

- The operating loads that the new system will put on existing infrastructures such as the LAN, WAN, or e-mail system
- The ease of integrating the new system with existing third-party or legacy systems that will pass data to or accept data from the new system
- The data model of the application database that shows whether the application has been efficiently designed for use with a relational database
- The reliability of the system and how much fine tuning or regular housekeeping is required to keep the system functioning in an optimal way

A CRP is also an opportunity to:

- Assess the skill level of vendor or third-party consulting resources used in the pilot
- See if your working relationship is likely to be smooth or difficult
- Identify staffers who become energized by the CPR and could make useful internal product consultants
- Monitor how thoroughly and quickly the vendor responds to problems and the show-stopper level of these problems

Contracts to acquire client/server accounting software should be contingent on a successful CRP—defining what success means is a critcal due diligence step. A show-stopper problem should not necessarily immediately halt the CRP because such problems may appear less significant as the CRP progresses. Factor plenty of time into the evaluation schedule to allow for analyzing the results of the CRP before proceeding with a full implementation.

(c) Use Consultants Wisely

Businesses may need or want to use consulting resources for some or all aspects of the implementation of a client/server accounting package. While it can be very comforting to use the one-stop shopping approach offered by big six accounting firms or large systems integrators, it may be more cost effective to use specialized resources to help with specific aspects of the package selection and implementation process. The main attraction of the bigger players is:

- The reputation and experience that the firm brings to the table
- The volume of resources they can bring to bear on your problem
- The non-stop availability of these resources for overtime or weekend work
- The range of selection and implementation services available under one roof
- That it may be able to take the hit if costs and timescales overrun
- That you have someone worth suing if things really go badly wrong

All this comes at a cost that can mean the evaluation is saddled with:

- Top-dollar daily rates especially for people with real experience

- Heavy T&E expenses for use of resources drafted in from other locations
- Inexperienced college graduates or recent MBAs who are learning on your dollar
- The prospect of an us-and-them mentality developing between the consulting swat teams and internal staffers

By dividing the software selection and implementation process into components it may be possible to use independents or mix and match independents with ongoing resources provided by the bigger players. A typical client/server accounting package selection process can be divided into at least these four phases:

Phase	*Description*
1 Business Objectives	
Business Background	Defining the business environment and objectives for the new system
Business Scenarios	Defining the business scenarios for which the new system must add value
Business Rollout	Defining where the new system will be implemented and who is to be involved
2 Vendor Selection	
Invite to Bid Document	Preparing document for inviting vendors to bid for the application business
Vendor Research	To ensure the bid document is sent to the optimum list of appropriate vendors
Vendor Shortlisting	To review and research vendor responses to narrow the vendors to a viable shortlist
3 Package Selection	
Scenario Teams	Defining the staffers to be responsible for defining and testing business scenarios

Business Scenarios	Defining the business scenarios against which the packages can be evaluated
Vendor Presentations	Managing the presentation of the packages; collating and reviewing the results of the sessions

4 Contract Negotiation

Lead Vendor Selection	Identifying lead vendor and backup vendor and carrying out precontract negotiations
Conference Room Pilot	Setup, execution, and review of conference room pilot to finalize package selection
Contract Negotiation	Establishing the terms and conditions for a purchase contract

While it is possible to use different consulting resources for each of these steps it usually makes sense to have continuity over at least the first three steps, especially as these can often can be accomplished by a single consultant rather than a team. Step 4, contract negotiation involving the CRP, is a circumstance in which a switch to a team or adopting a new implementation consulting resource can make good sense. The rationale is that this phase is simply more complex and resource intensive as well as a logical transition phase between the software selection and implementation stages.

(d) Implementation Realities

Many client/server accounting vendors estimate that implementing their packages can cost anywhere from one to fivc dollars and up in implementation expenses for every dollar of software expenses. It has been known for implementations to cost as much as ten dollars per dollar of software cost. Typically the proportion is higher as thc application configuration requires more modules and greater complexity. So implementing a fixed-assets system may cost a lower multiple of software expense than implementing a full suite of manufacturing modules. A key piece of information to ascertain from the vendor and the references provided is what the breakdown was between their software and implementation spend and then budget accordingly. These figures may be surprising. Packages such as SAP R/3 are infamous for their implementation costs, which are often as much a result of wholesale reengineering of underlying business practices and processes as of the cost of configuring and implementing the software itself.

CHAPTER TEN

Reengineering Accounting Transaction Processing

10.1 INTRODUCTION

Reengineering your accounting system is primarily about taking advantage of technology to improve the efficiency of your business processes. Since the personal computer became a business tool in the early 1980s, the mantra of the hardware and software technology sector has become "cheaper, faster, and better." Over the last fifteen years, many businesses will have changed their accounting system once or even twice, but few can claim that their systems have kept pace with the breadth and depth of technology change during this period. Accounting software vendors have had enough difficulty keeping up themselves. The fact that most accounting vendors now actively pursue partnerships with other complementary software vendors to deliver more technological value in their systems indicates that it is becoming unrealistic to expect any one vendor to deliver everything.

The key point is that anyone implementing an accounting system now will almost certainly be installing software that has been completely redesigned within the last five years. In general, these new client/server accounting systems are making much better use of technology than previous generations of accounting software, which presents an ideal opportunity to reengineer business processes to take advantage of new technological advances. In any case, you may have to use these systems to make your business processes more efficient and to justify the costs of client/server accounting. Many of these new systems demand higher infrastructure, application-module, implementation, and support costs than previous generations of accounting software. Client/server can sometimes be justified on a cost basis when it genuinely replaces a mainframe system but often its costs can only be justified by productivity gains, which are more difficult to pin down.

Outlined in this section are a number of reengineering opportunities that generally focus on changing the way a traditional business process is managed through your accounting system. Each section is tackled in a similar way:

- A business process problem is introduced.
- One or more reengineering approaches are discussed.
- References are made to vendor and product resources.

The vendor and product names referred to as resources do not imply any endorsement by the author of these vendors or their products, but rather that they are representative of the resources used to deliver the reegineering solutions discussed. The resources list is not exhaustive, but rather a means to point you in the right direction. You should note that in most cases the vendors will also bring in other system integrations or consulting resources to help implement these reengineering solutions. Many of the reengineering approaches discussed may be approached using one or more of the common solutions outlined below.

(a) The Internet Solution

The Internet (or intranet) solution depends on the accounting application providing a means of passing data to and from Internet Web servers; of entering, querying, or presenting data through Internet browser software; and of utilizing Internet e-mail to receive and pass messages. Often this is achieved by the accounting vendor providing Internet applets—mini applications written in new programming languages such as Java from Sun Microsystems that can be loaded into and used from Internet browser software. The basic architecture of an Internet solution is shown in Figure 10.1.

The advantages and disadvantages of Internet-based solutions can be summarized as follows:

Advantages

Inexpensive to Deploy	The Internet browser software required to run the accounting applets is either inexpensive or free and is expected to become part of standard desktop operating systems in the future. The Internet itself is essentially a low-cost, low-maintenance, wide-area network that can be used by business and consumer users alike.

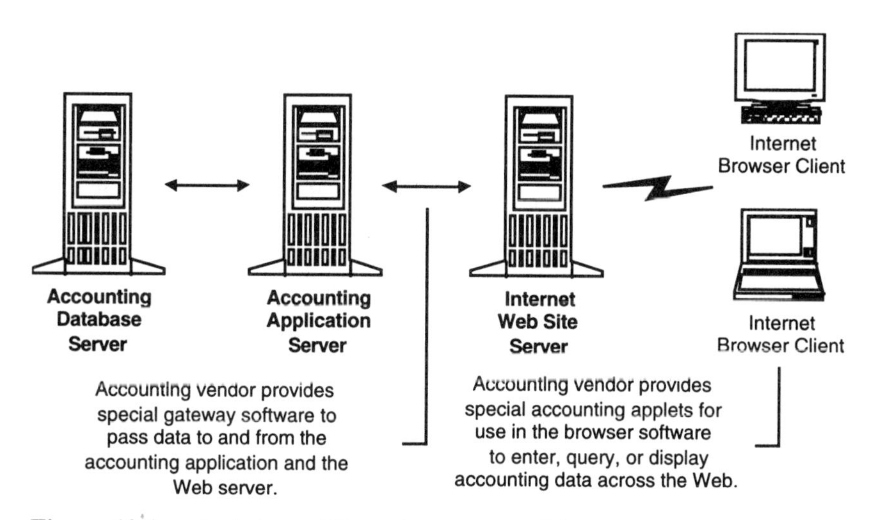

Figure 10.1. An Internet Reengineering Architecture.

Inexpensive to Acquire	The deployment of these solutions may not require the purchase of extra accounting-system client licenses but only specific Internet-enabled applets that may be provided free or at very low cost by the vendor relative to the cost of a full module license.
Easy to Maintain	Internet applets are stored on a central web server and are downloaded each time a specific document page is requested. Therefore there is only one place to update if the applet changes. This makes application maintenance easier and cheaper.
Extends Reach	Internet applets can be accessed at any time of day from anywhere in the world where there is an Internet connection. The applets can be accessed by any qualified user whether accounting or nonaccounting, internal to the corporation or an external partner. This extends the reach of the accounting application.

Disadvantages

Uncertain Security	The Internet is not yet regarded as a fully secure means of managing commercial transactions, although this is changing quickly as the electronic commerce market takes off. There always remains the possibility that your data could be hijacked by determined hackers located anywhere in the world and not under U.S. legal jurisdiction.

Slow Response Times	The rapid growth of the Internet and peaking of loads at various times of the day means that response times may suffer at the desktop browser level causing user frustration or occasionally dropped connections and possible data loss.
Increased Traffic	The use of Internet accounting applets may increase the traffic of casual users interacting with the accounting system, which may have an impact on the performance of the accounting system as a whole.
Increased Complexity	The use of an Internet accounting applet requires a web server plus the software that manages the transfer of data between the web server and the accounting application or database server to be in place. This adds more complexity to the system's plumbing and requires additional IS support.

(b) The Groupware Solution

The groupware solution depends on the accounting application providing a means to pass data to and from groupware software. Often this is achieved when the accounting vendor provides a special module that is designed to deliver integration services between the accounting system and the specific groupware software. System integrators who are proficient in both products then configure the integration module to handle the specific application task. The basic architecture of the groupware solution is shown in Figure 10.2.

The advantages and disadvantages of groupware-based solutions can be summarized as follows:

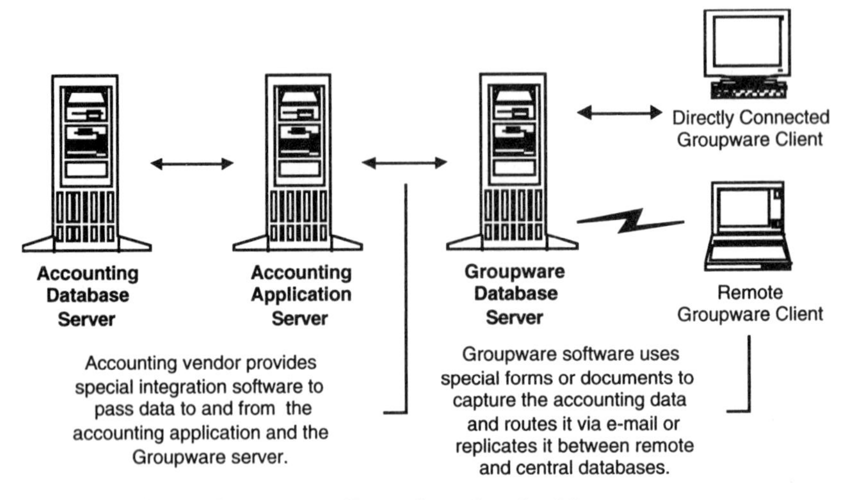

Figure 10.2. A Groupware Reengineering Architecture.

Advantages

Leverages Groupware	If the groupware software is already deployed in the organization, this approach leverages more value from that infrastructure by extending the use of the groupware system to handle accounting related tasks.
Extends Functionality	An existing groupware infrastructure provides an ideal mechanism for routing data around an organization outside the accounting system for use in reviewing or approving accounting related transactions. It does not require the accounting system to include any built-in workflow functionality.
Extends Reach	Groupware allows local and remote access to the groupware server that extends the reach of the accounting application beyond the accounting

	department and out to external or field based users.

Disadvantages

Expensive to Deploy	If the groupware is not already in place, the groupware solution may be expensive to deploy in an enterprise context, particularly when compared to doing the same job using an Internet-based approach.
Increased Complexity	The groupware solution may also be more complex to deploy when compared to an Internet-based approach. This is because accounting vendors are supplying preconfigured applets for the Internet, whereas you may have to build your own application in the groupware product. This transfers the cost of building and maintaining the application to your business rather than the vendor.

(c) The E-Mail Solution

The E-mail solution depends on the accounting application providing: access to an e-mail server for mail user directory and message routing services. The accounting application itself needs to include forms for creating mail messages and linking attachments (such as reports) to these messages, and provide access to electronic inboxes that are used to sort and manage electronic message queues. The basic architecture for an electronic mail solution is shown in Figure 10.3.

The disadvantages of e-mail solutions are: they may be expensive and complex to deploy if the e-mail infrastructure is not already in place; and they may not provide sophisticated manipulation of the

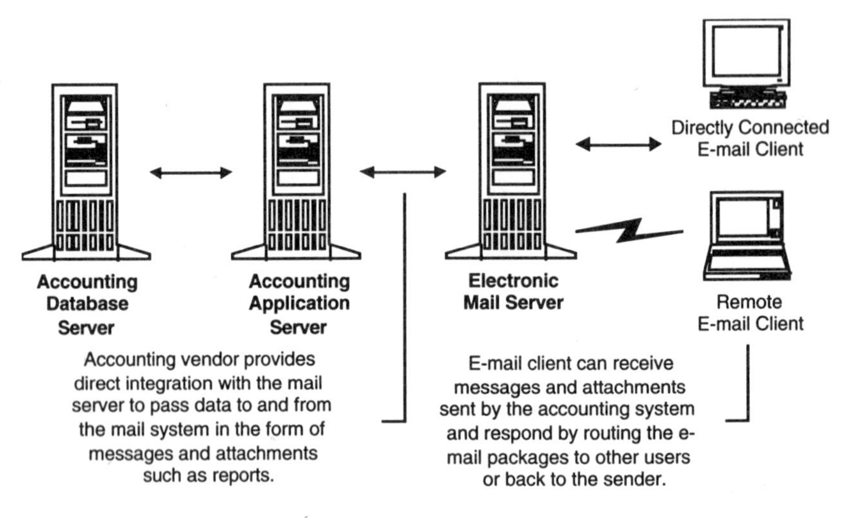

Figure 10.3. An E-Mail Reengineering Architecture.

accounting data before it is sent or received because the e-mail system is designed primarily to manage simple textual message data.

Advantages

Leverages E-Mail	If the e-mail software is already deployed in the organization, this approach leverages more value from that infrastructure by extending the use of the e-mail system to include accounting related tasks.
Extends Functionality	An existing e-mail infrastructure provides an ideal mechanism for routing data around an organization outside the accounting system to distribute reports or review accounting documents. It does not require a separate integration module as the groupware solution may, but it does require that the accounting system include mail enabling functionality

	such as a Send button as an output option when generating accounting reports.
Extends Reach	E-mail allows local and remote access to the mail server that extends the reach of the accounting application beyond the accounting department and out to external or field based users.

Disadvantages

Expensive to Deploy	If the e-mail is not already in place, the e-mail solution may be expensive to deploy in an enterprise context, particularly when compared to using an Internet-based approach in which e-mail may be hosted by an external provider of Internet mail services.
Adds Loading	If an e-mail system is already in place, using it for accounting-related routings may add significant extra load to the current mail system. Consequently new or more powerful mail servers may be required and more sophisticated selection and sorting rules defined to improve response in the mail client software.

(d) The ODBC Linking Solution

The ODBC linking solution depends on the accounting application providing read and/or write access to its accounting database via the ODBC data access protocols. The vendor may provide this ODBC data source driver for free or as a standard driver of the desktop operating system. Once the ODBC data source is registered by the operating system, the accounting database is potentially accessible to any ODBC-compliant application. These are usually query and reporting tools, EIS packages, or worksheets. The basic architecture of an ODBC solution is shown in Figure 10.4.

The advantages of the ODBC solutions are: they allow code and other lookup tables to be maintained in just one place (the accounting database) so they can be accessed by any ODBC-compliant tool; they are simple to set up if the desktop client environment uses Microsoft Windows and the ODBC data source is properly registered for use by client applications; and they are inexpensive to deploy because ODBC drivers essentially come free from either Microsoft or the accounting vendor.

The disadvantages of ODBC solutions are that: they may encourage too many desktop tools to be configured to provide access to the accounting data; or they may not provide the security or performance that is required for the application in question.

Advantages

Inexpensive and Easy — ODBC drivers to access the accounting database are usually provided free by

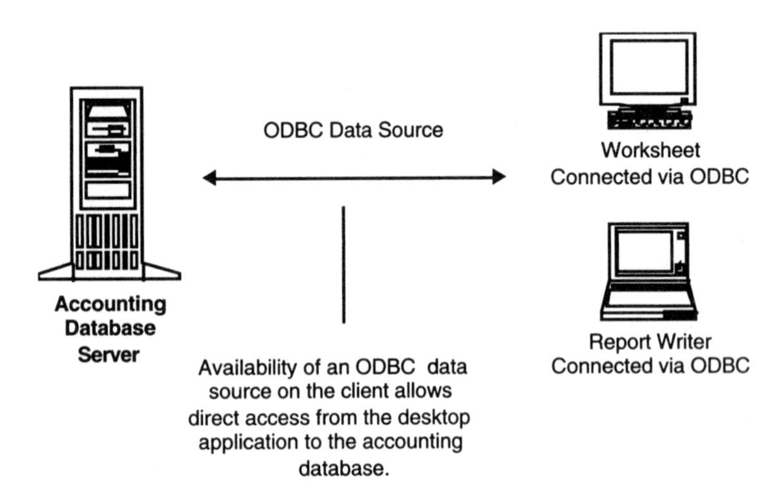

Figure 10.1. An ODBC Reengineering Architecture.

the vendor or as part of the desktop operating system (such as Microsoft Windows 95). Any third-party tool that is ODBC compliant can access the accounting data directly. Registering the availability of the ODBC data source is easy and only needs to be done once to make it available to any ODBC compliant application.

Real-Time Access	ODBC allows third-party tools to access the accounting data directly, in real time, just as if it were one of the accounting system's native users. There is no need to run any programs or batch interfaces to move data between the accounting database server and another application server.
One Data Source	Because ODBC-enabled solutions work directly against the accounting database, there is no need to maintain duplicate code and lookup tables in the desktop application. This ensures that all data is controlled from one place and that error-prone updates between two sets of lookup tables are not required.
Popular	ODBC is backed by Microsoft Corporation and has been widely adopted by the industry, including accounting vendors, as a common method of accessing data in relational and nonrelational sources. ODBC is being improved with every release and is likely to be around for some time to come. Other attempts at similar stan-

	dards, such as Borland's IDAPI have not proven as successful in the marketplace.
Read/Write Access	ODBC may allow read-only or read/write access to accounting data. This means that a third-party tool or custom application may be able to post directly to the accounting system using ODBC. Of course this may be regarded as both an advantage and a disadvantage.

Disadvantages

Slow Performance	Although ODBC is improving all the time, in many circumstances it may not perform as quickly or effectively as so-called native data access drivers that are designed to work directly against one specific database engine instead of providing access to many different database engines.
Security	While ODBC opens up the accounting database to many desktop tools it also opens up the possibility of bypassing accounting system access security or data integrity controls. Before any ODBC solution is considered, steps must be taken to ensure that the security and integrity of the accounting data cannot be breached.

(e) The Specialist Add-On Module Solution

The add-on module solution depends on providing read and/or write access to the accounting application's database, usually via ODBC data-access protocols, from a module that is external but complementary to the accounting system. In the past a major problem with this approach was that the specialist module had to maintain copies of certain accounting system code and lookup tables to function. Via a common data-access method such as ODBC this no longer necessary so it has become more viable for smaller, specialist vendors to release add-on modules that can work with multivendor accounting solutions. The basic architecture for an add-on module solution is shown in Figure 10.5.

Advantages

Solution Focus	These add-on modules are designed to solve a specific business problem and often provide broader or deeper functionality in their specialist area than can be expected from generic accounting packages. The add-on module can

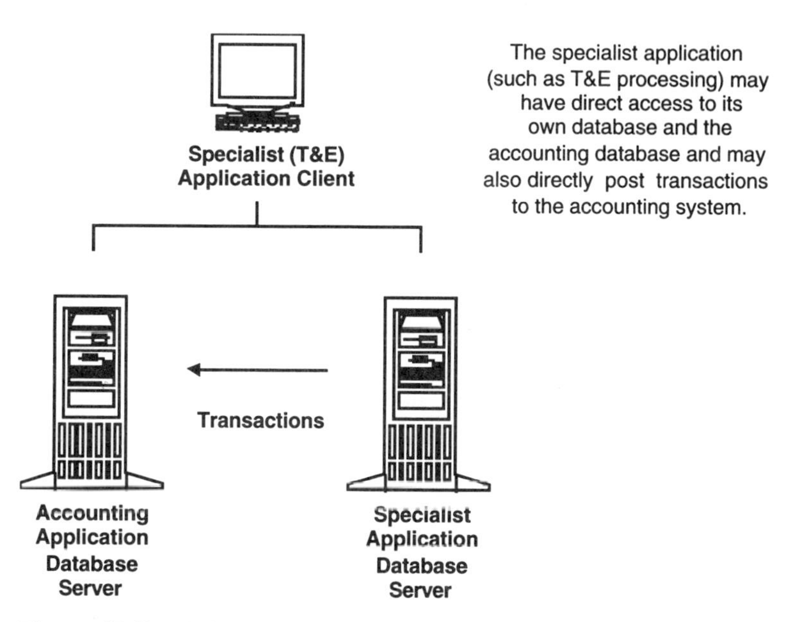

Figure 10.5. A Specialist Module Reengineering Architecture.

plug a gap or enhance an otherwise incomplete accounting system.

Real-Time Access	Using ODBC allows these add-on modules to access the accounting data directly, in real time, just as if it were one of the accounting system's native users. There may be no need to run any programs or batch interfaces to move data between the accounting database server and the add-on package's application server.
One Data Source	Because ODBC enabled solutions work directly against the accounting database, there is no need to maintain duplicate code and lookup tables in the add-on application. This ensures that all data is controlled from one place and that error-prone updates between two sets of lookup tables are not required.

Disadvantages

Expensive	Add-on modules may be expensive to acquire and may require the purchase of additional database or application servers. However, these modules are unlikely to be any more expensive than the cost of the accounting modules to which they link up.
Slow Learning Curve	The add-on modules are unlikely to be designed exactly like the accounting modules they complement. This may mean an additional learning curve that accounting users have to manage to become proficient in the new application.

(f) The Metadata Reporting Solution

The metadata solution depends on the use of an intermediary layer between the accounting system and a third-party query or reporting tool. This intermediary layer, the metadata—or data about data—acts as a mapping layer to allow one application to read and/or write data from/to another application. The metadata layer may be provided by the accounting system vendor as a means of describing the accounting database structures to a third-party application. Alternatively the metadata layer may be provided by the third-party tool vendor to describe the data structures from which their application needs to work. In the latter case, it is the responsibility of the accounting vendor or the user to manage the population of this layer with meaningful data to describe the underlying accounting system structures to be accessed. The basic architecture for a metadata solution is shown in Figure 10.6.

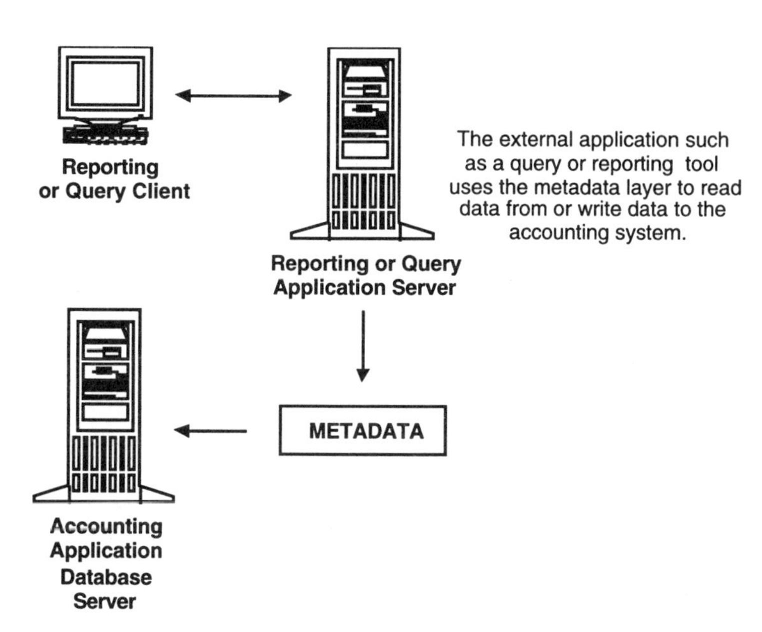

Figure 10.6. A Metadata Reengineering Architecture.

Advantages

Extends Functionality	The use of a metadata layer means that the accounting data can be accessed intelligently from query and reporting tools that may not themselves have any accounting-specific intelligence. These tools can then take advantage of balance and time-series data tables possibly provided by the metadata layer that would otherwise have to be defined from scratch by the IS department.
Secure	Working through a metadata layer can ensure that third-party applications do not work directly with accounting data but through views of the data. Use of such views secures sensitive data from prying eyes, restricts access to balance data rather than the original transactions, or ensures that data accessed is subject to other specific business rules coded in and used exclusively by the metadata layer.

Disadvantages

Difficult Setup and Maintenance	If the provided metadata layer is not already populated by the accounting or third-party application vendor then the user information systems department is responsible for populating the metadata itself. Furthermore as the structures of either the accounting system or the third-party system change, then the metadata layer may need to be changed also, requiring ongoing maintenance.

Performance	By working against the data through a metadata layer, there may be an impact on the performance of the third-party query or reporting tool because of the overhead of using the layer and complying with any business rules in the layer. However, depending on the design of the metadata layer and the third-party tool accessing it, performance may in fact be improved over using the accounting system's own tools because both the metadata and the third-party tool are optimized for a specific decision-support task.

10.2 TRANSACTION MANAGEMENT REENGINEERING

In this section, reengineering opportunities that relate primarily to changing the way accounting transactions are processed are outlined. An accounting transaction is a business process that has a life cycle.

Start of Life Cycle	End of Life Cycle
Sales order	Cash receipt
Purchase requisition	Cash payment
Customer activation	Delivery of goods or service
T&E submission	Employee expense check

(a) One Point-of-Entry Customer Activation

(i) Process Problem

Many businesses selling services or equipment contracts use field sales forces to sign up new customers and contract new and follow-on business from those customers. Many field salespeople are now equipped with laptop computers that are typically used for sales presentations, printing contracts or collateral, and contact management, rather than initiating the customer activation and order-taking process. While new customer data and orders may be captured at the point of sale, they are often printed and faxed back to a central accounting system to be rekeyed into the accounts receivable module by a clerk.

This process is made more efficient by using only one point of entry for recording new customer data and new or revised order data. This point of entry should be the field salesperson's laptop, which is the closest point to the customer. By using one point of entry the possibility of rekeying errors is reduced, the process can be fully managed electronically for faster throughput, and the central customer database can be as accurate as the last time the field salesperson visited the customer, thus preventing incorrect address or contact data being used by the accounting system for billing purposes.

(ii) Reengineering Approaches

Granular workflow-oriented software allows you to distribute the customer activation and order-entry aspects of the receivables process by locating only these functional components on the field salesperson's laptop. The data is captured locally through the same screen-based forms as it would be if processed centrally and stored in a local database. At predetermined times the laptop is connected using dial-up lines to transfer the local data to the central receivables database using a predefined workflow process with the appropriate business rules to manage the creation of new customers and recording of new or changed order data in the main receivables system database.

For this approach to work the software functionality must be able to be deployed as separate, isolated granules, support small footprint, local databases, operate on laptop platforms, and deliver a workflow engine that is sophisticated enough to handle the synchronization of data between the remote laptop application and the main receivables server application. The main benefit of this approach is that everything is handled by one application, namely the accounting software and no third-party software is required.

(iii) Resources

Vendor	Product
Computron Software (Rutherford, NJ)	Computron Financials
Dun & Bradstreet Software (Atlanta, GA)	SmartStream Financials
FileNet Corpation (Costa Mesa, CA)	Visual WorkFlo
Lawson Software (Minneapolis, MN)	Insight

So called groupware products that are designed for remote access to centralized information are another reengineering approach. Groupware consists of client and server application and database software that allows the local or remote client component to interact with the server component by replicating data to and from the groupware server database to the groupware client database and vice versa. In this approach, specially defined new-customer activation and order entry forms would be available on the laptop groupware client application to record the data at the point of sale. Whenever the laptop is connected back to the groupware server, this local data is copied back to the main groupware database using replication. Once it is in the central groupware database a separate process can automate the collection of this data and its transfer into the accounting system receivables database. A number of vendors are providing special integration modules for defining this process to link their accounting software databases with those of leading groupware products.

(iv) Resources

Vendor	Product
Great Plains Software (Fargo, ND)	Lotus Notes Integration Manager
Lotus Development Corporation (Cambridge, MA)	Lotus Notes
FileNet (Costa Mesa, CA)	Ensemble

The Internet or a corporate intranet may also be used as a reengineering solution. In this case a standard Internet browser package, such as Netscape Navigator, Spyglass Mosiac, or Microsoft Internet Explorer, is used to display special forms for collecting new customer or order data. The field salesperson connects to an Internet or intranet web site with the browser and loads the appropriate documents that contain the customer activation or order-entry forms. The data is entered, transmitted back to the web server, and then automatically transferred into the central receivables system by a link between the vendor's accounting server database and the web-server database. This means that new customers and order data can be transferred from anywhere that has Internet connection capability. Through Internet e-mail, this approach can also automatically inform the salesperson if there are problems with the customer activation, due to credit history issues for example, or to confirm that an order has been accepted or shipped. Many of the client/server accounting vendors are currently working on these types of systems and the availability of solutions is likely to increase considerably between 1996 and 1997.

(b) On-Line Sales-Order Entry

(i) Process Problem

Recording orders into order-entry systems is a laborious task in many businesses and requires hordes of telephone order takers or data-entry clerks whose sole job may be to rekey information from order forms and coupons, letters, and faxes. This introduces errors, makes tracking order status more time-consuming, and creates an artificial border between the customers and their supplier.

Moving the responsibility for order entries into the hands of the customer can ensure more accurate order taking and reduce the amount of human intervention required. By making the order-entry process more visual you can ensure that the customers have a better idea of what they are ordering. Then, by establishing an electronic connection to the customers you can keep them better informed about the status of their order.

(ii) Reengineering Approaches

For business-to-business sales orders, electronic data interchange (EDI) is a popular approach to solving this problem. A purchase order is created in your customers' procurement software and instead of being printed is output electronically in a format that your own EDI-enabled system can understand. This EDI file is then transmitted electronically to you from your customer, usually via a third-party value-added network (VAN) provider. When received it is converted into a sales order in your sales-order processing system, thus the whole order process is automated and managed electronically.

Drawbacks to EDI include requiring businesses to subscribe to more than one EDI VAN to allow customers to reach them, or customers' systems not being able to handle the creation of EDI documents themselves, making the whole process impractical. Currently, EDI is regarded as a more secure means of transferring business data than the Internet, however this perception is likely to change quickly as electronic commerce takes off on the Internet. At this point in time, many EDI software vendors are working on converting their systems to use the Internet instead of the third-party VANs to carry the EDI traffic and many big users of EDI, such as General Electric Corporation (GEC) are making the transition from traditional EDI to new Internet-based customer-supplier communication channels.

(iii) Resources

Vendor	Product
Premenos Technology Corporation (Concord, CA)	EDI/400 Templar
Sterling Commerce Inc. (Atlanta, GA)	CONNECT
TradeRights Inc. (Malibu, CA)	EDI Reference

For business-to-business and consumer-to-business sales ordering, the Internet and telephony are providing new solutions for automating the sales order process. As the Internet reaches more and more homes around the world it is fast becoming the most widespread direct link to consumers after television and the telephone. Because the Internet is already being integrated with televisions, it is likely to reach most homes that matter to business by the end of the 1990s. The Internet is ideal for consumer ordering because it is highly visual and can be easily kept up to date. The Internet allows businesses to maintain one electronic catalog in a central web server location and make it available to literally millions of consumers at any time of the day, anywhere in the world, instead of printing millions of paper catalogs, reissuing them every month, and mailing them to consumers.

Orders can be recorded in forms embedded in Internet browser software and transmitted to the central order database. This data is then fed directly into the order-entry module of the accounting system through automated links between the web server database and the accounting server database. Because an electronic link is established with each business or consumer placing orders across the Internet, a dialogue between customer and supplier can be maintained. This dialogue provides better customer service by keeping them informed of their order status via e-mail. Furthermore, this dialogue provides the vendor with a means of targeting customers with special offers and incentives that may increase a business's volume or profit.

(iv) Resources

Vendor	Product
SBT Internet Systems (San Rafael, CA)	WebTrader
Microsoft Corp. (Redmond, WA)	Merchant Server

If the items being ordered are simple and repetitive or services that do not depend on visual catalogs then using telephony technology makes sense. In this scenario, telephony is a means of allowing the telephone to transfer data into a database. Telephony is a basis for fax-on-demand services. This involves information being ordered via a toll-free number using a touchtone phone to select information from a database that is delivered to you as a fax document. Telephony software is used to translate the numbers and letters indicated by touchtone choices into information that can be used either to retrieve data from a database or store data in a database. It may also be used to store and even parse whole chunks of voice data such as when callers leave their name and address as voice messages, in order to store this as a contact record in a database. A telephony sales order system simply walks callers through a series of steps that describe the product or service they are ordering, and captures their contact data and payment information, usually a credit card number. After the caller hangs up this data can be translated into a valid sales-order transaction and automatically posted to an accounting system. If necessary a human operator may then call back to confirm, query, or reject the order but at this point the new customer and sales order data have been electronically captured, this time via a touchtone phone.

(v) Resources

Vendor	Product
Edify Corporation (Santa Clara, CA)	Electronic Workforce

(c) Automate T&E Processing

(i) Process Problem

Many accounting systems do not handle the processing of travel and entertainment (T&E) expenses very effectively. Often employees must be set up as if they are suppliers in the payables system, customers in the receivables system, or both. Sometimes there is no concept of the employee except as a part of the payroll system. Consequently much T&E accounting actually takes place outside of the accounting system through the use of worksheet forms that capture trip expenses. The data from these worksheets may be transferred using a batch program or may simply be rekeyed into the accounting system. As a result, T&E data often reaches the accounting system in summary form only, which makes it harder to analyze and investigate in the event of problems or meet demands for new ways of looking at the information.

(ii) Reengineering Approach

T&E automation may be achieved through the use of groupware or the Internet as described in section 10.1. In this case the groupware or Internet browser displays T&E collection worksheets from which data is passed back to the accounting system. The problem with this approach is that code tables used by the T&E data-entry forms may need to be maintained in two places: in the accounting system and remotely on the laptops used by employees to manage their T&E worksheets.

If you are using the worksheet approach already it may be worth considering enhancing your current collection of T&E data, by connecting these worksheets directly to your new accounting system database through an ODBC link. This avoids the two-step entry and post routine required when there is no ODBC link because the worksheet is connected directly to the accounting database and can post T&E transactions in real time if required. It also ensures that any codes used in the accounting system such as currency, department, or employee do not need to be maintained in two places because the ODBC enabled worksheet accesses the same code tables as the rest of the accounting system.

Another approach is to take advantage of new T&E expense or so-called employee payables applications that are being released. These packages are designed to specifically manage this type of accounting while providing the ability to read data from and post data to other accounting databases. The benefit of these types of packages is likely to be greater if the volume and complexity of the T&E problem is greater because they are designed to manage only this type of functionality.

These packages help to ensure that all T&E submissions meet corporate-wide compliance standards and business rules. They can maintain a single source for all corporate-approved expense categories, levels, hotels, airlines, and other vendors. Exception-processing rules can be defined so that expenses exceptions can be treated in a consistent manner but varied by employee or department. Expenses can be allocated to clients, jobs, projects, or cost centers for rebilling.

Employee payables packages may support a store-and-forward method of transmitting data from employee laptops or PCs to the central employee payables server via e-mail. This ensures that employees can complete their T&E worksheets remotely and then forward them to a T&E server on a regular basis. Employee payables packages are designed to treat T&E as a business process that requires entry, approval, and reimbursement stages so that the lifecycle of an expense can be tracked, queried, and reported in various ways on an ad-hoc basis.

(iii) Resources

Vendor	Product
Adisoft (San Leandro, CA)	Expense Report!
Captura Software Inc. (Bothell, WA)	Employee Payables
Portable Software Corporation (Bellevue, WA)	Xpense Management

(d) Enable Distributed Requisitioning

(i) Process Problem

Many organizations wish to maintain central control over their procurement process but allow distributed input to the system. Currently there are two ways this is being handled: by giving a wide range of users direct access to the accounting system's purchasing module, or by routing paper or electronic requisition forms to local, regional, or group purchasing departments.

Giving access to the accounting system is not ideal. Most users generating requisitions are casual rather than production accounting users. To give them all access to the accounting system is often functional overkill, can be costly in terms of licensing, may complicate the security required to manage all these casual logins, and will negatively impact system performance unnecessarily. Routing paper or electronic forms still means that a purchasing department clerk may have to rekey or otherwise manually consolidate requisitions for conversion into valid, approved, purchase orders.

Ideally the accounting system should provide functionality that extends the reach of the requisitioning process to users who, although they do not have access to the accounting system directly, are represented as addresses in the corporate e-mail system.

(ii) Reengineering Approach

Distributed requisitioning may be achieved through use of groupware or the Internet as described in section 10.1. In this case the groupware or Internet browser displays requisition entry forms from which data is passed back to the purchasing system. The problem with this approach is that code tables used by the requisition data-entry forms may need to be maintained in two places: in the accounting system, and remotely on the laptops used by employees to manage their requisition entry.

Another approach is to front-end the accounting system with a workflow to route requisitions through their approval process.

(iii) Resources

Vendor	Product
Dun & Bradstreet Software (Atlanta, GA)	SmartStream
Lawson Software (Minneapolis, MN)	Insight
SAP America Inc. (Wayne, PA)	R/3

(e) Automate the Approval Process

(i) Process Problem

Many accounting systems process a large number of transactions that require approval before they can be posted to the accounting database. These transactions include general ledger journals, sales and vendor invoices, and sales and purchase orders. Most accounting systems offer a hold-and-review process for approving these transactions that demands access to the accounting system itself often by a supervisor whose sole interaction with the system may be to approve transactions. Consequently many of these approval transactions are printed on paper forms and distributed by hand or fax to receive an approval stamp or signature. The forms use up paper, and can get lost or damaged in this manual approval process, and provide a poor way of recording data that illuminates the approval (or rejection) of the transaction.

(ii) Reengineering Approach

Instead of simply being put on hold, transactions requiring approval may be packaged into e-mail messages that can be routed via internal e-mail or the Internet to nonaccounting systems users for approval. These receiving users may simply be required to view the transaction data and check a box on an electronic form that records whether the transaction is approved or rejected. Users may also attach their own note to record more information about their decision. The transaction is then returned to the accounting system and the change of status recorded against the transaction record in the accounting database. This mail-driven approval process can be enhanced by the use of organization-driven distribution lists and special business rules that route specific types of transaction or transaction values to specific users in the distribution list.

Alternatively, a document-enabled accounting system may allow a scanned transaction document to be routed via e-mail for approval rather than some package of basic transaction data. The approving user can then view the original source document before approving or rejecting it. The document management software that manages this process may also allow the document to be annotated, be highlighted, have notes, or have an electronic approval signature attached before returning it to the sender. All this information remains attached to the document and can be viewed at any time by any user with permission to view the accounting transaction to which the document is attached. This document-driven approach provides a richer approval process than the e-mail approach but may be overkill in organizations in which the source documents themselves are not especially rich in information.

Using an external workflow package can also be a means of automating the approval process. This approach depends on the accounting transaction being initiated in the workflow package and its routing and approval stages being managed outside of the accounting system. Once the transaction is approved it can then be passed as a valid transaction to the accounting database. This can work well for purchasing or payables transactions for which the resulting accounting transaction is an invoice that is approved for payment, this being the stage in which a real accounting system is required to kick in. The drawback is that the information supporting that accounting invoice is being stored in an external application. This information may not be easy to access directly from queries or reports created in the accounting system thus making on-line investigation of exceptions more difficult to achieve unless special drillthrough functionality is provided.

(iii) Resources

Vendor	Product
FileNet (Costa Mesa, CA)	Watermark Enterprise Saros Mezzanine
FileNet (Costa Mesa, CA)	Visual WorkFlo Payables
FlexiInternational (Shelton, CT)	FlexiFinancials

(f) Link Images to Accounting Transactions

(i) Process Problem

Even in accounting systems, information context can be enhanced through the ability of users to see visual images. Examples of such images may be:

- Inventory catalog items
- Bill of material's parts-explosion diagrams
- Inventory goods receipt notes
- Photographs of fixed assets
- Asset, lease, or insurance documents
- Photographs of employees
- Source transaction documents (checks, invoices, etc.)
- Sales and purchase contracts

It makes sense for accounting users to have access to these images from within their accounting system rather than having to switch to a separate application that is not context sensitive to the current accounting record being viewed.

(ii) Reengineering Approach

Even though these types of images can usually be stored as a blob (binary large object) data type within the same databases used by client/server accounting systems, it may not efficiently store the data in the same database as other accounting data for performance reasons. Thus instead of always displaying a linked image with an accounting record, many vendors have opted for on-demand viewing of the image. This is achieved by linking third-party imaging management applications to the accounting system, often through use of Microsoft's OLE technology. In this case the accounting system becomes an OLE client that requests a specific image from the image management software that is performing the role of the OLE server.

By pushing a button on an inventory or employee maintenance form, for example, the image management package is loaded in a separate display window under the control of the accounting system. The user can then view and manipulate an image already linked to that employee or inventory record. Or if no image is linked, the user may click a scan button and scan in a new image that is automatically linked to the current record using an image identifier added to the accounting system record. Because the user is viewing the image from within the image management package, the image may be manipulated in any way that the specialist package allows—for example it could be printed or mailed to another user. Once the image viewing or manipulation is completed, the image application is closed down and the user returned to their current context in the accounting system.

(iii) Resources

Vendor	Product
FileNet (Costa Mesa, CA)	Watermark Enterprise Saros Mezzanine
FlexiInternational (Shelton, CT)	FlexiFinancials
Great Plains Software (Fargo, ND)	Dynamics C/S+

(g) Improve Performance Using Process Servers

(i) Process Problem

Many accounting transaction-related processes are resource intensive, that is they demand a high level of computing resource to manage carrying out processes such as:

- Batch posting of large transaction files from feeder systems
- Producing multireport packs as part of month-end reporting
- Closing a fiscal period or year and updating report balance files
- Number-crunching operations such as running currency revaluations
- Extracting transaction data for feeding to other systems

If more demands are put on these processes because the number of underlying transactions has increased, or the processes are being run by more users or more frequently by the same users, or the complexity of the process has increased, then overall system performance may degrade.

(ii) Reengineering Approach

By establishing process servers you can help to distribute the process load more efficiently over more computing resources. This approach requires that the accounting system's structure allow processes to be spun off to network server computers as designated by the user or system administrator. Not all systems have been designed with this level of granularity in mind but usually the ability to define process servers is a facility expected to be in three-tier client/server accounting systems.

These systems generally treat all batch-related postings and reporting programs as separately executable processes. The user that initiates the process may then optionally run the process on any one of many available process servers. These servers are simply computer network nodes whose address is known to the accounting system and on which software to manage the accounting process has been installed. The process server resources are then dedicated to a specific task such as validating import transactions, extracting a transaction feed, or running a report. The process task is of course run remotely in the background, allowing the initiating user to continue working without interruption. The availability of process servers also assists system managers in scheduling process jobs because they can be spread across multiple process servers and each server job queue managed to suit the business priorities. Adding process servers simply involves registering a server with the accounting system and copying any process management software to the server in question. Process-server-based financial reporting tools can also be used to essentially remove the whole reporting process burden onto separate reporting servers if required.

(iii) Resources

Vendor	**Product**
Great Plains Software (Fargo, ND)	Great Plains Dynamics C/S+
FRx Software (Denver, CO)	FRx Enterprise
SAP America Inc. (Wayne, PA)	R/3
SQL Financials (Atlanta, GA)	SQL Financials

CHAPTER ELEVEN

Reengineering Accounting Decision Support

11.1 INTRODUCTION

Outlined in this section are reengineering opportunities that relate primarily to changing the way decision support is managed from an accounting system. Accounting decision support relies on the system's capabilities to:

- Run flexible queries against the accounting database
- Generate formatted reports from the accounting database
- Extract business intelligence from the accounting database
- Distribute business intelligence to a wider audience
- Allow access to accounting data from third party decision-support tools

Recent surveys such as those sponsored by Deloitte & Touche LLP/Hyperion Software, and Price Waterhouse/Lawson Software have confirmed that many corporate financial managers are dissatisfied with the ability of their current systems to deliver useful decision-support information.

11.2 ESTABLISHING A DECISION-SUPPORT SERVER

(a) Process Problem

Accounting systems have traditionally been designed as transaction processors. The primary problem that high-end accounting software has to solve is how to manage the receipt-, validation-, and business-rule-driven posting of hundreds of thousands of transactions on a daily basis while maintaining system availability and transaction data integrity. Consequently many old-generation accounting systems concentrated their database design on transaction performance rather than information retrieval functionality.

Many traditional accounting report writers roll up individual transactions each time a report is run. While this method ensures the integrity of the report because it always reflects the transactions in the database at the time the report was run, it can lead to report generation times of hours or even days. At peak reporting times such as at month end, or for complex reporting such as multientity consolidations, system resources could be tied up and business processes put on hold while the system cranked out reports.

The use of balance files helps to reduce reporting times significantly but balance files are often rejected because to keep them updated detracts from transaction processing performance and once a balance file is corrupted, rebuilding it is another drain on system resources. Improvements in the performance, availability, and integrity of the database management systems used by modern accounting systems have meant that balance files are now common and often maintained almost in real time. In fact, many systems now include multiple-balance file structures that may be user defined in some cases to ensure that the balances being kept reflect the type of reports the user organization wants to run. However, even with balance files and user-defined balance rollups an accounting system may still not be able to align its database structures exactly to your business decision support needs. In any case, you may wish to separate decision-support activity and audiences from transaction processing for performance or security reasons for example.

(b) Reengineering Approach

Establishing a decision-support server can be a way to improve the quality of your decision-support information and its availability through desktop tools or to nonaccounting-oriented users. The role of the decision-support server is to act as a repository for information extracted from the transaction processing systems that has been optimized for decision-support analysis and reporting. This decision-support server may be an enterprise-wide data warehouse, a departmental or line-of-business datamart, or simply a separate database in which balance files and rollups are stored by the accounting system. By separating the decision-support activity from the transaction processing activity you are simply recognizing the need to divide the management of two essentially different processes, a decision that often leads to better performance for both processes.

The decision-support server may be one or more separate physical servers located on the network and it may run the same database model as the accounting transaction system or a different database model. Typical database configurations for transaction processing and decision-support servers are:

Accounting Platform	*Transaction Processing*	*Decision Support*
Mainframe, Midrange	VSAM, ISAM	Relational
PC LAN	ISAM, Btrieve	Relational/multidimensional
Client/server	Relational	Relational/multidimensional

Clearly if the same database is used for both transaction processing and decision-support this can be helpful as it takes better advantage of IS expertise and introduces a new database architecture into the organization. However, in many cases this may not be possible especially as many experts argue that the multidimensional database model is better suited for most types of decision support activity than the relational model. There are currently no accounting systems that use a multidimensional database for transaction processing as every client/server accounting vendor uses a relational database for this purpose.

For users of mainframe and midrange accounting systems, establishing a decision-support server is a very attractive way to move to client/server accounting in a controlled manner while continuing with the host systems for transaction processing and leveraging more value from the host data. Data is almost always staged to a decision-support server, a process that can be complex and require regular management by IS to ensure it proceeds smoothly and on a timely basis. Often this data staging involves the source transaction data being subject to one or more of these processes:

Process Type	Description
Data aggregation	Summarizing transaction data into higher-level balances such as activity by account by period
Data cleansing	Cleaning up data that has been coded incorrectly or ignoring transactions reversed to correct mispostings
Data mapping	Mapping multiple codes, such as customer codes, into a single, global customer code for analysis purposes
Data transformation	Transforming alpha codes into numeric IDs using separate lookup tables to improve processing performance
Data balancing	Checking that the data going into the decision-support server balances back to the source transaction data
Data reordering	Reordering the arrangement of data in a target table compared to the source table
Data combining	Combining data from multiple source table columns, such as last name and first name, into a single column

Data denormalization	Replacing numeric IDs in source table columns with full text descriptions in target table columns
Data calculation	Calculating new balances such as total period debits or credits in the target table from source table transactions
Data dimensioning	Combining data dimensions from many source tables such as product, rep, and location into one single target table

Setting up, maintaining, and processing this data staging is the biggest and most costly difficulty of using a decision-support server apart from the acquisition and integration of the decision-support server hardware and software. But there are other costs. Middleware software designed for data staging can also be expensive to acquire and maintain. Every desktop user that intends to make use of the decision-support server needs to be equipped with one or more decision-support query, report writing, OLAP, EIS, or worksheet add-in tools to enable access to the data. However there are many benefits to creating a decision-support server that for many organizations will outweigh the cost and maintenance drawbacks. These benefits include:

- Improving the overall performance of the accounting transaction system by offloading most decision-support processing onto another database and server computer
- Improving the availability of decision-support data by locating it on a database and server platform that is more accessible to desktop decision-support tools
- Improving the quality of decision-support information by ensuring it is organized in formats optimized for the ways the information is to be analyzed and reported
- Extending the life of legacy accounting systems by staging decision-support data to client/server platforms

- Extending the reach of decision-support data to an audience that does not want or need access to the accounting system for any other reason than data analysis
- Providing direct access to decision-support data that does not require running and printing of formal reports to view the data
- Providing a means to use a variety of desktop analysis tools for manipulating the data at the user's desktop for immediate assimilation of meaningful information

(c) Resources

Vendor	Product
Arbor Software (Sunnyvale, CA)	Essbase OLAP Server
The Dodge Group (Waltham, MA)	Financial Warehouse
Evolutionary Technologies, Inc. (Austin, TX)	ETI•Extract
Platinum Technology (Oakbrook Terrace, IL)	InfoPump
SAS Institute (Cary, NC)	CFO/Vision
Timeline Inc. (Bellevue, WA)	MetaView

11.3 CREATE A REPORT REPOSITORY

(a) Process Problem

While the introduction of a decision-support server is a strategic response to delivering improved decision support from accounting systems, there are a number of less demanding tactical ways to improve decision support. For some businesses, simply changing from a reporting process dominated by paper-to-digital reporting can deliver many operational benefits. For many organizations, financial reporting means printing reports, copying them, highlighting exceptions, creating distribution cover sheets, and routing these reports by internal mail, the postal system, courier, or fax. This is an expensive, environmentally wasteful and time-consuming process that can be largely obsoleted by moving to digital reporting.

(b) Reengineering Approach

Establishing a report repository is the first step in switching from paper to digital reporting. All modern accounting systems can store reports in digital file formats—this is how reports can be viewed on screen prior to printing. All a report repository does is collect these reports, store them in a database on a separate report server, and provide a means for the reports to be accessed and manipulated. Instead of printing reports, the default behavior of the accounting report writer is changed to storing reports in a specific file format and database at a specific network location.

Reports may be published to the repository in a number of formats depending on the nature and role of the repository. Reports published in standard ASCII formats, in delimited formats such as comma separated or in formats for use in specific worksheets (XLS for Excel or WKS for Lotus 1-2-3, for example) can be accessed from the report repository by a variety of desktop viewing, query, report writer, and worksheet tools. Reports published to the repository as HTML files can be accessed from standard desktop Internet browsers and navigated by users through the hypertext links embedded in the report files. If reports are being accessed by external users it may be useful for them to be published in compressed and encrypted formats for faster and secure transmission across the Internet.

A report repository may actually store the reports in a relational or object database and can be organized in various ways including:

- On a time series basis such as by date, period, quarter, or year

- On a line of business basis such as by marketing, finance, and operations
- On a user-group basis such as by supervisors, managers, or executives
- On a type of report basis such as aging, income, or balance sheets
- On some other rule-driven exception basis that reflects business priorities

The repository may be accessible to accounting and non-accounting users, across a LAN, WAN, the Internet, or an intranet. Document management software may be used to access the report repository to allow reports to be recalled from the repository and:

- Viewed on-screen through a report viewer
- Printed for a hard copy if required or faxed
- Converted to other file formats for example to load into a worksheet
- Digitally annotated, highlighted, or enhanced with added notations

A report repository may also be used as a collection point for reports prior to their routing to users via internal e-mail or Internet/intranet mail. The reports can be attached to e-mail messages and accessed through electronic mailboxes or inboxes. In this way the report repository can act as a means to isolate all users from running any reports against the source accounting data. Instead the reports are run from the accounting system under control of a batch program that outputs all reports to the report repository. In this scenario, the report repository may not be accessible at all to users but only to IS who manage the housekeeping of the repository and the distribution of reports using rule-based distribution logic. This approach ensures that digital reports are automatically pushed to the relevant users on a workflow basis, driven by defining user roles and report rules and routes in workflow management software that uses the reports in the repository as the workflow items to be routed around the organization.

(c) Resources

Vendor	Product
FileNet Corporation (Costa Mesa, CA)	Ensemble
FRx Software (Denver, CO)	FRx Enterprise
Lotus Development Corporation (Cambridge, MA)	Notes
Microsoft Corporation (Bellevue, WA)	Exchange Internet Information Server
Novell (Provo, UT)	GroupWise
ViewStar Inc. (Alameda, CA)	Process Architect

11.4 LEVERAGE REPORT MINING

(a) Process Problem

Reports from accounting systems often contain a great deal of information that is only useful to a selected audience and may further generate useful data if compared to previous or other report data. Traditionally, organizations rely on human intervention to highlight report exception data manually or to analyze paper reports for signs of trends or useful comparative data that is specific to the business context of the report. There is no guarantee that every report will be analyzed in this way or that the same standards will be applied each time the report is analyzed. This means that critical business data may be missed literally due to human error or lack of training. In low-volume, low-complexity business environments this is unlikely to be an issue but in high-volume, high-complexity environments such as utilities, telecommunications, or retail this can result in missed opportunities or unnecessary cost overruns.

(b) Reengineering Approach

Once reports are stored electronically in digital formats they can be mined by tools that are programmed to search out exception data. Traditional financial systems regard the production of a report as the end of a process; modern accounting systems regard a report as just a step in the overall process of managing a business. Paper-based reporting has always been a dead end because once committed to paper the data is dead and cannot be reused. Report mining is the concept of extracting maximum value from the report information by analysis either using specialized report mining engines provided by the accounting system or by users through tools on their desktop.

Report-mining engines or software agents use advanced analysis and artificial intelligence techniques to sift through the report data to automatically make decisions such as:

- Who needs to be made aware of this report information?
- How much of the information is relevant to specific users?
- What are the exceptions in this report information?
- In what format should the data be delivered to users?
- Should the system take any specific action based on the report data?

Once the engine has finished doing its report mining it may then generate a wide range of activities automatically (see Figure 11.1) without any user intervention, including:

- Sending report packages to users via e-mail
- Queuing report snapshots for eventual download to remote users

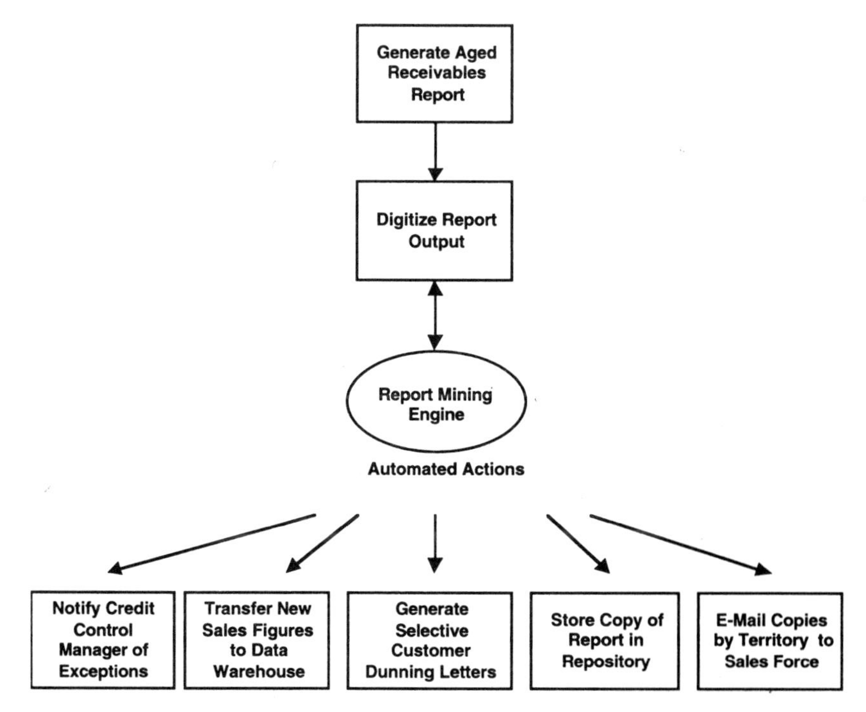

Figure 11.1. Report Mining.

- Transferring summary report data into a decision-support server
- Creating a copy of the report for on-line access from the report repository
- Generating alert messages to distribute to managers or executives
- Generating other system documents such as letters or bills
- Initiating other system tasks that depend on the report data

(c) Resources

Vendor	Product
Angoss Software (Toronto, ON)	KnowledgeSeeker
Computron Software	Computron Workflow

(Rutherford, NJ)	
DataMind (Redwood City, CA)	DataMind

11.5 DELIVER INTELLIGENT REPORT SNAPSHOTS

(a) Process Problem

Even when reports are stored and delivered electronically they may be simply static views of the data, unsuitable for further analysis or for use to build personalized views of the business. As organizations employ more workers on a telecommuting or mobile basis it becomes important for these users to have access to more than just the report format but also to the data underlying the report. This data can then be analyzed, accumulated into local databases residing on laptops or home PCs, or loaded into worksheets for further analysis. Remote users become more productive and the report data is leveraged more completely without wasteful rekeying or complex parsing of report data to get it into a usable analysis format.

(b) Reengineering Approach

To manage report snapshots, use a report writer that supports the architectural decoupling of the report viewing and analysis functionality from the production of the report itself. This requires a component-based application design. The report viewer component can then be deployed separately from the main report writing engine that manages the definition and running of report instances. A separate local report database is required to receive the data downloaded from a central report server so the report data can be manipulated locally. Replication technology can help ensure that each time a remote report user logs in to a central reporting server, the latest copies of their personalized report book can be copied to their workstation or laptop. Using a report writer that can generate packages of report formatting information plus the underlying data and provide access to report data via a viewer tool that supports report navigation and drilldown allows remote users real flexibility to analyze the latest data off-line on their personal workstation.

Alternatively the report package may be a file designed for loading into a worksheet for further analysis. Worksheets are frequently used to analyze financial report data, so this approach simply makes the publishing of report data into worksheets as easy as possible to avoid rekeying and parsing of the report data. Some accounting report writers are now able to generate intelligent worksheet files that can take advantage of a wide range of new features found in the latest versions of popular desktop worksheets. Instead of delivering just raw data that has to be formatted manually by the user to fit the destination worksheet, these files include formatting data that allows them to automatically build:

- Multiple worksheets with original report formatting such as borders, shading, and boxes still intact
- Tabbed worksheet workbooks that organize the data logically using worksheet tabs to represent individual report instances
- Navigable summary and detail reports using worksheet outline controls that can expand or collapse the display of report lines and totals

Delivery of financial information into worksheets can also be enabled through the use of special worksheet add-ins that turn spreadsheets into front ends for accounting systems to extract data directly into financial report templates. In this scenario, the add-in supplements the standard worksheet menus with additional options for extracting data from accounting databases and formatting it into financial statements or consolidations. The report templates can use the built-in sophistication of the spreadsheet to enable data drilldown, report expansion and collapse, multisheet consolidations, and e-mail distribution.

(c) Resources

Vendor	Product
FRx Software (Denver, CO)	FRx Enterprise
Synex Corporation (Vancouver, BC)	F9
Timeline (Bellevue, WA)	MetaView Analyst

11.6 BUILD BUSINESS INTELLIGENCE AND ALERT MONITORS

(a) Process Problem

Accounting systems are an information asset in which a lot of business intelligence is archived. Also because accounting systems are usually heavy transaction processors the information is being increased and enriched on a daily basis. Some of this information, such as the cash balances or currency exposure at any given point in time, can be mission critical for business such as financial services. Monitoring business thresholds, financial ratios, and key performance indicators can help line-of-business managers avoid problems, identify opportunities, and exploit unexpected trading conditions. However, the traditional way to get this type of data has been to run paper reports and then use business analysts to analyze and synthesize the data in worksheets before presenting it to management. This approach is labor intensive and lacks the immediacy of pulling such data directly from the accounting system or having alerts pushed to the appropriate managers.

(b) Reengineering Approach

Accounting databases that support triggers can be used as the foundation for a business alert system that uses e-mail as a means to alert managers to exception conditions in the accounting system. Triggers are small programs stored in the database itself that are fired automatically in response to a specific database-managed event taking place, such as the insertion, updating, or deletion of an accounting transaction. The trigger may contain code that checks for a specific condition such as whether the receipt of a new sales order causes a customer credit limit to be within 10 percent of its limit or whether an expense claim contains any item over $1,000. If the condition is met then the trigger can generate a message which is passed to a local or Internet e-mail system and ends up as a special flagged alert entry in a manager's electronic inbox.

Triggers can include relatively sophisticated conditional processing, because they can be used to initiate multiple database-stored procedures, and can cause messages or other information to be passed to other complementary systems. Triggers are ideal for monitoring and responding to exception conditions because triggers are always fired in response to specific database events and the exception logic is stored in the database so it is always applied consistently and can be easily maintained. While complex triggers do have a drawback in terms of overall database performance because their use incurs a processing overhead, they are still a simple way to generate simple alert messages and actions from exception conditions that are database driven.

Business indicators, alerts, and ratios can also be monitored using EIS or digital dashboard tools that provide the means of graphically displaying exception data, ratios, and so on through the use of maps, business charts, and other visual dashboard controls such as slider bars, needle indicators, and speedometers. These dashboards use queries against the accounting database to poll the database on a regular, schedule-driven basis to check for thresholds being exceeded, to update ratio calculations, or to report specific balances or comparative information. When the user loads their own personalized dashboard they see a view of the business that reflects their management needs. Visual cues such as color coding, flashing traffic lights, or animated alarm bells can be used by these dashboards to highlight important alert or exception data. The dashboard can always be refreshed at the push of a button to get the most up-to-date picture of the business intelligence stored in the accounting system.

(c) Resources

Vendor	Product
Microsoft Corporation (Bellevue, WA)	SQL Server 6.5
Oracle Corporation (Redwood Shores, CA)	Oracle Alert
Platinum Technology (Oakwood Terrace, IL)	Forest & Trees
SBT Internet Systems (San Rafael, CA)	WebAlert

CONCLUSION

Client/server accounting has provided a useful shot in the arm for both accounting-system vendors and users.

For vendors, client/server accounting provides:

- A valid rationale for restructuring and reengineering their accounting applications on a ground-up basis
- A window of opportunity to enter the accounting applications market or to reach up or down from their current market positioning
- A chance to build in the many wish-list items that have been delayed in the past
- A way to extend the reach of accounting applications by integrating them with a number of complementary technologies
- The ability to broaden and deepen their product functionality by taking advantage of new or more mature development methodologies

For users, client/server accounting provides:

- An opportunity to modernize their antiquated accounting systems and to bring them into line with the technology used by the rest of the organization
- A catalyst for undertaking overdue process reengineering throughout the business
- A means of leveraging other new technology infrastructures more effectively
- A vehicle for transforming the accounting department into a value-added information provider for the organization's information consumers
- A way of introducing the new-generation applications that can embrace new technologies such as workflow, software agents, and the Internet more successfully than old host systems
- A valuable means of maintaining competitive edge through more productive, more empowered end users, extended enterprise transaction processing, and improved decision support

While the combination of business objects components, software agents, workflow, and the Internet already promise to spawn a whole new generation of accounting applications, client/server accounting represents the state of the art in business management software in the mid 1990s.

APPENDIX

Client/Server Accounting Vendor Contact List

American Software
470 East Paces Ferry Rd.
Atlanta, GA 30305
Telephone: (404) 264-5296
Fax: (404) 264-5206
Web Site: http://www.amsoftware.com
Product: Ensoft

Apprise Software Inc.
3121 Route 22
Somerville, NJ 08876
Telephone: (908) 725-6000
Fax: (908) 725-9555
Web Site: http://www.apprisesi.com
Product: Apprise Financials

Baan Company
4600 Bohannon Drive
Menlo Park, CA 94025
Telephone: (415) 462-4949
Fax: (415) 462-4953
Web Site: http://www.baan.com
Product: Baan IV

Big Software
1601 South De Anza Boulevard
Cupertino, CA 95014
Telephone: (408) 725-7200
Fax: (408) 725-7205
Web Site: http://www.bigsoftware.com
Product: Big Business

CODA Inc.
1155 Elm Street
Manchester, NH 03101
Telephone: (603) 647-9600
Fax: (603) 647-2634
Web Site: http://www.codainc.com
Product: CODA Financials

Computer Associates International Inc.
One Computer Associates Plaza
Islandia, NY 11788-7000
Telephone: (516) 342-2245
Fax: (516) 342-4864
Web Site: http://www.cai.com
Product: Masterpiece/2000

Computron Software Inc.
301 Route 17 North
Rutherford, NJ 07070
Telephone: (201) 935-3400
Fax: (201) 935-7678
Web Site: http://www.ctronsoft.com
Product: Computron Financials

Concepts Dynamic Inc.
1821 Walden Office Square, Suite 500
Schaumburg, IL 60173
Telephone: (847) 397-4400
Fax: (847) 397-0575
Web Site: http:/ www.conceptsdyn.com
Product: CDI Control Series

Deltek Systems
8280 Greensboro Drive
McLean, VA 22102-3841
Telephone: (703) 734-8606
Fax: (703) 734-1146
Web Site: http://www.deltek.com
Product: Costpoint

Design Data Systems Corporation
11701 S. Belcher Road, Suite 105
Largo, FL 34643-5116
Telephone: (813) 539-1077
Fax: (813) 539-8042
Web Site: http:// www.designdatasys.com
Product: SQL*Time

Dun & Bradstreet Software
66 Perimeter Center East
Atlanta, GA 30346-1805
Telephone: (404) 239-2000
Fax: (404) 239-4933
Web Site: http:// www.dbsoftware.com
Product: SmartStream Financials

FlexiInternational Software Inc.
Two Enterprise Drive
Shelton, CT 06484
Telephone: (203) 925-3040
Fax: (203) 925-3044
Web Site: http://www.flexi.com
Product: FlexiFinancials

FourGen Software
115 NE 100th Street
Seattle, WA 98125-8098
Telephone: (206) 522-0055
Fax: (206) 522-0053
Web Site: http://www.fourgen.com
Product: Enterprise

Fourth Shift
7900 International Drive, Suite 450
Minneapolis, MN 55425
Telephone: (612) 851-1500
Fax: (612) 851-1560
Web Site: http://www.fs.com
Product: Manufacturing Software System (MSS)

FRx Software Corporation
4949 South Syracuse Street, Suite 620
Denver, CO 80237
Telephone: (303) 741-8000
Fax: (303) 741-3335
Web Site: http://www.FRxsoft.com
Product: FRX Enterprise

GeacVisionshift
3707 West Cherry Street
Tampa, FL 33607
Telephone: (813) 872-9990
Fax: (813) 876-8786
Web Site: http://www.geac.com
Product: Vision*Shift*

Global Software
1009 Spring Forest Rd.
Raleigh, NC 27615
Telephone: (919) 790-4457
Fax: (919) 876-8205
Web Site: N/A
Product: Global System

Great Plains Software
1701 SW 38th Street
Fargo, ND 58103
Telephone: (701) 281-0550
Fax: (701) 281-3700
Web Site: http://www.gps.com
Product: Dynamics C/S+

Hyperion Software Corporation
900 Long Ridge Rd.
Stamford, CT 06902
Telephone: (203) 703-3000
Fax: (203) 968-9319
Web Site: http://www.hysoft.com
Product: Hyperion Financials

J D Edwards
8055 East Tufts Avenue
Denver, CO 80215
Telephone: (303) 488-4000
Fax: (303) 488-4842
Web Site: http://
www.jdedwards.com
Product: One World

JBA International
3701 Algonquin Rd., Suite 100
Rolling Meadows, IL 60008
Telephone: (708) 590-0299
Fax: (708) 590-0049
Web Site: http://www.jba.com
Product: Business/400

Lawson Software
1300 Godward Street
Minneapolis, MN 55413-3004
Telephone: (612) 379-8086
Fax: (612) 379-7141
Web Site: http://www.lawson.com
Product: Insight

LIBRA Corporation
4001 S. 700 East, Suite 301
Salt Lake City, UT 84107-2177
Telephone: (801) 281-0700
Fax: (801) 284-9180
Web Site: N/A
Product: Perspectives by LIBRA

Macola Inc.
333 East Center Street
PO Box 1824
Marion, OH 43301-1824
Telephone: (614) 382-5999
Fax: (614) 382-0239
Web Site: http://www.macola.com
Product: Progression Series

Maconomy NE Inc.
124 Anderson Road
Marlborough, MA 01752
Telephone: (508) 460-8337
Fax: (508) 460-6327
Web Site: http://www.maconomy-usa.com
Product: Maconomy Series

MTX International Inc.
98 Inverness Drive East, Suite 110
Englewood, CO 80112-5108
Telephone: (303) 790-1400
Fax: (303) 790-4058
Web Site: http://www.mtxi.com
Product: MTX Accounting

Navision Software US Inc.
One Meca Way
Norcross, GA 30093
Telephone: (770) 564-8000
Fax: (770) 564-8010
Web Site: http://www.navision-us.com
Product: Navision Financials

Open Systems Inc.
7626 Golden Triangle Drive
Eden Prairie, MN 55347
Telephone: (612) 829-3950
Fax: (612) 829-1493
Web Site: http://www.osas.com
Product: Traverse

OpenPlus International Inc.
3925 West Braker Lane, Suite 305
Austin, TX 78759
Telephone: (512) 328-1231
Fax: (512) 328-1491
Web Site: http://www.openplus.com
Product: OpenPlus Financials

Oracle Corporation
500 Oracle Parkway
Redwood Shores, CA 94065
Telephone: (415) 506-4176
Fax: (415) 506-7132
Web Site: http://www.oracle.com
Product: Oracle Financials

Orange Systems
13577 Feather Sound Drive, Suite 450
Clearwater, FL 34622-5539
Telephone: (813) 571-1606
Fax: (813) 571-1703
Web Site: http://www.alcie.com
Product: ALCIE

PeopleSoft
4440 Rosewood Drive
Pleasanton, CA 94588-3031
Telephone: (510) 225-3000
Fax: (510) 225-3100
Web Site: http://www.peoplesoft.com
Product: PeopleSoft Financials

Platinum Software Company
195 Technology Drive
Irvine, CA 92618-3308
Telephone: (714) 453-4000
Fax: (714) 453-4091
Web Site: http://www.platsoft.com
Product: Platinum SQL

PowerCerv
400 N Ashley Drive, Suite 2700
Tampa, FL 33602
Telephone: (813) 222-2378
Fax: (813) 222-0886
Web Site: htp://www.tampa.powerCerv.com
Product: Intergy

QSP Inc.
3200 Atlantic Avenue
Raleigh, NC 27604
Telephone: (919) 872-4036
Fax: (919) 872-4015
Web Site: http://www.qspinc.com
Product: Universal OLAS

Ramco Systems Corporation
2201 Walnut Avenue
Fremont, CA 94538
Telephone: (510) 494-2964
Fax: (510) 494-2979
Web Site: http://www.ramco.com
Product: Marshal

Ross Systems Inc.
1100 Johnson Ferry Rd.
Center Two, Suite 750
Atlanta, GA 30342
Telephone: (404) 851-1872
Fax: (404) 257-0434
Web Site: http://www.rossinc.com
Product: Renaissance

SAP America Inc.
701 Lee Road
Wayne, PA 19087
Telephone: (610) 725-4500
Fax: (610) 725-4555
Web Site: http://www.sap.com
Product: R/3

SAS Institute
SAS Campus Drive
Cary, NC 27513-8008
Telephone: (919) 677-8000
Fax: (919) 677-8123
Web Site: http://www.sas.com
Product: CFO Vision

Scala North America Inc.
601 South Lake Destiny Road, Suite 200
Maitland, FL 32751
Telephone: (407) 875-6999
Fax: (407) 875-9957
Web Site: http://www.scala.se
Product: Scala

Skylight Systems
135 Greencote Ave.
Wyncote, PA 19095
Telephone: (215) 576-1001
Fax: (215) 576-1527
Web Site: http://www:skylightsystems.com
Product: Relational Financial System (RFS)

Software 2000 Inc.
25 Communications Way, Drawer 6000
Hyannis, MA 02601
Telephone: (508) 778-2000
Fax: (508) 778-5420
Web Site: http://www.s2k.com
Product: Infinium

Solomon Software
200 East Harbor Street
Findlay, OH 45840
Telephone: (419) 424-0422
Fax: (419) 424-3400
Web Site: http://www.solomon.com
Product: Solomon IV for Windows

SourceMate Systems Inc.
20 Sunnyside Avenue
Mill Valley, CA 94941-1928
Telephone: (415) 381-1011
Fax: (415) 381-6902
Web Site: http://www.sourcemate.com
Product: Visual AccountMate

SPFC
PO Box 163
Madison, NJ 07940
Telephone: (800) 676-7732
Fax: (201) 765-0791
Web Site: N/A
Product: SQL Accounting for Windows

SQL Financials International Inc.
Two Ravinia Drive
Atlanta GA 30346
Telephone: (770) 390-3900
Fax: (770) 390-3999
Web Site: http://www.sqlfinancials.com
Product: SQL Financials

State Of The Art Software Inc.
56 Technology
Irvine, CA 92718
Telephone: (714) 753-1222
Fax: (714) 753-0930
Web Site: http://www.stateoftheart.com
Product: Acuity Financials

Synon Corporation
1100 Larkspur Landing Circle, Suite 180
Larkspur, CA 94939
Telephone: (415) 461-5000
Fax: (415) 461-4239
Web Site: http://www.synon.com
Product: Synon/Financials

System Software Associates Inc.
500 West Madison
Chicago, IL 60661
Telephone: (213) 258-6000
Fax: (312) 479-7500
Web Site: http://www.ssax.com
Product: BPCS Client/Server

Systems Union Inc.
10 Bank Street
White Plains, NY 10606
Telephone: (914) 948-7770
Fax: (914) 948-7399
Web Site: http://www.systemsunion.com
Product: SunSystems

The Dodge Group Inc.
404 Wyman Street
Waltham, MA 02154
Telephone: (617) 672-8600
Fax: (617) 672-8632
Web Site: http://www.dodge.com
Product: OpenSeries/Financial Warehouse

Timeline
3055 112th Avenue NE, Suite 106
Bellevue, WA 98004
Telephone: (206) 822-3140
Fax: (206) 822-1120
Web Site: http://www.timeline.com
Product: MetaView

USL Systems
8227 Old Courthouse Road
Vienna, VA 22182-9923
Telephone: (703) 790-2754
Fax: (703) 790-3396
Web Site: http://www.uslsystems.com
Product: USL Financials

Walker Interactive Systems
Marathon Plaza Three North
303 Second Street
San Francisco, CA 94107
Telephone: (415) 495-8811
Fax: (415) 543-6338
Web Site: http://www.walker.com
Product: APTOS

Glossary

3GL (Third Generation Language) A traditional programming language such as COBOL or FORTRAN. Many nonclient/server accounting systems are written in COBOL.

4GL (Fourth Generation Language). The successor to programming languages such as COBOL. 4 GLs automate much of the basic application building tasks so the source code is smaller and easier to manage. Some client/server accounting systems are built using 4GLs.

ABC (Activity-Based Costing) Used to determine the true cost of a business activity by analyzing all the relevant direct and indirect costs attributable to that activity.

Access A popular database management and application-development tool for building small to medium business accounting systems from Microsoft Corporation.

AIX (Advanced Interactive Executive) The IBM version of UNIX that runs on its RS/6000 series and other computers. A number of client/server accounting systems use the RS/6000 as a server platform.

ANSI (American National Standards Institute) The main body for setting computing standards in the United States. SQL-92 is an ANSI standard.

AS/400 The minicomputer range that replaced the IBM System/36 and System/38 minicomputers. Many AS/400 accounting vendors are re-writing their accounting applications for client/server platforms such as UNIX and Microsoft NT.

ASCII (American Standard Code for Information Interchange) The codes used to represent standard written characters. All accounting systems can output reports as an ASCII file—a file of data stored in ASCII code representation.

Back End Used to indicate a source of client/server application logic or data (aka Server).

BackOffice A suite of Microsoft server applications including networking, relational database, e-mail, Internet, system management, and host connectivity services.

Balance files/tables Database files or tables that store summary balances for combinations of information dimensions such as account and period.

Bandwidth Bandwidth determines the ability of the network to process larger individual packets of information, more of them, or both. Bandwidth largely determines the speed and capacity of the network to process information.

Batch Posting Used to describe accounting applications that post transactions in batches so all modules or accounts impacted by the transaction are updated at specific intervals. The opposite of real-time posting.

Benchmark A suite of tests that formally establish the performance of a specific task using a specific combination of hardware and software. A number of client/server accounting vendors have released performance benchmarks for their systems. *See also* TPC.

Best of Class A marketing term that indicates high functional depth but low functional breadth. It often means the vendor can only supply a restricted range of application modules. (aka Best of Breed)

Best Practices Best practices are performance measurements obtained by a market leader for a specific business process that other businesses, often in different market sectors, try to emulate.

BLOB (Binary Large Object) A database data type that can hold large amounts of data for storing objects such as images, sound, or video. All leading relational databases used by client/server accounting systems can support BLOB data.

BPR (Business Process Reengineering) A term popularized by Michael Hammer that refers to a method of reengineering based on business processes rather than functional departments. Workflow-enabled client/server applications can help with BPR.

Brokers Software used to manage application objects in a networked environment by passing messages between objects and routing objects to applications that request to use them.

Btrieve A popular data file manager from Pervasive Inc. supported by many PC LAN accounting vendors.

Business Alert A warning message, usually delivered by e-mail to alert an application user to the fact that a business event has occurred that violates a business rule. For example, "inform the credit controller if a customer has exceeded their credit limit."

Business Event An application event such as inserting a new order or deleting an account code that triggers a specific processing response.

Business Objects Functional components designed to interact with other business objects to solve a business problem.

Business Process A process that usually involves the movement of a unit of work along a workflow that may cross functional and system boundaries before completing its lifecycle.

Business Rules Rules that are used by the application as the basis for deciding whether to take a specific action such as rejecting an order or alerting a manager to an exception condition.

C-ISAM A popular data-file management system for applications written for use on UNIX platforms.

C/C++ Traditional programing languages associated with the UNIX operating system. C++ is based on C and allows the use of object-oriented structures and functions. Many client/server accounting systems are written in C or C++.

CA-Ingres A popular RDBMS system from Computer Associates supported only by a few accounting vendors.

Client Usually a desktop PC or workstation that processes information requested from a local or remote server. (aka Front End)

Client/Server A computing architecture that divides work between desktop clients and local or remote servers. Most host-based accounting software has been rewritten for use on client/server architectures.

Closing Closing a fiscal accounting period, a process that may involve running report packs and posting various automated and manual transactions to the accounting database

COBOL (Common Business-Oriented Language) A popular 3GL for writing accounting systems and other business management applications. Popularized by the MicroFocus COBOL products.

COBOL-ISAM A popular data file management system used by many COBOL accounting vendors.

Codd, E. F. The originator of the relational database model and, more recently, the 10 rules of on-line analytical processing (OLAP).

COM (Component Object Model) Microsoft's proposed object standard based on object linking and embedding (OLE).

Continuous Improvement Quality initiatives designed to ensure that a specific business process is subject to continuous improvement over time.

CORBA (Common Object Request Broker Architecture) A standard sponsored by the Object Management Group (OMG) for managing distributed objects over a network. This standard is critical for accelerating the momentum towards object-oriented accounting software.

Core Competencies The focus of the business or where the business makes money. Noncore competencies are often outsourced to maintain the focus.

CPU (Central Processing Unit) A computer processor or microprocessor such as the Intel 486 or Pentium. Most client/server accounting systems require a 486 or better CPU for their client computers.

Cross Platform Software that can be run on more than one computer platform such as a PC or a Mac. Many client/server accounting packages offer a range of deployment options.

Data Dictionary A table or group of tables that provides more information about a system, an application, or its data. Usually data dictionaries contain metadata, or data about data. Accounting systems with a data dictionary are usually easier to customize.

Data mining Using specialized software for analyzing large databases to identify hidden trends, patterns, and relationships in the data that can be used to business advantage.

Data Warehouse A separate repository of data copied from multiple transaction systems and rearranged for faster access by decision-support users. Often used as a means of providing wider access to data from legacy accounting systems.

Datamart A more specialized version of a data warehouse typically focused on a particular business function such as sales and marketing or a specific audience such as VP level executives.

DB2 IBM's relational database management system (RDBMS) that runs on mainframe and nonmainframe platforms. Some client/server accounting vendors support DB2 as a data source.

dBase A popular database management and application development tool for building small to medium business accounting systems. From Borland.

DBMS (Database Management System) Software for creating and maintaining a database. Today's leading DBMS products use the relational model for storing and managing data (*see* RDBMS)

DDE (Dynamic Data Exchange) A Microsoft API for interapplication communication and exchange of information frequently used to pass data between accounting applications and spreadsheets.

Deadlock When two or more users are trying to access the same information at the same time and the database locking manager cannot resolve the contention.

DEC (Digital Equipment Corporation) The DEC VAX minicomputer used to be a popular accounting platform. Now DEC is making a comeback with its new Alpha servers for client/server accounting on Microsoft NT.

Designed for Windows 95 A Microsoft logo and certification process for applications that comply with certain Windows 95 attributes.

Dimension A unique information element such as an account code or document identifier that is used to sort and select information for decision support purposes.

Distribution Distribution is used to refer to modules such as inventory, sales order entry, and billing used to manage the distribution of goods to customers.

Document Management Managing of documents in electronic formats to allow them to be imaged, routed, edited, output, and archived. Many client/server accounting systems now support document management, allowing documents to be tagged to accounting transactions.

Downsizing Reducing managerial and clerical redundancy in organizations through business process reengineering or the efficient application of technology. Usually associated with cost cutting and head count reductions.

Drilldown Navigating data from summary balances to detail transactions or source documents.

Drillthrough A drilldown that crosses system boundaries in which the drilldown may start in one system such as the general ledger and end in another such as payroll.

DSS (Decision Support System) A system designed to provide access to information rather than manage high volumes of transactions.

Dumb Terminal A screen with no local processor or disk resource that is simply used to view and enter data managed by a host-based (mainframe, mini, UNIX) application.

EDI (Electronic Data Interchange) A set of standards for exchanging business documents such as sales or purchase orders electronically.

EIS (Executive Information System) An application for presenting information to senior executives using highly graphical information panels, dashboards, or briefing books.

E-mail (Electronic Mail) Software for managing the creation and routing of electronic messages across computer networks.

ER (Entity Relationship) A popular method for visually modeling relational database structures consisting of related tables and columns.

Essbase A popular multidimensional OLAP database server from Arbor Software Corporation.

Excel A popular spreadsheet program from Microsoft Corporation for analyzing financial data.

Extended Enterprise An enterprise consisting of internal business units, outsourced business units, suppliers, customers, and other business partners.

Extended Transaction A transaction of a long duration that may span many functional systems such as a transaction that begins life as a sales order, passes through manufacturing, finished goods inventory, and shipping, and ends up as a receivable.

Fat Client A term used to indicate an application that does the majority of its processing on the client, requiring a more powerful desktop client computer.

File Server Usually a PC on a local area network in which files shared by network users are stored. File servers simply deliver files across the network to users on their local PC. This file transfer can result in an inefficient use of network bandwidth.

Firewall Security software for protecting internal corporate intranet data from access by unauthorized Internet browsers and hackers.

FoxPro A popular database management and application development tool from Microsoft Corporation for building small to medium business accounting systems.

Front End Usually a desktop PC or workstation that processes information requested from a local or remote server. (aka Client)

Gateway A device, often a PC or other server, that provides connection services between dissimilar devices or applications.

Granularity The term used to indicate the how finely or coarsely an application has been designed to be broken down into separate functional components. Highly granular applications are typically more cost effective and offer better scaleability and deployment options.

Granules Functional components at a finer level of granularity than traditional modules that can be used to construct more flexible applications.

GUI (Graphical User Interface) User interfaces used by applications that mix text with graphics and icons to make the interface more interesting and understandable. For example: Microsoft Windows, Apple MacOS, and OSG/Motif.

Hooks Hooks are specific points in the packaged application source code in which calls may be made to user-defined programs or procedures. For example, to insert a custom line discount calculation into a sales order entry application.

Host A computer that centralizes the management of the applications by managing all software and data from one host operating system such as a mainframe, mini, or UNIX-based host.

HP-UX Hewlett Packard's version of UNIX for its HP 9000 series computers. HP-UX is a popular server platform for client/server accounting systems.

Image-Enabling Adding functionality to an application that allows it to capture, display, and manipulate image data such as documents or pictures.

Imaging Managing the scanning of images such as photographs or forms and attaching those images to accounting data such as an inventory, fixed-asset, or invoice transaction record.

Informix A popular RDBMS from Informix Corporation supported by a number of client/server accounting vendors.

Integrated Integrated accounting applications share common information such as account, department, or employee codes. It is possible to trace transactions back to their source for complete audit trails.

Integrity A term used to describe the accuracy of data stored in a database. All database systems provide some techniques for ensuring data integrity is maintained.

Interfaced Interfaced accounting applications do not share common information such as account, department, or employee codes. Each module is an information island and depends on batch processes to update information between modules.

Internet An international communications network that allows any server to be accessed by any client.

Intranet An internal corporate network or server connected to the Internet that protects access to its servers through use of a security firewall to restrict user access.

ISAM (Indexed Sequential Access Method) A popular data file format that stores data records in ascending or descending order based on a primary key index. Used by many accounting systems written in COBOL or C.

ISO 9000 (International Standards Organization) ISO 9000 is an international standard for quality that has been awarded to some client/server accounting vendors for their software development processes.

ISV (Independent Software Vendor) A business that resells software, often from many vendors.

Java A programming language used primarily to build compact applications for use across the Internet. (From Sun Microsystems)

JIT (Just-In-Time) Focuses on reducing waste in inventory control by ensuring rapid replenishment of inventory when reorder points are reached, and by use of production methods that are order driven.

Join A term used in connection with linking two or more tables in a relational database. Joins are based on a common key value such as the customer ID used to join a customer table with an order table for example.

Key A key is a value in a database table row or file record used to index or order the data contents. Every record or row usually has one primary key to uniquely identify its content.

LAN (Local Area Network) Multiple computers linked for the purposes of sharing data and peripherals, and passing messages between them.

Locking The mechanisms and rules used by the database manger to ensure that only one person is working with one version of the data at any one time. Locking is used to prevent data corruption due to simultaneous access to data in multiuser systems.

Log A record kept by a database management system of specific activities in the database. A log is used in transaction rollback to undo incomplete transactions. Logs add a performance overhead to most database activities.

Lotus 1-2-3 A popular spreadsheet program from Lotus Development Corporation for analyzing financial data.

Mainframe A large and expensive computer designed to support hundreds or thousands of users that centralizes the management of the applications by managing all software and data from one host operating system (aka Host). IBM mainframes dominate the market.

MAPI (Mail Applications Programming Interface) A Microsoft messaging standard that is supported by most client/server accounting vendors for routing data and reports using e-mail.

MDI (Multiple Document Interface) MDI allows multiple windows to be displayed simultaneously using the Microsoft Windows GUI. More than one accounting form can therefore be shown on screen at once.

Metadata Data about data, usually stored in a data dictionary and used by other applications to read and write data to the system described by the metadata. Accounting vendors are providing metadata to assist decision support tools to access accounting data.

Middleware Application interfaces and protocols used to connect client and server applications. Microsoft open database connectivity (ODBC) is an example of middleware used by many accounting software vendors to connect their applications to data sources.

Minicomputer A scaled down and less expensive version of a mainframe, such as an IBM AS/400, DEC VAX or HP 3000 computer that centralizes the management of the applications by managing all software and data from one host operating system (aka Host).

MIPS (Millions of Instructions Per Second) One measure of a processor's operating performance in terms of how many discrete software instructions it can manage in a second. A higher number is faster.

MRP (Manufacturing Resource Planning) Integrated applications that manage manufacturing and inventory.

MS-DOS (Microsoft Disk Operating System) The world's most popular operating system for PCs using Intel processors.

MVS (Multiple Virtual Storage) An IBM mainframe operating system.

NetWare The market's leading PC LAN operating system for file and print sharing using PCs from Novell Corporation. All leading workgroup accounting applications run on Novell NetWare LANs and most use the Btrieve file manager for data storage.

Network A combination of software and hardware that provides a means for computers to communicate with each other. (*see* LAN and WAN)

Notes A groupware application from Lotus Corporation that supports collaborative, document-based work processes, and data replication between Notes servers and clients.

NT Microsoft's successor to MS-DOS, a 32-bit operating system available for deployment as a client or a server operating system.

OAG (Open Applications Group) A group of client/server accounting and manufacturing vendors working to standardize interapplication transaction processing using a business document model. The aim is to allow users to combine best-of-class applications.

Object A building block in constructing component-based applications. Objects encapsulate both data and the methods used to manipulate that data.

OCX (OLE Custom Extension) Custom controls (user defined objects) that comply with Microsoft's object linking and embedding object model.

ODBMS (Object Oriented Database Management System) A database designed to store objects, rather than just data. Often used for storing complex data such as maps, diagrams, or documents that can be manipulated in different ways from text and numeric data.

ODMA (Open Document Management API) A standard for sharing documents between applications.

Office A suite of Microsoft desktop applications including word processing, spreadsheets, presentation graphics, data management, scheduling, and e-mail.

Office Compatible A Microsoft logo and certification process for applications that can integrate closely with the Microsoft Office suite.

OLAP (On-Line Analytical Processing) A marketing term invented by Arbor Software to describe ad-hoc decision-support applications that manipulate data stored in a multidimensional database.

OLE (Object Linking and Embedding) A Microsoft object component standard that allows an object managed by one application to run within another application. OLE is used to enable document management in accounting applications, for example.

OLTP (On-Line Transaction Processing) Typically real-time systems used by banks, airlines, or telemarketing businesses that place a heavy emphasis on the input of short, regular, transactions such as ATM withdrawals, reservations, or telephone orders.

OMG (Object Management Group) A body that is defining standards for object-oriented computing development and deployment, one of which is the influential CORBA standard supported by a multi-vendor consortium.

OO (Object Oriented) Used to classify development tools, programming language, methodologies, and applications that make use of objects, inheritance, polymorphism, and encapsulation. There are few OO client/server accounting packages released as of 1996.

OOP (Object-Oriented Programming) Usually used in reference to object-oriented programming languages such as Smalltalk or C++.

Open Systems A term used to describe systems that have an API in the public domain and are therefore more likely to collaborate with other systems. Often used to describe systems that run on the UNIX operating system.

OpenDoc A competing component object standard to Microsoft's Component Object Model (COM) based on OLE. OpenDoc is supported by IBM, Apple, Novell, and others.

ORACLE A popular RDBMS from Oracle Corporation supported by a number of client/server accounting vendors.

OS (Operating System) A program required on all computers to manage routine tasks such as accepting keyboard input, managing screen display, and data input/output to memory and disk.

OS/2 A client and server operating system from IBM that competes with

Microsoft NT and UNIX. OS/2 has not proven as popular as a platform for client/server accounting applications by comparison with either NT or UNIX.

OS/400 The combined operating system and database that runs on IBM's AS/400 computers.

OSF (Open Systems Foundation) Founded by UNIX vendors competing with AT&T and Sun Microsystems, the OSF is known primarily for the Motif GUI. Now known as Open Systems Group.

Outliner A means of displaying a linked hierarchy of information such as a chart of accounts or organization reporting structure. The outliner can be collapsed or expanded using the mouse to show more or less information in the outline. (aka Browser)

Outsource To contract work to an external consultant or systems integrator. Payroll is the type of function that is typically outsourced by accounting departments.

Parallel Processing Processing transaction entry, query, or processes across multiple processors rather than one. Parallel processing offers the potential for high levels of scalability and performance. Few accounting systems take advantage of parallel processing.

Pivot Rotating the axis of a two-dimensional matrix to show a different view of the data being analyzed.

Portability The ability of accounting applications to be run on different combinations of server operating system, database engine, and user interface.

Posting Posting is the insertion of correct and balancing accounting data into the accounting database. Each posting usually generates some form of unique transaction number or ID.

PowerBuilder A popular 4GL from PowerSoft Corporation for building client/server applications.

Process Server A physically separate networked server used to run specific processes such as transaction posting, data feeds, or financial reporting without burdening other application and database servers.

Query A query is an inquiry against the database to retrieve specific information based on the parameters included in the query.

RAM (Random Access Memory) The volatile memory used for temporary storage of data and programs that is cleared when the computer is switched off.

RDBMS (Relational Database Management System) A database management system that manages data stored using the relational model.

Real-Time Posting The term used to indicate accounting applications that post transactions in real time so that all modules or accounts impacted by the transaction are posted at once. The opposite of batch posting.

Reengineering The analysis and redesign of business processes to achieve measurable performance improvements. Reengineering is often made practical in accounting software through the use of workflow functionality.

Referential Integrity How the database manager ensures that data stored in related tables is kept in synchronization.

Relational A data storage model in which data is broken down into a logical model of related tables, table columns, and indexes. The data is accessed by applications through the structured query language (SQL). All client/server accounting systems use relational data.

Replication The mechanism for managing the copying and synchronization of data between databases. There are many replication models depending on the business needs driving the replication. Few client/server accounting systems have yet to make use of replication.

RFP (Request For Proposal) A document detailing application specifications and requirements often sent to vendors to determine whether they should be included in a selection process.

RISC (Reduced Instruction Set Computing) Computer chips with limited instruction sets designed to process simple instructions very rapidly. Most servers running the UNIX operating system are based on RISC chips.

ROLAP (Relational On-Line Analytical Processing) A term invented to counter OLAP by vendors who provide decision support software designed to work against data stored in relational databases.

Rollback Relational databases that support rollback can undo incomplete transactions and rollback the database to its consistent state prior to the transaction being accepted. Rollback depends on the use of a transaction log.

RPC (Remote Procedure Call) A means of requesting a remote computer to execute a specific procedural program. A request by a client application to execute a server-based, stored procedure is an example of an RPC.

RPG (Report Program Generator) A 3GL used on IBM minicomputers such as the AS/400 for running processes or producing reports.

SAG (SQL Access Group) A group of vendors and users promoting SQL and database access standards.

SAP AG The world's leading accounting applications vendor (by revenue), based in Walldorf, Germany.

Scalable SQL A database from Pervasive Inc. supported by some client/server accounting vendors.

Scaleability The ability of an accounting application to handle increasing transaction volume, user connections, and functional sophistication.

SCO UNIX (Santa Cruz Operation) A popular UNIX variant that provides multiuser computing to workgroups. Many workgroup accounting vendors support versions of SCO UNIX to run their applications.

Screen Scraper Replacing a dumb terminal interface to a host application with a graphical user interface running on a PC. Usually a stopgap measure to improve the look and feel of a mainframe application.

Silo A term used to describe applications that are poorly integrated and difficult to access for decision support (aka Stovepipes).

Smalltalk A popular object-oriented programming language considered one of the few pure OO languages.

Solaris Sun Microsystem's variant of the UNIX operating system.

SPARC (Scalable Processor Architecture) A proprietary chip architecture used in Sun Microsystems computers.

SQL (Structured Query Language) Now the de facto standard for querying data in relational databases. SQL is neither a complete programing language nor completely standard because vendors have added their own extensions for commercial advantage.

SQLBase A popular RDBMS from Centura Software Corporation supported by a number of client/server accounting vendors.

SQL Server A popular RDBMS from Microsoft Corporation supported by a number of client/server accounting vendors.

SQL Windows A popular 4GL from Centura Software Corporation for building client/server applications.

Stored Procedure A piece of code that is stored as an object in the database. A stored procedure can be run only by being called from an application program. Stored procedures are efficient, preparsed, and preoptimized SQL programs.

Suite A bundle of software products such as financials, supply chain, or manufacturing consisting of multiple integrated or interfaced modules.

Supply-Chain Management Used to refer to modules such as inventory, purchasing, and sales-order entry used to manage the chain of processes between customers and suppliers.

Sybase A popular RDBMS from Sybase Corporation supported by a number of client/server accounting vendors.

T&E Travel and entertainment expenses, a business process that is just recently being fully automated.

Tab Folder A means for displaying and managing linked information maintenance forms using a single container window with multiple tabs. When a tab is clicked a new form is displayed that is often linked to a master form.

Table A two-dimensional array used to represent data stored in a relational database. Tables are related through the use of join keys—common data stored in both tables.

TAPI (Telephony API) A Microsoft standard that helps to integrate telephone systems with computers. Telephony has been exploited mostly by HR application vendors providing employees with telephonic access to their payroll and benefits information.

TCP/IP (Transmission Control Protocol/Internet Protocol) A set of network and application protocols originally developed by the United States Department of Defense. A de facto standard for use with UNIX systems and client/server and Internet/intranet applications.

Telephony Technology for integrating telephone systems with computers. In client/server accounting, telephony has been exploited most by HR application vendors providing employees with touchtone access to their payroll and benefits information.

Terminal A visual display unit attached to a host system used to interact with applications stored on the host.

Thin Client A term used to indicate an application that does the majority of its processing on the server, requiring a less powerful desktop client computer.

TPC (Transaction Processing Council) A group of vendors who coordinate the benchmarking of software tools and applications using published benchmarks such as TPC-C.

Transaction A unit of work such as a GL journal, a purchase order, or a cash receipt. Transactions may be simple or complex, discrete or distributed. An incomplete transaction may also be rolled back by an RDBMS to maintain database integrity.

Transaction Monitor Software that manages the routing, status, integrity, and optimization of distributed or extended transactions that cross applications connected across a network.

Trigger A piece of code that is stored as an object in the database and fired automatically in response to certain events, notably data insertion, updating, or deletion. Triggers can be used to audit access, update balances, or enforce referential integrity.

Two/Three-Tier Architecture Terms used to describe how client/server applications can be distributed over two or three physical deployment tiers depending on the granularity of the application partitioning.

Ultrix Digital Equipment Corporation's version of the UNIX operating system.

UNIX An operating system that is not exclusively controlled by any one vendor and forms the basis for so called Open Systems.

VAN (Value-Added Network) An external network that delivers a specific service to its customers such as the management of electronic data interchange (EDI).

VAR (Value-Added Reseller) A reseller of software and hardware that provides integration, implementation, and support services.

VAX A family of midrange minicomputers from Digital Equipment Corporation (DEC).

View A virtual table that combines data from one or more tables into a single logical view. Views can be used to limit user access to information from the database. Views are often read-only and may not have their information updated or deleted.

Visual Basic A popular graphical programming language from Microsoft Corporation for building workgroup applications.

VBA (Visual Basic for Applications) A Microsoft scripting and application programming language that is being licensed to third parties such as SAP AG for inclusion in client/server applications.

VMS (Virtual Memory System) The operating system used by Digital's VAX minicomputers and now known as OpenVMS.

WAN (Wide Area Network) A group of geographically dispersed hardware and software networked together. A WAN may link multiple local area networks (LANs).

WfMC (Workflow Management Coalition) A group of users and vendors focused on developing standards for workflow applications and the management of cross-application business processes.

Windows The world's most popular graphical user interface and the standard front-end for client/server accounting packages.

Workbook A Microsoft Excel function for bundling multiple worksheets and displaying them as a single tabbed worksheet. Each tab is clicked to display the worksheet linked to the tab.

Workflow The management of business documents and electronic transactions through software that uses rules, routes, and roles.

Worksheet A two-dimensional electronic notepad and calculator used for analyzing financial data.

Workstation A generic term for a desktop computer usually running a graphical user interface and configured to a high specification of CPU memory and disk resource.

Bibliography

Bochenski, Barbara. *Implementing Production Quality Client/Server Systems.* New York: John Wiley & Sons, Inc., 1994.

Champy, James and Nitin Nohria. *Fast Forward: The Best Ideas on Managing Business Change.* Boston: Harvard Business School Press, 1996.

Cronin, Mary J. *The Internet Strategy Handbook.* Boston: Harvard Business School Press, 1996.

Fingar, Peter. *The Blueprint for Business Objects.* New York: SIGS Books, 1996.

Hammer, Michael and James Champy. *Reengineering the Corporation.* New York: HarperCollins, 1993.

Harmon, Paul and Curtis Hall. *Intelligent Software Systems Development.* New York: John Wiley & Sons, Inc., 1993.

Jacobson, Ivar, Maria Ericsson, and Agneta Jacobson. *The Object Advantage.* New York: ACM Press, 1995.

Kalakota, Ravi, and Andrew B. Whinston. *Frontiers of Electronic Commerce.* New York: Addison-Wesley, 1996.

Keeling, Denis. *Corporate Accounting Packages.* London: Ovum Ltd., 1995.

Keen, Peter G. W. and Ellen M. Knapp. *Every Manager's Guide to Business Processes.* Boston: Harvard Business School Press, 1996.

Koulopoulos, Thomas M. *The Workflow Imperative.* Boston: Delphi Publishing, 1994.

Loomis, Mary E. S. *Object Databases: The Essentials.* Reading, MA: Addison-Wesley, 1995.

Pendse, Nigel and Richard Creeth. *The OLAP Report.* Norwalk, CT: Business Intelligence, 1995.

Purdum, Jack. *Accounting and Finance Developer's Guide.* Indianapolis: SAMS Publishing, 1995.

Savage, Charles M. *5th Generation Management.* Newton, MA: Butterworth-Heinemann, 1996.

Siebel, Thomas M. and Michael S. Malone. *Virtual Selling.* New York: Simon & Schuster, 1996.

Taylor, David A. *Object Oriented Technology: A Manager's Guide.* Reading, MA: Addison-Wesley, 1990.

Taylor, David A. *Object Oriented Information Systems: Planning and Implementation.* New York: John Wiley & Sons, Inc., 1992.

Taylor, David A. *Business Engineering with Object Technology.* New York: John Wiley & Sons, Inc., 1995.

Watterson, Karen. *Client/Server Technology for Managers.* Reading, MA: Addison-Wesley, 1995.

Index